# The Rochester Mob Wars

Blair T. Kenny

Blair Publishing

The Rochester Mob Wars



3rd edition

5th Printing June 2017

ISBN: 978-1-5323-4126-7

# Acknowledgements

I would like to acknowledge the following people:

Patti Scherzi, my girlfriend, for putting up with my long days and nights of research and writing. There were many days that I woke up before dawn to work on the book, neglecting my normal day to day responsibilities. Patti picked up the slack for me and never complained despite working a full time job herself.

Wendy Post, for proof reading a chapter of another book that I was researching and writing about, The History of the Rochester Teamsters. Wendy encouraged me to change directions and focus on the Rochester Mafia itself instead of just its influence on organized labor. Wendy was a great source of encouragement to me during the entire process, often giving me her time and expertise as a professional newspaper editor herself.

Finally, I would like to thank my good friend Ed Kelly's mother, Barbara Kelly, a retired English teacher, for editing my book. Mrs. Kelly corrected many grammatical errors that I was unable to see myself. Her time and efforts are greatly appreciated.

# Forward

The Rochester Mob Wars is the result of years of researching the Rochester Mafia and its influence on organized labor. The book was derived entirely from two Senate hearings, many court documents and approximately 1000 newspaper articles. Most of the newspaper articles came from the Democrat and Chronicle in Rochester, New York.

When the information is presented in a chronological fashion, like it is in the book, it creates a clear picture of the Rochester Mafia and all of their activities over a forty year time period. The Rochester Mafia began to exert their influence over gambling and organized labor in the fifties and sixties. That influence lasted nearly four decades and came to an end only when the majority of the Organizations' members were imprisoned in the eighties and Teamsters Local #398 was dissolved by the government for lifetime affiliation with the Mafia in 1997.

Several names have spelling variations due to the names being spelled two different ways either in court documents or newspaper articles. For the most part I left them as they were in each particular document. I apologize for the inconsistencies. Any spelling errors are unintentional.

# Table of Contents

# Introduction

The "**Rochester Mob Wars**" was a term used to describe a bloody gang battle that raged in the streets of Rochester, New York and its outlying suburbs during the late 1970's and early 1980's. The participants of this "war" were two opposing factions of the same organization, the Rochester Mafia. There were so many participants on both sides of this war that law enforcement had a hard time keeping track of who was on each side. Terms like the "A Team" and "B Team" were established to keep track of which side each participant was on. Sometimes it was not even clear to the mobsters themselves where everyone's loyalties lay.

The term "A Team" was used to identify the long established Rochester Mafia leaders, Samuel Russotti, Rene Piccarreto and Sammy Gingello, and those still loyal to them. The term "B Team" was used to identify the opposing faction of the Rochester Mafia headed by Thomas Didio and those who became loyal to Didio while the "A Team" mob leaders were in prison. Members of the "B Team" included Sonny Celestino, Rosario Chirico, Anthony Chirico, Frank Frassetto and others.

In 1976, the "Boss," "Underboss," both "Capos" and several "Soldiers" of the Rochester Mafia were convicted of murder, conspiracy and racketeering for the 1973 killing of Vincent "Jimmy The Hammer" Massaro and other gang related crimes. They were all sentenced to lengthy prison terms.

In their absence, the "Boss" of the Rochester Mafia, Samuel "Red" Russotti, left Thomas Didio temporarily in charge. Didio was the cousin of Russotti's "Capo," Thomas Marotta, who also was in jail for the Massaro murder. Since Thomas Didio was considered to be somewhat "slow witted," Russotti felt that he would have no problem controlling Didio from his prison cell, but once Thomas Didio had been in power for a while, he became less and less receptive to taking orders from Russotti.

Because of Didio's contempt for the established hierarchy of the mob, a decision was made to remove him from the position of "Acting Boss" after he had been in that position for about nine months. A formal meeting was called at the Blue Gardenia for that purpose. Attending that meeting for the "B Team" were Thomas Didio, Angelo Vaccaro and Dominic "Sonny" Celestino.

# Introduction

When they arrived, they were confronted by "A Team" loyalists who greatly outnumbered them, including John Fiorino, Joseph Rossi, Thomas Taylor, Joseph LoDolce and others.

It was at this meeting, that Thomas Didio was informed that his temporary promotion to "Acting Boss" of the Rochester Mafia had been rescinded. Didio's response was probably not that well thought out. He informed the "A Team" representatives that he had no intention of stepping down as "Boss." He was then severely beaten and thrown out of the restaurant along with Vaccaro and Celestino. At one point during the confrontation, Joseph LoDolce, mob "Soldier," placed a loaded gun in the mouth of Angelo Vaccaro, according to witness Anthony Oliveri. Immediately following that incident, the entire "B Team" went into hiding.

If one specific event could have been identified as being the actual start of the Mob Wars, it would have been that meeting, with Didio's stated refusal to relinquish control and the severe beating that followed that decision.

Had Thomas Didio conformed and complied with the orders given to him by his superiors and relinquished control of the Mafia as he was told, things would have been much different. It would have been back to business for the Rochester Mob and there would be half a dozen or so more people still alive. They all could have continued to gamble and make money together like they had already been doing for decades. Instead, the vast majority of the established Mafia in Rochester ended up dead, in jail or in the Federal Witness Protection Program.

Coincidentally, within months of that meeting, all the mobsters in prison for the murder of Vincent "Jimmy The Hammer" Massaro were released from prison when it was discovered that police had fabricated the evidence that was used to convict them at their murder trials.

What followed next was nothing short of a "war" that raged in the streets of Rochester and its suburbs like Greece and Irondequoit where innocent bystanders lived and worked. Over the next several years, murders, bombings and shootings became so frequent in the fight for control of Rochester's rackets, that the gang war was dubbed by police and the media alike as the "**Rochester Mob Wars**."

# *Chapter 1*
# The Rochester
# Mob War Begins

## Didio Refuses To Step Down and The "B Team" Gets A Beating

In **September 1977**, after refusing to relinquish control of the Rochester Mafia when ordered to do so, "B Team" members Thomas Didio, Angelo Vaccaro and Dominic "Sonny" Celestino were confronted by a larger contingent of "A Team" loyalists including John Fiorno, Joseph Rossi, Thomas Taylor, and others not identified, at the Blue Gardenia Restaurant, in Irondequoit, N,Y.

At the direction of Sammy Gingello and the other imprisoned mob bosses, Didio and his followers were advised that they were "all done;" Didio's temporary promotion to "Acting Boss" of the Rochester Mafia had just been rescinded. An altercation then occurred. Didio, Vaccaro, and Celestino were severely beaten and ejected from the restaurant by the "A Team" faction. Didio and his group, who were greatly outnumbered, then went into hiding.

Almost coincidental to that incident were indications that the entire mob leadership including Samuel Russotti, Rene Piccarreto, Sammy Gingello, Thomas Marotta, and Richard Marino might be released from jail due to discrepancies in witness testimony at their murder trial. **(6)**

## The "B Team" Holds Daily Meetings

It was once stated that the war could have ended here before it began. If the "B Team" had taken its "licking" for their disobedience and had fallen back into line, it is possible that the coming bloodbath could have been avoided completely. Unfortunately the "B Team" had no intention of falling back into line. Instead, they went on the offensive.

From **October 1977** through **January 1978**, the "B Team" had held almost daily clandestine meetings at the

Vineyard Restaurant, Pittsford, N.Y. Those meetings were attended by Thomas Didio, Angelo Vaccaro, Rosario "Ross" Chirico, Dominic "Sonny" Celestino, " William Barton, and a small number of other participants who remain unidentified.

One of the unidentified participants, described as a small, elderly man, virtually controlled the conduct of the meetings. When he raised his hand, everyone would stop speaking, and he would point or nod to the participants when he wanted them to voice their ideas or opinions.

## The "B Team" Attempts To Blow Up Joseph "The Hop" Rossi.

After months of strategy meetings, the "B Team" developed a plan. Their plan included the use of explosive devices as a means of execution. In **December of 1977** Dominic "Sonny" Celestino, William Barton, Angelo Vaccaro, and Thomas Didio attempted to place a remote control dynamite pipe bomb under the vehicle owned by "A Team" member Joseph "The Hop" Rossi.

While attempting to place the device, they were discovered by "A Team" members, and a running gun battle erupted, including a high speed car chase through the streets of Rochester. The explosive device fell off Rossi's vehicle and was later discovered and dismantled by a 12- year-old boy who subsequently reported finding the device to the police.

In late **December 1977** "B Team" member Rodney Starkweather approached Earl Merritt, a member of the Hell's Angels motorcycle club, and told Merritt that he was attempting to purchase quantities of explosives. Shortly thereafter, Merritt took Starkweather to the residence. (7)

Chronology of the mob war

Here is a list of events police have linked to the mob war:

**Dec. 27** — An unexploded pipe bomb found near the Social Club of Monroe, a gambling parlor on Clifford Avenue.

**Jan 2.** — Molotov cocktail thrown through window of Yahambas Social Club, a gambling parlor on Franklin Street.

**March 2** — Pipe bomb explodes in parking lot of the Blue Gardenia restaurant on Empire Boulevard, where Salvatore "Sammy G" Gingello was having lunch.

**April 23** — Gingello killed when a remote-control dynamite bomb explodes underneath his car in a downtown Rochester parking lot.

**May 19** — Social Club of Monroe pipe-bombed, minor damage.

**May 22** — Dynamite bomb closes 1445 Club, a gambling parlor on University Avenue.

**May 24** — Rosario Chirico, identified by police as a leader of the "B" Team, is wounded in the arm by a sniper.

**June 2** — Discount Furniture Store, Goodman Plaza, pipe-bombed.

**June 8** — Dynamite bomb closes Social Club of Monroe.

**June 28** — Cache of explosives found in Greece, at Mt. Read Boulevard and Maiden Lane. Rodney Starkweather and Anthony Chirico, son of Rosario Chirico, arrested on charges of illegally storing the explosives.

**June 29** — Federal prosecutor identifies Starkweather in court as a suspect in Gingello's slaying.

**July 1** — Police raid a Smith Street house that Starkweather had listed as his home address.

**June 6** — Didio found dead in a Victor motel.

**July 6** — Angelo Vaccaro, identified as a "B" Team leader, arrested and charged with criminal possession of loaded guns.

**The news paper article above was taken from the July 7, 1978 edition of the Rochester, New York Democrat and Chronicle.**

# The "B Team" Starts Bombing the Gambling Parlors

**On December 27, 1977,** an unexploded pipe bomb was found near the Social Club of Monroe, a gambling parlor on Clifford Avenue in Rochester. The picture below shows exactly where the bomb was found.

The picture below that shows the location of other known Mob-controlled gambling spots in the city of Rochester in 1977.

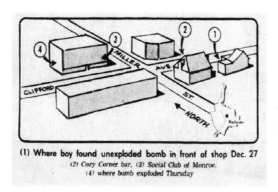

**(1) Where boy found unexploded bomb in front of shop Dec. 27**
*(2) Cozy Corner bar, (3) Social Club of Monroe,*
*(4) where bomb exploded Thursday*

**The Social Club of Monroe is Located at 1262-1266 Monroe Avenue**

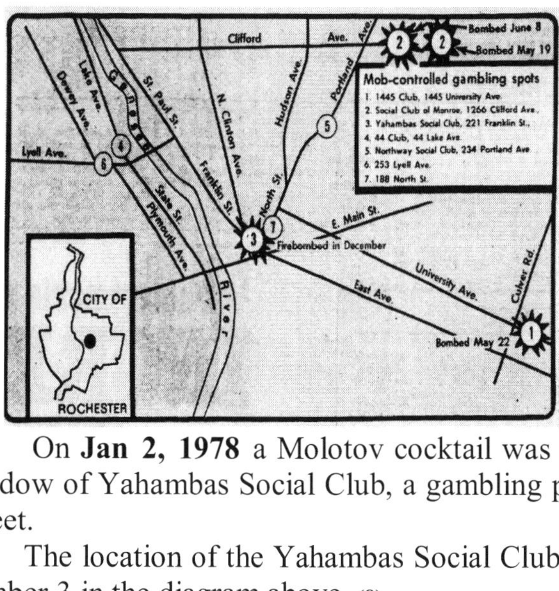


**Known mob controlled gambling spots in Rochester in 1977**

On **Jan 2, 1978** a Molotov cocktail was thrown through a window of Yahambas Social Club, a gambling parlor on Franklin Street.

The location of the Yahambas Social Club is marked by the number 3 in the diagram above. **(8)**

**Loren Picaretto,** son of mob "Consigliore" Rene Picaretto.

## "A Team" Members Loren Piccarreto and Leonard Stebbans Are Ambushed

Shortly after the bombing incident in early **January 1978**, "B Team" members Dominic "Sonny" Celestino, William Barton, and Rodney Starkweather ambushed a vehicle containing "A Team" members Leonard Stebbins, Loren Piccarreto (son of Rene Piccarreto) and others unidentified. The vehicle was riddled by shotgun blasts and handgun fire but, miraculously, all occupants escaped without injury.

## Rochester Mobsters are Released From Jail When Their Convictions Are Overturned

On **January 26, 1978**, the murder convictions of the imprisoned "A Team" mobsters were reversed due to irregularities in trial testimony. The evidence that led to the convictions of the leaders of the Rochester Mafia, was fabricated by the police. The detectives had lied.

Within days, on **January 31, 1978**, Samuel Russotti, Rene Piccarreto, Salvatore Gingello, Thomas Marotta, and Richard Marino were released from prison and returned to Rochester, N.Y., where they once again assumed leadership of an organization that was seriously divided and now being subjected to outside influences.

Democrat and Chronicle

Regional

5 convicted in murder freed; 2nd detective faces charges

Convictions dismissed for false testimony

Malsegna pays bail

Chavez ends boycott

**Democrat and Chronicle Feb. 1, 1978**

# *Chapter 2*
# The Murder of Sammy Gingello

## "B Team" Meets With Stanley Valenti At His Home And Prepares for Frank Valenti's Prison Release

In late **February 1978**, "B Team" members Thomas Didio, Angelo Vaccaro, Dominic "Sonny" Celestino, William Barton, Frank Frassetto, and Rodney Starkweather met with Stanley Valenti at his residence in Victor, N.Y.

The discussion centered around the fact that there would be no active involvement of other organized crime families in the current power struggle between the "A Team" and the "B Team," and if the "B Team" emerged victorious, they would have the support of organized crime interests in Pittsburgh, Pa.

Also, Rodney Starkweather was directed by the other "B Team" members to secure more explosives. Starkweather traveled to Auburn, N.Y., and purchased another quantity of blasting caps and KinePak stick from Timothy Ryan. Ryan, a member of the Hackers motorcycle club, acquired the Kinepak stick and blasting caps along with a Hell's Angels club member in Georgia and Tennessee, and brought them back to New York State.

KinePak stick was a binary explosive consisting of a two-part mix. The two parts do not constitute an explosive material until mixed together. Kinepak stick is not a regulated substance under the Federal Explosives Control Act of 1970, Public Law 91-452.

After the release of the "A Team" hierarchy from prison, almost daily meetings were conducted by "B Team" members in Rochester, N.Y. Present at these meetings were "B Team" members Thomas Didio, Angelo Vaccaro, Dominic "Sonny" Celestino, Rosario "Ross" Chirico, William Barton, Frank Frassetto, and Rodney Starkweather. It was during these meetings that the decision was made to kill Salvatore "Sammy G" Gingello.

# The Plot to Murder Sammy Gingello

Gingello was selected for elimination for many reasons, 1) Gingello was at one time a favorite protege of Frank Valenti, and his position within the organization was enhanced by that relationship. Valenti's influence was responsible for Gingello's quick rise through the ranks to the position of "Capo." Frank Valenti was greatly upset when he became aware that Gingello was one of the individuals responsible for the confrontation which forced him into retirement.

2) Thomas Didio and Stanley Valenti were aware that although relatively new as an "Underboss," Gingello had successfully succeeded in uniting various factions of the organization. As a result of his personality and generosity to his underlings, Gingello commanded the loyalty of his subordinates. The untimely death of Gingello would create dissension within the "A Team" ranks.

3) Gingello was a highly visible and readily identified member of organized crime in Rochester, N.Y. He reveled in playing the role of the "top mobster" in Rochester and surrounded himself with attractive women and bodyguards. Gingello spent lavishly and was chauffered about in expensive cars, unconcerned that he was identified publicly as an upper echelon organized crime member. It was the consensus of opinion among the "B Team" that killing Gingello would most impress upon the gamblers and operators of illicit enterprises the courage and determination of the "B Team" faction to retain control of the organization. (9)

4) Individually, many of the "B Team" members had personal motives for seeking the death of Salvatore "Sammy G" Gingello. Rosario "Ross" Chirico was the brother of Dominic Chirico, who was killed at the direction of Gingello in 1972. Anthony Chirico, the son of Rosario Chirico, was the nephew of Dominic Chirico. Angelo Vaccaro sponsored both Dominic and Rosario Chirico upon their entry into the organization and had strong personal ties to both men. At the direction of Gingello, Dominic "Sonny" Celestino had been beaten and ejected from the mob by Gingello in 1974, and was not allowed back into the organization until Thomas Didio assumed control.

The "B Team" was unable to get sufficiently close to Gingello to enable them to effect his murder by conventional means (that is, gun or knife). Due to that problem, it was determined that explosives would have to be utilized. By constructing a device that could be remotely detonated, the “B Team” members could remain far enough away to go undetected by Gingello or his bodyguards.

Among schemes proposed was a plan whereby a “B Team” member would secrete a remote control explosive device in a child’s toy, such as a "big wheel," and leave it on the walkway of Gingello's apartment. Upon seeing Gingello leave the premises and approach the toy the device would be remotely detonated. This plan was abandoned for fear that a child might walk off with the toy and “B Team” would lose the bomb.

The concern for safety of the child was not paramount, but the loss of the device was inexcusable. Due to the expense of manufacturing the remote control device (the component electronic equipment cost in excess of $350), the technical expertise required to modify the transmitter and receiver, and the scarcity of explosives, the “B Team” could not afford to lose any remote controlled explosive devices.

Another plan which was formulated involved lowering a remotely controlled device down the chimney of Gingello’s apartment, and then detonating it when Gingello was present. At the last moment, it was discovered that Gingello’s apartment did not have a chimney into which a device could be lowered.

Also considered was filling a traffic cone with explosives and remotely detonating it when Gingello's vehicle approached. This plan was apparently abandoned because the possibility existed of damaging the car but not killing Gingello.

## “B Team” Fails To Kill Sammy Gingello

On or about **February 24, 1978**, “B Team” members Didio, Vaccaro, Celestino, Barton, and Frassetto devised and attempted to carry out a plan to kill Sammy Gingello inside the Blue Gardenia restaurant. Frank Frassetto (who was not at that time identified as a “B Team” member) entered the restaurant carrying a remotely controlled pipe bomb inside an attache case. After determining that Gingello was present, Frassetto was to go to the pay phone inside the restaurant and place a call to William “Billy” Barton and advise him that Gingello was present. Frassetto would then leave the attaché case by the telephone and proceed to the bar area of the restaurant. Barton would then place a call to Celestino, Didio and Vaccaro, who were at a pay phone near the shopping plaza and could observe the front of the Blue Gardenia restaurant.

Barton would advise the other “B Team” members that Gingello was in the restaurant and they in turn would prepare to remotely detonate the explosives from the parking lot. Barton was then to call the pay phone at the Blue Gardenia restaurant and ask for Gingello. Frassetto, upon observing Gingello approach the telephone, would then leave the premises as a signal for his cohorts to detonate the device which was left by the phone booth in the attache case.

If this plan had been successful, numerous patrons and employees of the restaurant would have been killed or severely injured upon the detonation of the device. The plan, however, failed to work because when Frassetto attempted to telephone Barton, he consistently got a busy signal. It was later determined that this was due to Barton having an extended conversation on the telephone with his girlfriend.

During the months of February and April of 1978, five unsuccessful attempts to kill Gingello by means of explosives were made. Salvatore "Sammy G" Gingello was known to frequent the Blue Gardenia restaurant in Irondequoit, N.Y., which was located in a busy suburban shopping center. “B Team” members hid remotely controlled devices in snowbanks surrounding the restaurant, with the intention of detonating the bombs as Gingello approached the premises. On two occasions Gingello failed to show up, and on the other occasion the devices failed to detonate. **(10)**

## Rochester Mobster John Fiorino Is Appointed to Trustee of Local #398

In **February 1978**, reputed Rochester mobster, John Fiorino, "A Team", was appointed to the position of Trustee of Teamsters Local #398. (17)

## Bomb Explodes But "B Team" Fails Again To Kill Gingello

On **March 2, 1978**, the "B Team", returning to less elaborate plans, planted a remotely controlled device in a snowbank in front of the Blue Gardenia restaurant. Frank Frassetto was in the parking lot of the shopping center, with Dominic "Sonny" Celestino secreted in the trunk of the vehicle with the remote radio signaling device required to detonate the explosives. A hole had been drilled in the trunk of Frassetto's car so that the antenna for the radio device could be extended outside the vehicle to insure detonation of the device.

Salvatore "Sammy G" Gingello arrived at the Blue Gardenia in a vehicle operated by John Fiorino. Stepping in front of the restaurant, Gingello got out and approached the front door, at which time Celestino detonated the explosive device. Due to the manner in which the device was placed, Gingello was blown into the air but miraculously escaped serious injury. Shrapnel from the device caused damage to the front of the restaurant and adjoining buildings.

In late **March 1978**, "B Team" members Didio, Vaccaro, Celestino, Frassetto, and Starkweather met with Stanley Valenti at his residence in Rochester, N.Y. Stanley Valenti advised them that his brother, Frank Valenti, would be released from jail soon, and that "Rochester should be ready when Frank gets out." (11)

## "B Team" Votes To Murder "Billy" Barton

Also discussed at one of the "B Team" meetings was the group's displeasure with co-conspirator William Barton, who had been excluded from the meeting. The "B Team" members were upset about Barton's absence from recent meetings, and his apparent propensity to foul up their attempts to kill Gingello. Additionally, it was believed that Barton had contacted Gingello and attempted to ingratiate himself with him. The "B Team" members feared that Barton would identify Frank Frassetto as a "B Team" member, and divulge the participation of Stanley Valenti in the conspiracy. A vote was taken, and it was recommended that William Barton be killed. This task was assigned to Rodney Starkweather. During **March** and the early part of **April 1978**, "B Team" members Didio, Celestino, Vaccaro, and Frasstto made trips to West Virginia for the purpose of acquiring explosives.

## Mafia Informants

On Sunday, **March 12, 1978**, a series of newspaper articles appeared in Rochester, New York's morning newspaper about Rochester Mafia informants being placed into the Federal Witness Protection Program. By March of 1978, eight witnesses and their families had already entered into the Federal Witness Protection Program, not counting Al DeCanzio. Before the mob wars were over, more than 14 people and their families would enter into the program, all of them testifying as to the inner workings of the Rochester Mafia. **(12)**

Without the Federal Witness Protection Program, there would be no informants. ***The Justice Department says it lost 25 informants to the mob between 1961 and 1965. Some of the dead witnesses had dead canaries in their mouths.*** The idea of protecting witnesses through identity changes came under Atty. Gen. Robert F. Kennedy in 1961 and grew gradually under the Johnson and Nixon administrations. The program took shape as the Justice Department formed its strike force against organized crime. The first strike force was sent to Buffalo in 1967.

Pasquale "Paddy" Calabrese of Buffalo was the first man selected by the strike force for a change of identity. Calabrese, an armed robber, was convicted of robbing the treasurer's office in Buffalo's City Hall. He threatened to talk if the mob didn't finance his appeal. The mob countered by forcing his pregnant wife to pose naked in bed with his best friend, Frank Miele. (13)

Other Informers' new identities have been cracked through only a casual check of public records. One of them was among the eight protected witnesses from the Rochester area. The eight from the Rochester area were Angelo and Charles Monachino, John Galvin, William "Zeke" Zimmerman, Joseph "Spike" Lanovara, Joseph Zito, Jean Lupo and Marshall Snow.

All but Snow and Mrs. Lupo were arrested and turned informants against the mob. Snow and Mrs. Lupo are under protection soley because they testified against mobsters. The Monachinos, Zimmerman and Lanovara, were key informants in jailing six Mafia members for murder.

## “B Team” Murders “Sammy G” Gingello

In the early morning hours of **April 23, 1978,** “B Team” members Thomas Didio, Angelo Vaccaro, Dominic "Sonny" Celestino and Frank Frassetto placed a remote control device under Salvatore "Sammy G" Gingello's vehicle, which was parked in a lot in front of Ben's Cafe Society, at Main and Stillson Streets in Rochester, N.Y.

Blast kills Sammy Gingello

2 survive car bomb

Night crowd flocks to scene of bombing

Moro party hints it may negotiate

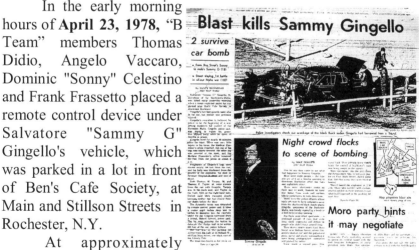

**April 23, 1978**
**Democrat & Chronicle**

At approximately 2:30 a.m., Gingello and his two “A Team” bodyguards, Thomas Taylor and Thomas Torpey, returned to the vehicle. As Gingello and his associates entered the vehicle, the device was remotely detonated.

Democrat and Chronicle

Sammy Gingello's car after bombing in April 1978 that killed him and slightly injured Thomas Taylor and Thomas Torpey

**Democrat & Chronicle April 23, 1978**

The force of the explosion amputated Gingello's right leg and nearly severed his left leg at the thigh. Within 20 minutes, Gingello died at Genesee Hospital as a result of the severe injuries suffered in the explosion. Thomas Taylor and Thomas Torpey suffered less extensive injuries. The following day Dominic "Sonny" Celestino was reputed to have stated that if he had placed the bomb properly, he would have "gotten all three of them bastards." **(14)**

# *Chapter 3*
# Peace Agreement Fails, The War Continues

## Peace Agreement Fails and Bombings Continue

Within days after the death of Salvatore "Sammy G" Gingello, "B Team" member Dominic "Sonny" Celestino met with "A Team" representatives at Lloyd's Restaurant in Rochester, N.Y., in an attempt to negotiate a settlement between the two opposing factions. It was suggested that the city be divided in half and split up between the two factions, with the river or Main Street being the dividing line. The "A Team" found this acceptable but the "B Team" did not. Primarily opposed to this idea was Sonny Celestino. **(52)**

Apparently unhappy with the outcome of the meeting, Celestino and the other "B Team" members decided to embark on a bombing campaign directed at gambling establishments operated by the "A Team." It was believed that if the "A Team" gambling establishments could be closed down, the resulting loss in revenue would require the "A Team" to settle their differences with the "B Team" .

To further terrorize the "A Team", Rodney Starkweather offered to furnish a Mr. Ryan with a dirt bike, bulletproof vest, and hand grenades, if Ryan would ride the motorcycle on the sidewalk and throw the grenades through the window of T. & T. Talent, 253 Lyell Avenue. T. & T. Talent was a theatrical booking agency operated by "A Team" members Marvin Pizzo and Thomas Torpey. Starkweather said he would pay Ryan $1,000, but Ryan refused the offer.

On or about **May 11, 1978**, "B Team" member Anthony Chirico broke into an explosives magazine at Genesee Explosives, Rochester, N.Y., and stole a quantity of explosives. Those explosives were delivered to Dominic "Sonny" Celestino and Frank Frassetto, at the Frassetto residence, Greece, N.Y. **(15)**

# "A Team" Gambling Parlor (Social Club of Monroe) Is Bombed "Mob War Revives With a Bang"

On **May 19, 1978**, "B Team" members Celestino, Starkweather and Bates threw a pipe bomb through the window of a known "A Team" gambling establishment called The Social Club Of Monroe located at 1264-1266 Clifford Avenue, Rochester, N.Y.

The club, which was owned and operated by Rochester Mafia member Donnie Paone (A Team), was full of patrons when the pipe bomb detonated. Fortunately, there were no reported injuries. **(16)**

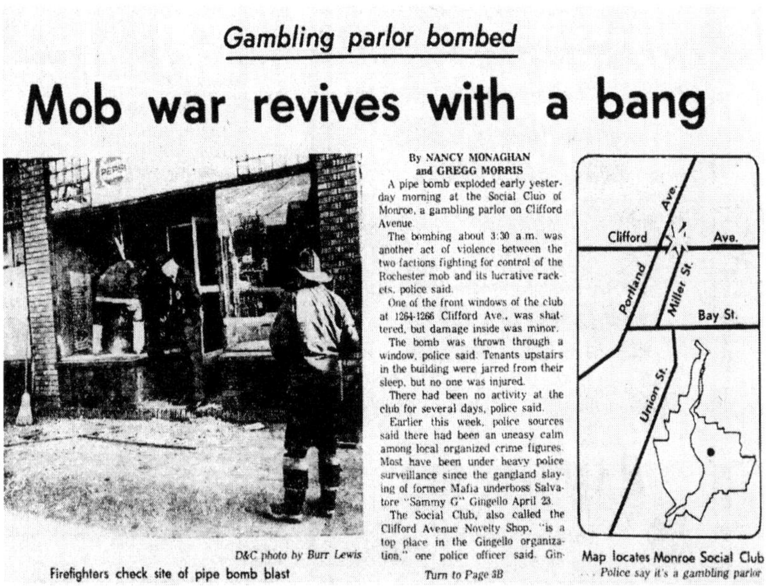

*Gambling parlor bombed*

## Mob war revives with a bang

By NANCY MONAGHAN and GREGG MORRIS

A pipe bomb exploded early yesterday morning at the Social Cluo of Monroe, a gambling parlor on Clifford Avenue.

The bombing about 3:30 a.m. was another act of violence between the two factions fighting for control of the Rochester mob and its lucrative rackets, police said.

One of the front windows of the club at 1264-1266 Clifford Ave., was shattered, but damage inside was minor.

The bomb was thrown through a window, police said. Tenants upstairs in the building were jarred from their sleep, but no one was injured.

There had been no activity at the club for several days, police said.

Earlier this week, police sources said there had been an uneasy calm among local organized crime figures. Most have been under heavy police surveillance since the gangland slaying of former Mafia underboss Salvatore "Sammy G" Gingello April 23.

The Social Club, also called the Clifford Avenue Novelty Shop, "is a top place in the Gingello organization," one police officer said. Gin-

Turn to Page 3B



D&C photo by Burr Lewis
Firefighters check site of pipe bomb blast

Map locates Monroe Social Club
. . . Police say it's a gambling parlor

**The Social Club Of Monroe located at 1264-1266 Clifford Avenue, Rochester, N.Y. was bombed May 19, 1978**

# The 1445 Club Is Bombed

On the evening of **May 21, 1978**, "B Team" members Celestino, Frassetto and Starkweather placed a time bomb near the entrance of an "A Team" gambling establishment located at 1455 University Avenue Rochester, N.Y. This device detonated at about 5:30 a.m. on **May 22, 1978**, while the club was in operation and full of patrons. No personal injuries were reported, but extensive damage was done to the exterior and interior of the building.

In May 1978, a bomb went off in front of door to 1455 Club on University Avenue

**The picture above was in the July 7, 1978 edition of the Rochester, New York Democrat and Chronicle. It shows the damage done by a bomb at the 1445 Club, a gambling parlor on University Avenue in Rochester. Below, police inspect the scene of the dynamite bombing.**

Police inspect scene of dynamite bombing at 1455 Club, 1455 University Ave.

Bomb ripped apart fence, heavily damaging front entrance

**Close up photo of the front entrance to the 1445 Club gambling parlor.**

# Latest mob blast rocks local club

*By a D&C Staff Writer*

Sixteen men who had just placed their blackjack bets survived a bomb-blast early yesterday morning at a University Avenue gambling parlor.

Fourteen of the players were thrown from their seats as shattered glass rushed past them on the floor, one of the players said.

Within minutes the men were led in groups of four to waiting patrol cars as city police took them downtown for questioning. All seemed stunned. None was injured.

The 5:50 a.m. blast at 1455 University Avenue was the third bombing since the gangland war for control of Rochester's lucrative gambling and numbers rackets escalated a month ago.

"It was the talk that it (another bombing) was going to happen," one of the 1455 Club's regular patrons said yesterday afternoon.

Debris from the dynamite bomb — hunks of insulation, twisted pieces of ductwork from the heating system, glass and splintered wood — was strewn 30 yards across University Avenue.

Police officers painstakingly picked up each piece of that debris, as they had last Friday and April 23. "We've got so much of this stuff we've had to open a second property office," Chief of Police Thomas Hastings said.

Passersby shook their heads in disbelief. "Why don't the police just let them blow each other up," said one man who lives two blocks from the bombed carriage-house. He sipped a coke. "They can't do anything anyway."

On April 23 the first major mob-related bombing rocked downtown Rochester. Eight sticks of dynamite placed under a black Buick and detonated by remote control killed Salvatore "Sammy G" Gingello, the mob's flamboyant underboss.

It was obvious then, police said, that an insurgent group was prepared to take over.

Then early last Friday morning a pipe-bomb was tossed through the front window of the Social Club of Monroe, also called the Clifford Avenue Novelty Shop, at 1264 Clifford Avenue.

"Things are going to get hot," a police detective said on Friday.

Gingello loyalists operate the Clif-

Turn to Page 3A

## Blasts don't involve him, Russotti says

*By A D&C Staff Writer*

Samuel "Red" Russotti spent part of yesterday cleaning up.

Russotti wasn't cleaning up after a bomb blast. In fact, Russotti said he didn't known anything about the bomb blasts.

Instead, Russotti, the reputed chieftain of local organized crime, spent yesterday washing his cars, sweeping his driveway, and clipping the grass around his neat beige brick and white clapboard home at 52 Creekside Drive, Irondequoit.

The alleged crime boss just brushed off reports that recent bombings of two city gambling clubs were warnings to Russotti.

"Tell them I don't know what the hell they are talking about," Russotti said yesterday while standing in his driveway.

Although by all outward appearances Russotti, 62, is just another retired Irondequoit homeowner, police

Turn to Page 3A

**" Sixteen men who had just placed their blackjack bets survived a bomb blast at a University Avenue gambling parlor. Fourteen of the players were thrown from their seats as shattered glass rush passed them on the floor," one of the players said.** (18)

Any of 7 could be next target

**May 23, 1978**
**Democrat and Chronicle**

Police believe that the dynamite bomb was thrown from a passing car, over a 6 foot fence, to the front door of the club. The explosion blew a two foot crater in the ground and ripped out a four foot section of fence that shielded the door from the street.

Both of the heavy steel doors at the entrance were blown into the building, police said. (19)

The article on the right appeared in the May 23, 1978 edition of the Democrat and Chronicle, the day after the bombing that closed the 1445 Club on University Avenue.

The article was a warning in a sense that any of the 7 known mafia gambling establishments in the city of Rochester, New York could be the next victim of the ongoing mob war there. **(20)**

# “B Team” Member Rosario Chirico Is Shot

**Rosario Chirico**

On **May 25, 1978**, “B Team” member Rosario "Ross" Chirico was fired upon by a sniper with a high-powered rifle while driving his pick up truck near his residence, along Kuhn Road towards Long Pond Road in Greece, N.Y.

Chirico was hit in the forearm and only superficially wounded. The sniper escaped through a wooded area on a motorcycle. (21)

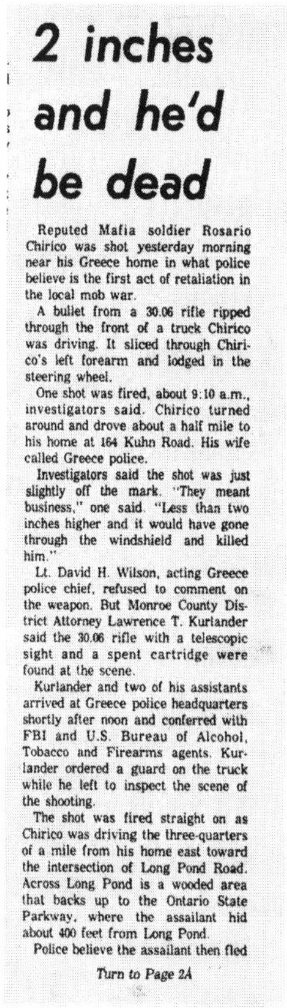

## 2 inches and he'd be dead

Reputed Mafia soldier Rosario Chirico was shot yesterday morning near his Greece home in what police believe is the first act of retaliation in the local mob war.

A bullet from a 30.06 rifle ripped through the front of a truck Chirico was driving. It sliced through Chirico's left forearm and lodged in the steering wheel.

One shot was fired, about 9:10 a.m., investigators said. Chirico turned around and drove about a half mile to his home at 164 Kuhn Road. His wife called Greece police.

Investigators said the shot was just slightly off the mark. "They meant business," one said. "Less than two inches higher and it would have gone through the windshield and killed him."

Lt. David H. Wilson, acting Greece police chief, refused to comment on the weapon. But Monroe County District Attorney Lawrence T. Kurlander said the 30.06 rifle with a telescopic sight and a spent cartridge were found at the scene.

Kurlander and two of his assistants arrived at Greece police headquarters shortly after noon and conferred with FBI and U.S. Bureau of Alcohol, Tobacco and Firearms agents. Kurlander ordered a guard on the truck while he left to inspect the scene of the shooting.

The shot was fired straight on as Chirico was driving the three-quarters of a mile from his home east toward the intersection of Long Pond Road. Across Long Pond is a wooded area that backs up to the Ontario State Parkway, where the assailant hid about 400 feet from Long Pond.

Police believe the assailant then fled

*Turn to Page 2A*

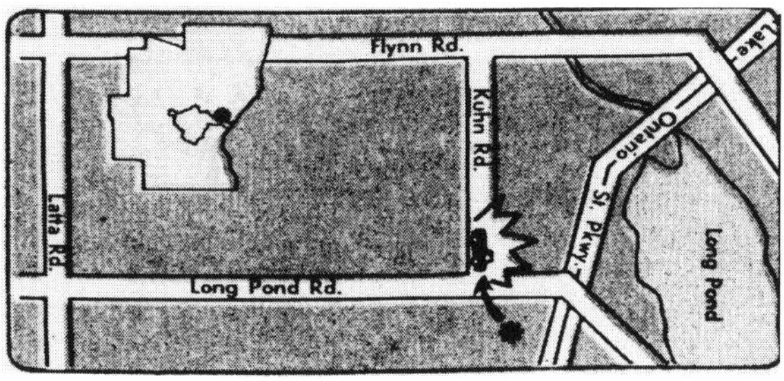


**Photo above shows the location of the shooting- May 26, 1978 Democrat and Chronicle**

On **June 2, 1978**, Discount Furniture Store in Goodman Plaza was pipe-bombed.

# Gambling Parlor Bombed Again

On **June 6, 1978**, “B Team” members Celestino, Frassetto Chirico and Starkweather decided to place another device in the “A Team” gambling establishment at 1264-1266 Clifford Avenue, Rochester, N.Y. After a few aborted attempts to break into the basement of the premises, entry was finally gained and a timed device was placed in the basement directly under the office area of the operator of the club. This device apparently malfunctioned, and failed to detonate.

On **June 7, 1978**, “B Team” members Celestino, Frassetto, and Starkweather returned to the premises and placed a second timed device next to the device they had placed the night before.

On **June 8, 1978**, at approximately 1:30 p.m., the second device detonated, causing an immediate sympathetic detonation of the original device. The blast caused a volume of debris and shards of glass to fly into a busy intersection shortly before scores of schoolchildren were to be excused from a nearby grade school. Extensive damage was caused to the building, which contained commercial space on the street level and occupied apartments on the second floor. The structural damage done to the building was so severe that the building was immediately condemned. A number of occupants in the gambling establishment were injured.

Gambling parlor bombed again

D&C photo by Joe Watson
Officer M.J. Sands in front of bombed social club.

• Narrowing choices (1B)

By GREGG MORRIS
D&C Staff Writer

A Clifford Avenue gambling parlor was heavily damaged by a dynamite explosion yesterday. It was the second bombing of the building within a month.

Police said the explosion burst through floors of the Social Club of Monroe, 1262-1266 Clifford Ave. It shattered large plate glass windows and weakened the building.

Police said it was the seventh organized crime bomb incident in five months.

Three persons who were in the gambling parlor when the dynamite exploded about 1:31 p.m. weren't injured.

Police said the bomb ruptured gas lines in the basement. Police, using dogs trained to find explosives, did not enter the building until the gas was cut off by a crew from Rochester Gas and Electric Corp.

Major Anthony Fantigrossi, chief of detectives, said dynamite was planted in an I-beam in the building's basement. It was placed just left of the center of the building, he said.

He said the building would be closed until its structure has been checked. Police said the front of the building could collapse.

Police said yesterday's explosion apparently is part of the continuing battle between warring factions of organized crime that are competing for lucrative profits from gambling, loan sharking and prostitution.

So far, one man, organized crime underboss Salvatore "Sammy G" Gingello, has been killed by a bomb and

Turn to Page 3A



**Democrat and Chronicle June 9, 1978 reported that The Social Club of Monroe located at 1262-1266 Clifford Avenue in Rochester was bombed again the day before June 8, 1978.**

# Bomb Threat Empties Bar

The Cozy Corner Bar, which was located across the street from the Social Club of Monroe, received a bomb threat emptying the bar. The bomb threat came just two days after the Social Club of Monroe, a known mafia gambling parlor was bombed. The threat appeared to be a hoax. **(22)**

## Mob war? Clubs' neighbors play it cool

By GARY GEREW

The underworld and police may be concerned about a mob war. But, if people who live and work near gambling parlors that have been or might be bombing threats are worried, they don't say so to strangers.

"Worried" Not me. As long as they don't bomb me, I don't care," said the operator of a furniture store a few yards away from the Northway Social Club at 234 Portland Ave., which police say is a mob-controlled gambling spot.

"None of our customers have said anything about it," he said. "There's not much talk about it in the neighborhood."

One man in the store pointed his head toward the club up the street, smiled and said. "Why don't you ask them what they think?"

While two of the three men in the store talked about the price of furniture, the other, who just smiled and shook his head when asked questions, made a phone call from the back room.

He returned with the results of a horse race. "Sorry we can't help you," one of the clerks said. "It's just been business as usual."

A hint of worry is found in peoples' reluctance to give their names.

"I don't even want to see what I told you in the paper, let alone my name," a man on Portland Avenue said. He said he wasn't worried about the bombings. They didn't involve him, he said.

Police cordoned off Clifford Avenue at Portland Avenue yesterday to investigate a bomb threat at a bar across from the Social Club of Monroe, 1226 Clifford Ave., the site of Thursday's bombing and one last month. The surrounding side streets were quiet and empty.

But at the corner of Clifford and Portland, a few people waited for something to happen and told newcomers what was going on.

"It's really close," a service station attendant said. "The police are look-

*Turn to Page 2B*

## Bomb threat empties bar

By GREGG MORRIS

The Cozy Corner Bar and Restaurant, across the street from a gambling parlor that was dynamited Thursday, was evacuated yesterday after a telephoned bomb threat. Police said it was a hoax.

Police said three persons were in the Cozy Corner at 1271 Clifford Ave. about 1 p.m. when a telephone caller told a waitress that a bomb would explode in the building at 1:25 p.m.

Police dogs and bomb squad members searched the building after the deadline passed, but no explosives were found, police said.

The bar is on a corner diagonal from the Social Club of Munroe at 1262-1266 Clifford Ave., which was heavily damaged Thursday by a dynamite explosion.

Police blocked off Clifford Avenue from Portland Avenue to Spiegel Park while they searched the bar.

Police said they have kept gambling parlors in the city under surveillance but add they can't do it 24 hours a day.

They said the Cozy Corner has no organized crime connections.

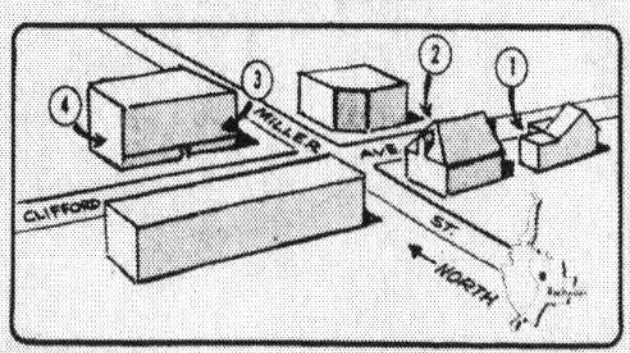


(1) Where boy found unexploded bomb in front of shop Dec. 27
*(2) Cozy Corner bar, (3) Social Club of Monroe, (4) where bomb exploded Thursday*

**Democrat and Chronicle June 10, 1978**

# Frassetto and Celestino are Arrested for Illegal Weapons

On **June 18, 1978**, local police officers conducting surveillances of "A Team" and "B Team" members in an attempt to curtail the violent bombings, observed "B Team" members Dominic "Sonny" Celestino and Frank Frassetto in a vehicle. A surveillance was initiated, but apparently the police vehicles were spotted. The vehicle operated by Frassetto attempted to elude the surveiling officers and a high-speed chase ensued.

A sawed-off M-1 carbine was recovered along the route of the chase, and it is assumed that the firearm was thrown out of the vehicle by Frassetto and Celestino. Celestino and Frassetto were then arrested. After the arrest, Frassetto telephoned Starkweather and asked him to go to Frassetto's house to pick up any "stuff" that was there.

Starkweather went to the house and was given a garbage bag by Betti Frassetto, which contained a New York State dealer's license plate and other items that were not identified at the trial. Apparently certain incriminating evidence had already been moved from Frassetto's house. Starkweather testified that sometime between **June 8, 1978** and **June 18, 1978**, Frassetto had told him that he had moved "the stuff" from his basement to the back of a Wise Potato Chip truck. The truck, which Frassetto had bought for use in surveillance of the Gingello faction, was generally kept either at Frassetto's house or at a certain Arco service station. On or prior to **June 28, 1978**, Frassetto made several abortive attempts to have the truck moved from the service station.

ATF agents located the Wise Potato Chip truck parked at a nearby service station. Suspecting that the vehicle was used to hide the illegal cache of "B Team" explosives and firearms, a 24-hour surveillance of the truck was immediately initiated.

On **June 28, 1978** two agents from the Bureau of Alcohol, Tobacco, and Firearms ("ATF") approached the attendant at the Arco station, Frederick Ledtke, to ask who owned the Wise Potato Chip truck. The attendant did not know, but put the agents in touch with the owner of the station. The owner later called Vincent Frassetto, Frank's brother, and asked how he could contact Betti Frassetto. Vincent Frassetto called his home, where Betti and Frank Frassetto had been staying, and relayed the station owner's telephone number to his wife, Margaret.

Margaret Frassetto testified that she gave the message to Betti and that in her presence, Betti made a telephone call, and asked who was asking about the truck. Margaret testified that Frank Frassetto asked Betti to go to the Arco station to see what was going on, and Betti said she would. At Frank's request Margaret got permission from her neighbor to use the neighbor's telephone, because Frank feared the Frassettos' phone was tapped. Betti made a call on the neighbor's telephone, then borrowed the neighbor's car, a green Dodge with a vinyl top.

Ledtke, the service station attendant, testified that between 11:30 a. m. and 12:30 p. m. on **June 28, 1978** he received a telephone call from a woman whom he did not know, asking who was making inquiries about the truck. When Ledtke responded that the inquirers were special agents, the woman said that she would be right down.

A short time later, a woman arrived at the station in a green car with a vinyl top. The woman asked Ledtke if he was the person she had spoken to, and asked again about the men who had questioned him about the truck. Ledtke asked the woman if she had the keys to the truck. According to Ledtke, the woman said she too was looking for the keys, and then kind of under her breath she said, "How am I going to move the truck?" The woman then left the station.

At the trial, Ledtke was unable to identify the woman in the green car as anyone in the courtroom. An ATF agent who had been watching the station on **June 28, 1978** testified that shortly after noon, a woman arrived in a green car, got out, and walked around the truck inspecting it.

Later that day, Frassetto finally got Starkweather and Anthony Chirico to go to the Arco station, remove a beer cooler from the truck, and throw it into the bushes behind the service station. Starkweather and Chirico were followed from the station by ATF agents and apprehended. The cooler was recovered by ATF agents; in it were found explosives, blasting caps, timing devices, and electrical boosters.

ATF agents arrested Rodney Starkweather and Anthony Chirico for violation of federal explosives and firearm laws. Under the front seat of the vehicle they occupied were fully loaded handguns. It should be noted that no further bombings occurred after the seizure of explosives and related items in the Wise Potato Chip truck.

As the investigation continued, Timothy Ryan was developed as a suspect in connection with furnishing explosives to Starkweather. Extensive attempts to locate Ryan failed, until it was learned that a $10,000 contract had been put out for his death. Ryan then cooperated with the authorities and was relocated into the Federal Witness Protection Program.

Information was also developed that Gary Haak may have been involved in the construction of the devices used in the bombings. Haak, a former business associate of Rosario "Ross" Chirico, was located and interviewed, but he denied any knowledge of the bombing incidents. Haak eventually admitted his involvement in the manufacture of destructive devices, firearms silencers and the alteration of firearms for "B Team" members. Haak was also relocated in the Federal Witness Protection Program. **(23)**

# Explosives Found on June 28, 1978

***"The chest contained a cache of explosives, detonators, blasting caps and timers, sufficient to blow off the map the four corners of Maiden Lane and Mount Read."***

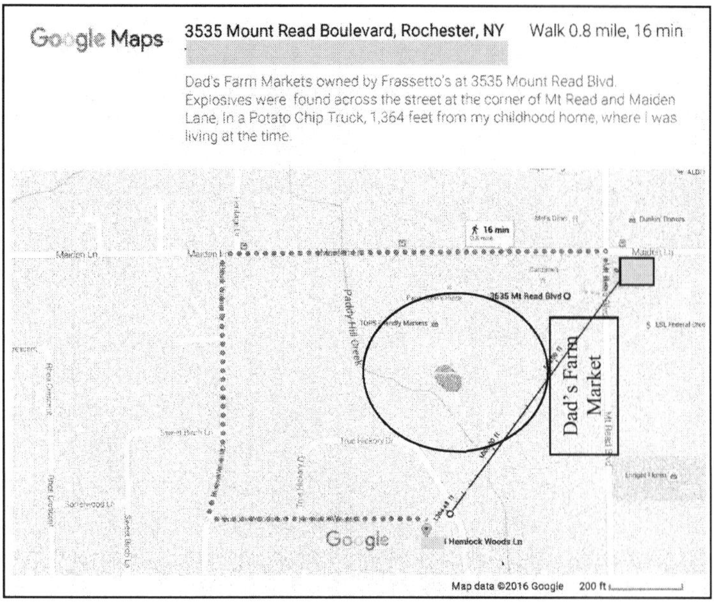


Bombings were a regular part of the "B" Team's strategy in the Rochester Mob War. Five unsuccessful attempts were made at blowing up Sammy Gingello before they were finally successful. Bombings of after hours gambling houses became "normal" as well.

Rochester Mafia member, Frank Frassetto (B Team), owned Dad's Farm Market on the corner of Mount Read and Maiden Lane in Greece, New York. Across the street from his Farm Market was a cache of all the "B" Team's unused explosives. The explosives were discovered on **June 28, 1978**. **(12)**

At the time that these explosives were found, I was 17 years old. The dot next to the word "Google" is my childhood home, where I was living at the time. The square is where the explosives were found. The distance between the two is 1364 feet. The circle is the woods and the farmers field where I played my entire childhood. I also drank in those woods as a teenager. There is a pretty good chance that I was in those woods on the exact day the explosives were found, I would have been there several times in the days and weeks preceding the discovery.

Besides the van full of explosives, there were four gas stations at that corner in 1978, one on each corner.

## 2 Men Arrested, Explosives Found

On **June 29, 1978** police arrested Rodney Starkweather and Anthony Chirico and charged them with possession and storage of explosives. The explosives were found behind a gas station in Greece the previous day.

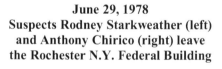

*D&C photo by Burr Lewis*

Agents follow as suspects leave federal building.
*. . . Starkweather is on left and Chirico on right.*

**June 29, 1978**
**Suspects Rodney Starkweather (left) and Anthony Chirico (right) leave the Rochester N.Y. Federal Building**

*D&C photo by Jim Shee*

Monroe County deputy carefully places object into a box on trailer.
*... police sealed off area and later would not allow pictures to be taken.*

**Monroe County Deputy carefully places object into box on trailer. Police sealed off the entire area and later would not allow pictures to be taken.**

# *Chapter 4*
# The War Takes a Turn, Didio Is Murdered

Thomas Didio

## "B Team" Leader Thomas Didio is Machine-gunned To Death

A former driver and bodyguard of Sammy Gingello's, Thomas Didio (B Team) was machine-gunned to death at the Exit 45 Motel on **July 6, 1978**, for refusing to relinquish control of the Rochester Mob after his former bosses were all released from jail.

Didio was appointed to "Acting Boss" of the Rochester Mafia Family in 1977 when Piccarreto, Russotti, Gingello, Marotta and Richard Marino were jailed for the Massaro murder.

Instead of stepping down upon the release from prison of his bosses, Didio forged an alliance with deposed and imprisoned Mafia don Frank Valenti. Didio tried in vain to keep control of the crime family, a futile attempt, which ultimately ended in his death.

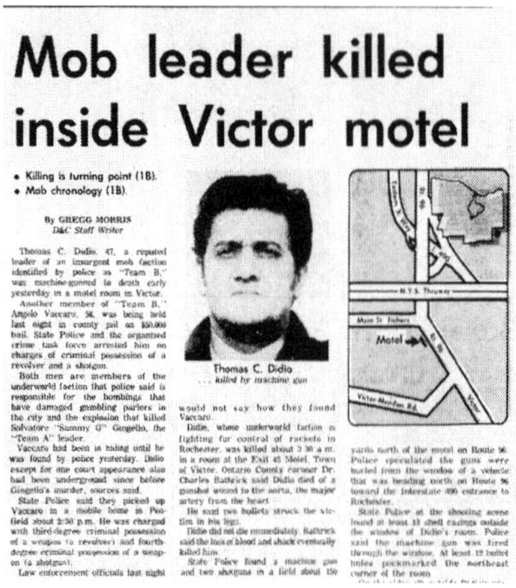

Mob leader killed inside Victor motel

- Killing is turning point (1B).
- Mob chronology (1B).

By GREGG MORRIS
*D&C Staff Writer*

Thomas C. Didio, 47, a reputed leader of an insurgent mob faction identified by police as "Team B," was machine-gunned to death early yesterday in a motel room in Victor.

Another member of "Team B," Angelo Vaccaro, 58, was being held last night in county jail on $50,000 bail. State Police and the organized crime task force arrested him on charges of criminal possession of a revolver and a shotgun.

Both men are members of the underworld faction that police said is responsible for the bombings that have damaged gambling parlors in the city and the explosion that killed Salvatore "Sammy G" Gingello, the "Team A" leader.

Vaccaro had been in hiding until he was found by police yesterday. Didio except for one court appearance also had been underground since before Gingello's murder, sources said.

State Police said they picked up Vaccaro in a mobile home in Penfield about 2:30 p.m. He was charged with third-degree criminal possession of a weapon (a revolver) and fourth-degree criminal possession of a weapon (a shotgun).

Law enforcement officials last night would not say how they found Vaccaro.

Didio, whose underworld faction is fighting for control of rackets in Rochester, was killed about 3:30 a.m. in a room at the Exit 45 Motel, Town of Victor. Ontario County coroner Dr. Charles Bathrick said Didio died of a gunshot wound to the aorta, the major artery from the heart.

He said two bullets struck the victim in his legs.

Didio did not die immediately. Bathrick said the loss of blood and shock eventually killed him.

State Police found a machine gun and two shotguns in a field about 150 yards north of the motel on Route 96. Police speculated the guns were hurled from the window of a vehicle that was heading north on Route 96 toward the Interstate 490 entrance to Rochester.

State Police at the shooting scene found at least 13 shell casings outside the window of Didio's room. Police said the machine gun was fired through the window. At least 12 bullet holes pockmarked the northeast corner of the room.

Thomas C. Didio
. . . killed by machine gun



Democrat and Chronicle
July 7, 1978

Several Teamsters Local #398 Officers and Stewards were indicted for murder and conspiracy as a result of this murder. A short distance from the scene of the homicide, a Thompson submachine gun and two sawed-off shotguns were recovered. The Thompson was identified as the firearm used to kill Didio, and it is assumed that the three weapons had been abandoned by the perpetrators of the homicide. Near Didio's body in the motel room was a loaded handgun which he apparently was attempting to reach when he was gunned down. (24)

# Didio's Death Weakens Mob Insurgents

The article on the right appeared the day after Tom Didio's death, on **July 7, 1978**. The article describes how Didio was the leader of the insurgent faction of the Rochester Mafia dubbed by police as the "B Team."

Didio was reported to have been not only the brains but the main muscle behind "B" Team's grab for control of the underworld, police sources say. **(25)**

The picture of the man covering his face is Angelo Vaccaro who was arraigned for criminal possession of loaded guns.

Local B

This Morning

City school talks at an impasse

Didio's death weakens mob's insurgents

BOCES staffers slow to pay center for car repair bills

Receiver requested for 'home'

Chronology of the mob war

75 demand settlement of contract

**Democrat and Chronicle**
**Rochester, N.Y.,**
**Friday, July 7, 1978**

## Anthony Chirico and Rodney Starkweather Indicted

Grand jury indicts 2 mob suspects

By JIM ROWLEY

A federal grand jury yesterday indicted Rodney J. Starkweather and Anthony M. Chirico on charges of illegally storing high-order explosives.

Starkweather and Chirico are charged in a three-count indictment with conspiracy to violate federal firearms law. They are accused of illegally possessing and storing unregistered explosives. Conviction of the charges carries a maximum 10-year sentence.

The two were arrested June 28 after a three-day surveillance of a panel truck outside a Greece service station by U.S. Bureau of Alcohol, Tobacco and Firearms agents.

Starkweather also was arrested yesterday by city vice squad detectives and charged with selling alcoholic beverages without a license.

They had a warrant that stemmed from a raid July 1 at an after-hours drinking place at 437 Smith St. Twenty-five persons were arrested for being inmates of an improper place.

Police said Starkweather told them the place was his home. He wasn't there when the others were arrested in the raid.

According to the federal charges, agents saw Chirico and Starkweather at an Arco gas station at the corner of Mt. Read Boulevard and Maiden Lane June 28.

Agents saw Starkweather open the rear door of a 1973 Mac truck parked near the gas station and toss a container on the grass, according to court papers. Agents found high-order explosives in the container.

The two were arrested by agents who followed them to a restaurant on Stone Road.

Yesterday's indictment was handed up an hour before the scheduled preliminary hearing in the case. U.S. Organized Crime Strike Force attorney Gregory A. Baldwin was granted a two-hour delay in the hearing to allow the grand jury to complete its work on the case.

An hour after the adjournment was granted by U.S. Magistrate Stephen Joy, the grand jury returned the indictments.

The preliminary hearing would have required Baldwin to present evidence of probable cause why the defendants should be charged with the crime. The issuing of the indictment provided Baldwin with a legal way around conducting the preliminary hearing.

*Turn to Page 6B*

Rodney J. Starkweather
*New liquor sale arrest*

Anthony M. Chirico
*Leaving Federal Building*

Anthony Chirico and Rodney Starkweather were indicted on **July 19, 1978** for "illegally storing high end explosives behind a gas station at the corner of Mt Read Blvd. and Maiden Lane." **(26)**

# "B Team" Member Rodney Starkweather Is Shot

On **July 30, 1978**, "B Team" member Rodney Starkweather, who was out on bail on the pending federal charges, was ambushed by two unidentified men wearing ski masks, who approached him on a dark street and shot him three times. Starkweather was rushed to Strong Memorial Hospital in serious condition and eventually recovered from his wounds.

The attempt on his life, and the awareness of the government's case against him, convinced Starkweather to provide testimony against his co-conspirators. Starkweather subsequently pled guilty to pending federal charges and was relocated into the Federal Witness Protection Program.

Continued investigation determined the involvement of James Bates as a co-conspirator with other "B Team" members. Bates subsequently agreed to cooperate with authorities and render truthful testimony concerning his knowledge of "B Team" activities. Bates pled guilty to federal charges and was relocated in the Federal Witness Protection Program.

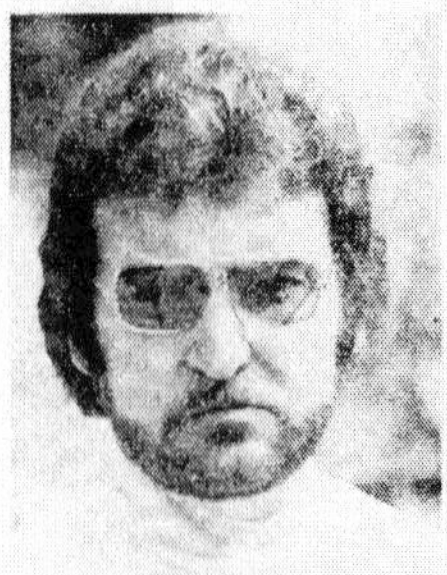

Rodney J. Starkweather

**Starkweather 'satisfactory'**

By BRIAN ROONEY
*D&C Staff Writer*

Rodney J. Starkweather, whom police have identified as a suspect in the mob killing of Salvatore "Sammy G" Gingello, was in satisfactory condition yesterday in Strong Memorial Hospital after he was shot in the abdomen Sunday night.

Despite his improved condition, police said they were unable to interview Starkweather yesterday and couldn't piece together the events surrounding the shooting.

Greece police Lt. David Wilson said no major evidence was uncovered yesterday. He said no witnesses to the shooting were identified.

Police believe Starkweather was shot with a small caliber weapon about 9:30 p.m. Sunday in or near a vacant lot at Lee Road and Ridgeway Avenue in Greece.

It isn't known whether Starkweather was shot in a car or in the vacant lot, police said. They said it's possible Starkweather knew the person who shot him and that there's an outside chance the shooting wasn't

*Turn to Page 3A*

**The Democrat and Chronicle August 1, 1978 article reporting the Starkweather shooting.**

## Guns, Silencers and Explosives Seized

On **August 29, 1978**, ATF special agents executed a federal search warrant at Trolley Collision, 5 Fromm Place, Rochester, N.Y., an auto collision shop operated by "B Team" members Rosario "Ross" Chirico and his son, Anthony Chirico. Seized at the premises were a firearm silencer, literature on how to manufacture firearms silencers, assorted firearms, a quantity of safety fuse, and miscellaneous component parts utilized in the construction of destructive devices.

# Mob pressures drive 2 away

By JIM ROWLEY
D&C Staff Writer

Teamsters Construction Local 398 vice-president Samuel C. Campanello and James Cannarozzo, the union's business agent resigned their union jobs on the same day and put their homes up for sale because of Mafia pressure to leave the Rochester area, local and federal law enforcement officials said yesterday.

Campanello, 45, of 419 Whipple Lane, has been identified by mob informants as a member of local organized crime and a powerful figure in the union that authorities have identified as being infiltrated by reputed Mafia members.

Union President Philip Koch said Campanello and Cannarozzo resigned in early September. Koch said neither gave any reason. Koch denied his union has ties to organized crime.

Cannarozzo, 41, of 183 Kings Gate South, Irondequoit, is a convicted counterfeiter who has been identified as a close associate of local mobsters.

Cannarozzo and Campanello were unavailable for comment when a reporter visited their homes last night. Both homes had "For Sale" signs outside.

Campanello stood trial in 1976 with six reputed Mafia members accused of the 1973 slaying of Vincent "Jimmy the Hammer" Massaro. His indictment was dismissed during the trial. Police believe he ran the local underworld while his co-defendents were serving time for the murder.

Convicted of the killing were: Rene Piccarreto, Salvatore (Red) Russotti, Richard J. Marino, Thomas Marotta, Eugene DiFrancesco and the late Salvatore "Sammy G" Gingello. Their convictions were overturned Jan. 31 when a sheriff's detective admitted he fabricated evidence used against them.

Sources say Piccaretto and Russotti were dissatisfied with Campanello because he didn't properly protect the rackets from being taken over by a rival mob faction.

Police officials weren't sure where

Samuel C. Campanello
. . . resigns Teamsters post

Campanello's allegiance was when mob warfare broke out last spring. The conflict surfaced with a series of bombings, including the April 23 dynamite blast which killed Gingello in a downtown parking lot.

Law enforcement officials believe Campanello is being ordered to leave because he was too close to the insurgent faction believed responsible for Gingello's death.

*Turn to Page 3A*

In **September of 1978**, two Teamster Local #398 Officers, Vice-President Sam Campanella and Business Agent James Canarozza, both quit their jobs on the same day. Then they both put their houses up for sale and moved out of town, because of Mafia pressure that was put on them after the Didio murder.

Campanella was indicted in 1976 for the Massaro murder but his indictment was dismissed. He was supposed to share in the responsibilities with Thomas Didio of overseeing the Rochester Mob activities while the bosses all remained jailed for that killing. Russotti, Piccarreto, Gingello and others were then released from prison the following year, after it was discovered that police had fabricated evidence presented at their trials.

Thomas Didio, a cousin to Thomas Marotta had been left "temporarily" in charge but when the other mob bosses were released from prison, Didio refused to relinquish control of the Rochester rackets, and was then killed for his disobedience. Sometime while the other mob leaders were still in prison, Campanella and Canarozza had switched their allegiances and had become loyal to Didio.

After the murder of Thomas Didio, Campanella and Canarozza were both given a rare opportunity to retire from the Rochester Mafia and leave town without being killed themselves, (27) an opportunity that both men wisely took.

# 5 plead innocent to bomb charges and obstruction

By JIM ROWLEY

Reputed mob associate Rodney J. Starkweather is accused of obtaining explosives which he knew would be used to kill Mafia underboss Salvatore "Sammy G" Gingello, according to an indictment opened yesterday in U.S. District Court.

Starkweather and four others are variously charged in the eight counts with conspiring to make and possess explosives, and to obstruct the federal grand jury's investigation of bombings last spring.

Two counts specifically charge Starkweather with obtaining blasting caps and chemical explosives "knowing and intending" they would be used to injure or kill Gingello.

Because Gingello died in the April 23 bomb blast, Starkweather could be sentenced to life in prison if convicted of either of these counts.

Also named in the indictment is reputed Mafia member Rosario F. Chirico, 52, of 164 Kuhn, Greece; Chirico's son, Anthony Chirico, 26, of 67 Carthage St.; Francesco Frassetto Jr., 29, of 190 Lida Lane, Greece; and his wife, Betti, 28.

Mrs. Frasetto is charged with conspiring with the other defendants to obstruct the grand jury's investigation.

All five pleaded innocent during arraignment.

The obstruction of justice charge claims that Mrs. Frassetto, her husband, Anthony Chirico and Starkweather conspiring to move a truck containing explosive devices from a Greece service station.

The indictment claims that the conspiracy took place after the Frassetto's were served on June 19 and 22 with federal grand jury subpoenas.

Starkweather, 31, of 59 Tacoma St., and Anthony Chirico were arrested by federal agents on June 28 after they were seen at the Arco service station at Mt. Read Boulevard and Maiden Lane.

Agents said Starkweather was seen removing explosives from the back of the truck and leaving in a car driven by Chirico.

The two were followed and later arrested by agents for the U.S. Bureau of Alcohol, Tobacco and Firearms. They were charged with possession of explosives.

The new indictment incorporates those earlier charges and ultimately will replace them, said Marty Stein-

Turn to Page 2B

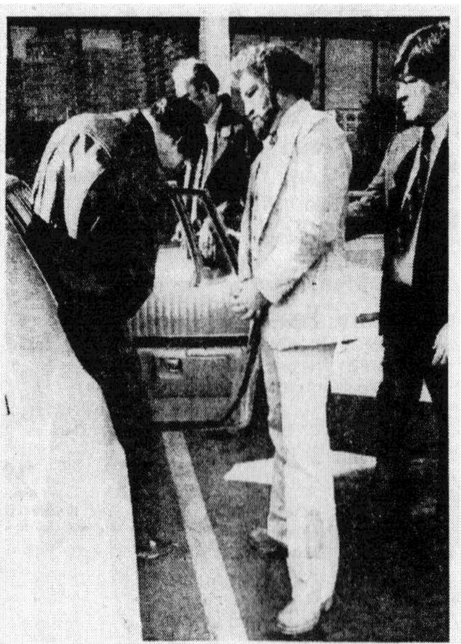

D&C photo by Jim Sheehan

Rodney Starkweather (center) waits to enter car as Francesco Frassetto Jr. maneuvers himself inside for transportation to jail

**November 17, 1978 Democrat and Chronicle**

## 5 Plead Innocent To Bomb Charges

Francesco Frassetto (getting into car above) and Rodney Starkweather are being transported to jail after being arraigned on charges of conspiring to make and possess explosives.

The charges were in connection to the explosives found across the street from Frassetto's Farm Market in Greece several months earlier. Also named in the indictment were Frassetto's wife Betty, Rosario Chirico and Anthony Chirico. (28)

## Rochester Mobster John Fiorino Becomes Local #398's New Vice-President

Reputed Rochester La Cosa Nostra family member John Fiorino became the new Vice-President and Business Agent of Teamsters Local #398, replacing Sam Campanella who resigned. When the opening was created, Fiorino told the President of Teamsters Local #398, Phil Koch, "I am taking that job."

Koch noted in his testimony to the New York State Police, "the Executive Board of Teamsters Local #398 approved Fiorino for the two positions because *no one dared to object*." **(29)**

The openings on Local #398's Executive Board were created when local organized crime leaders in Rochester forced James Canarozza and Sam Campanella to leave town, according to law enforcement sources.

There was an election, but no one in their right mind would dare run against the Mafia members, so they ran unopposed and were technically elected.

Also elected that day were Mafia "Underboss" Richard Marino and his brother-in-law Angelo Misuraca. **(30)**

**Teamsters officers**

A close friend and former business partner of the late Mafia underboss, Salvatore "Sammy G" Gingello has been elected vice-president of Teamsters Construction Local 398.

John Fiorino a former partner of Gingello's in SJ Trucking Inc., was elected vice president without opposition in elections held last week.

Fiorino, 41, of 78 Venice Circle, Irondequoit, was elected to a three-year term as vice-president. In that job he also serves as a paid business agent for the union.

Also elected to the union's executive board was reputed Mafia underboss Richard J. Marino and Marino's brother-in-law, Angelo Misaraco.

The election was held to fill a vacancy created in September by the resignation of Vice President Samuel C. Campanello. According to law enforcement sources, Campanello, a reputed Mafia soldier, and his union business agent James Cannarozzo, were ordered to leave town by local organized crime leaders.

**Fiorino Elected to V.P. of Teamsters Local #398 Democrat and Chronicle December 1, 1978**

# Teamsters Local #398 Members Joseph LaDolce and Anthony Oliveri Are Inducted Into the Rochester Mafia

**Joseph LoDolce**

According to eye witness testimony that would not be available for many years to come, from self admitted Rochester La Cosa Nosa member Anthony Oliveri, both he and Joseph LaDolce were inducted into the Rochester Mafia on the same day in **December of 1978**. They both were members of Thomas Marotta's crew. Teamsters Local #398 Business Agent and Rochester Mafia Captain, Dick Marino, was also present at this induction ceremony. **(31)**

## James Bates Becomes Latest Informant

# Informant could link Mafia to bombings

By NANCY MONAGHAN
D&C Staff Writer

• Mob who's who (3A)

A Rochester man who officially turned state's evidence yesterday is expected to be a crucial link in the investigation of last year's Mafia bombings and other organized crime activities.

James D. Bates, 23, also known as "Carlos," became an informant late last week. He pleaded guilty yesterday to criminal possession of explosives and then spent the afternoon giving statements behind closed doors in the Monroe County District Attorney's office.

Bates, of 141 Grand Ave., is a long-time friend and former employee of Francesco Frassetto, investigators said. Frassetto has been identified as an important figure in last year's underworld power struggle that was marked by bombings and shootings.

Frassetto is the only man known by police to have secretly switched his allegiance from the established Mafia members, dubbed the A Team by police, to the insurgent faction, called the B Team. Frassetto and Bates moved freely within the A Team until police and the A Team discovered Frassetto's loyalty to the B Team last June 18.

On that day Frassetto was arrested with Dominic "Sonny" Celestino, a reputed B Team leader, after a high-speed car chase by a city police investigator assigned to organized crime surveillance. Frassetto and Celestino were both arrested on charges of possession of a dangerous weapon involving a switchblade knife. It was the authorities' first break in the investigation of the gangland war.

There were no further gambling parlor bombings — which police had attributed to the B Team — after Frassetto's arrest. Within two weeks police began a string of arrests of reputed B Team members.

It is expected Bates will give information on Frassetto's activities with both the A Team and the B Team, investigators said.

Bates is the second man in three weeks to cooperate in the bombing investigation. Later this week he is expected to be relocated with a new identity under the Federal Witness Protection Program.

The first to cooperate was Rodney Starkweather, who left Rochester with a new identity Feb. 13. He, too, gave authorities information on the bombings.

They are the first major Mafia informants to cooperate since 1975 when then-Mafia soldier Angelo Monachino turned informant for the

Turn to Page 3A

James Bates leaves courtroom
. . . spent afternoon talking to cops

**Democrat and Chronicle March 6, 1979**

On **March 5, 1979**, James Bates officially turned state's evidence after his conviction on criminal possession of explosives. He spent the afternoon giving statements behind closed doors in the Monroe County District Attorney's office. He was a friend and former employee of Francesco Frassetto.

Bates was expected to disclose information on Frassetto's activities with both the "A Team" and the "B Team." When he was done testifying, he was relocated with a new identity into the Federal Witness Protection Program. (32)

## "A Team" Members Anthony Oliveri and Anthony Columbo Attempt To Whack Angelo "Oskie" DeMarco

On **March 14, 1979**, officers of the Gates Police Department observed a suspicious vehicle in the vicinity of the residence of Angelo "Oskie" DeMarco. DeMarco, operator of one of the "A Team" gambling establishments, had cooperated with federal authorities in the bombing investigation. As police officers approached, the vehicle left the scene at a high rate of speed and a chase ensued. The vehicle was eventually apprehended and the two occupants were identified as "A Team" members Anthony Oliveri and Anthony Columbo.

Retracing the route of the chase, police officers recovered a sawed-off shotgun, a loaded handgun, a ski mask and a pair of black leather gloves. Neither Oliveri nor Columbo had any identification on their person. It was later determined that the vehicle that they were operating was fictitiously registered, in that the person to whom the vehicle was registered was nonexistent. It was speculated that Angelo "Oskie" DeMarco was slated to be killed as a result of his cooperation with federal authorities.

On **April 12, 1979**, “B Team” members William "Billy" Barton, Anthony Chirico, Rosario "Ross" Chirico, Dominic "Sonny" Celestino, Frank Frassetto, Angelo Vaccaro, Stanley Valenti, and Betti Frassetto were named in a 14-count federal indictment. The indictment alleged violations of federal firearms, explosives and conspiracy statues.

Most “B Team” members other than Betti Frassetto were charged with possession of destructive devices and with malicious damage to buildings. All defendants except Betti Frassetto were charged with conspiring to perform the above acts in violation of 18 U.S.C. § 371 (1976), and to conduct the affairs of an enterprise through a pattern of racketeering activity in violation of the Racketeer Influenced and Corrupt Organizations Act (RICO).

## Mahoney From Top Cop To Prison

“Backroom Bill” Mahoney, the Sheriff's Chief of Detectives, was indicted the same day, on **April 12, 1979**, by a federal grand jury on five counts of civil rights violations involving the prosecution of 14 persons, including 11 reputed members of the Rochester Mafia.

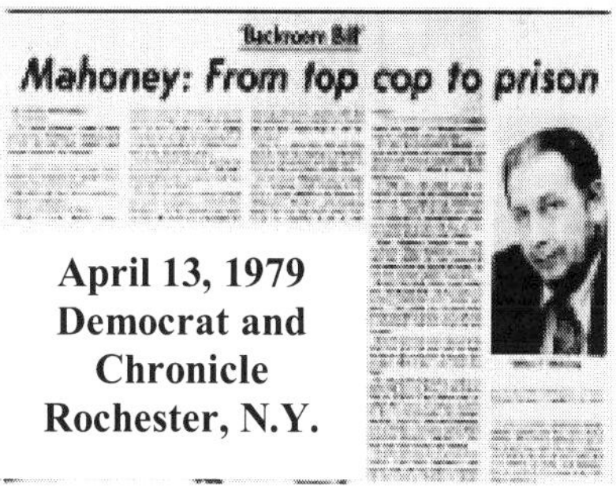
Backroom Bill
Mahoney: From top cop to prison

**April 13, 1979**
**Democrat and Chronicle**
**Rochester, N.Y.**

It was 1974 when Mahoney got the top detective's job in the county. His boss, Sheriff William M. Lombard, told him to go after the Mafia. The Chief's vigorous pursuit earned him a new nickname, “Backroom Bill” Mahoney for the publicity his work attracted.

When Mahoney retired from the Rochester Police Department to work with the sheriff, he had earned 20 commendations for his police work. He had also earned another nickname. Behind his back other cops called him "Backroom Bill" for his tactics in getting confessions from crime suspects. Four times the rumors were strong enough to prompt local officials to investigate, and four times he was cleared.

Many times there were rumors of his close ties with the mob and an association in the restaurant business with gangster Billy Lupo, who later was slain. He socialized downtown, where he dined with his wife Betty at the Rascal Cafe or Eddie's Chop House and accepted the praise of citizens grateful for his crime-busting.

On Sunday morning. April 23, 1978, the Mahoneys were at Eddie's moments before Mafia "Underboss" Salvatore "Sammy G" Gingello was slain across the street.

'I had faith,' Piccarreto says

The Monachinos sang for freedom

$50 million in lawsuits

Cops against cops and the mob went free

**Rochester, New York Democrat and Chronicle Tuesday, Apr. 13, 1979**

It now appeared that "Backroom Bill" was headed off to prison himself for his role in the fabrication of evidence that temporarily imprisoned the leadership Rochester's Cosa Nostra.

The Democrat and Chronicle newspaper in Rochester had a field day with the arrest of Bill Mahoney, the recent news about the mafia informers and then the cops getting caught fabricating evidence. These articles were only some of the many mob related articles that dominated the newspaper that day. (33)

## New Informant, James Bates, Leads to Bombing Indictments

### (The Who's Who of Characters In Bombing Probe)

The cast of characters involved in the investigation resulting in a federal grand jury bombing indictment was unsealed on **April 16, 1979**. James D. Bates, was the newest informant who turned against the mob, Bates, 23, was an air-conditioning mechanic who worked with and was a good friend of Francesco Frassetto.

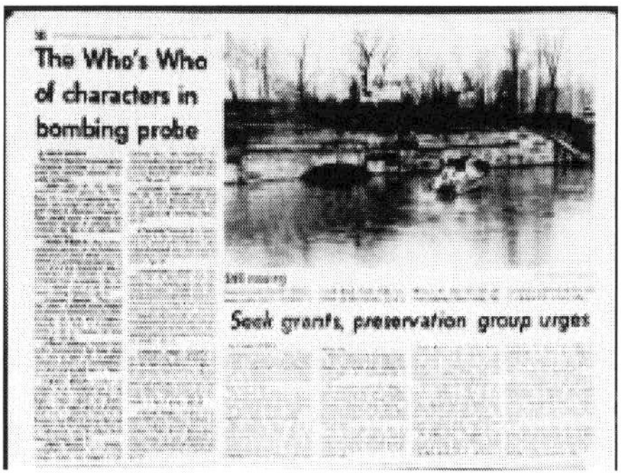
The Who's Who of characters in bombing probe

Seek grants, preservation group urges

**ROCHESTER DEMOCRAT AND CHRONICLE**
**Tuesday, Apr. 17, 1979**

Bates pleaded guilty to weapons and conspiracy charges in exchange for testimony that led to the indictment opened the previous day.

William B. Barton was a heavy equipment operator for the Rochester Department of Public Works and had worked as a gambling club doorman. In April 1974 he was acquitted of federal conspiracy and extortion charges stemming from accusations that he was a muscle man in the Broome County vending industry.

Dominic Celestino was 42 years old; they called him "Sonny." A former mason, he was charged and cleared in the Columbus Day 1970 bombings. His arrest with Francesco Frassetto in June of 1978, in Irondequoit, proved a key in cracking the mob bombings.

Anthony Chirico, age 27, was arrested with Rodney Starkweather in June of 1978 when they were on their way to recover explosives stored in an abandoned potato chip truck parked near a Greece service station.

Rosario Chirico, age 48, father of Anthony, was considered to be one of the leaders of the insurgent Mafia "B Team." Police believed his Trolley Collision auto repair shop on Fromm Place was a meeting place for "B Teamers." On May 24, 1978, he was shot and wounded when he stopped his truck at an intersection near his Kuhn Road home in Greece.

Thomas C. Didio, age 53, a middle-management mobster, also had charges against him dropped. Didio became the leader of the insurgent "B Team" and he was machine-gunned to death on July 6, 1978 at the Exit 45 Motel on Route 96 in Victor.

Betti Frassetto, Francesco's wife, ran a now-bankrupt farm market on West Henrietta Road. She was named in bomb indictments in the fall of 1978 and charged with obstructing justice.

Francesco Frassetto Jr., age 28, was considered to be loyal to the incumbent "A Team," until his arrest with Celestino. Information developed after that arrest led authorities to the explosives cache in Greece.

Rodney J. Starkweather, age 29, formerly ran an after-hours club and worked as a heating and air-conditioning mechanic. He was arrested in June of 1978 for possession of high-order explosives and named as a suspect in the bombing death of mob boss Salvatore "Sammy G" Gingello. He later was shot in the arm and stomach. In February 1979 he became a protected government witness after pleading guilty to conspiracy and weapons charges.

Angelo Vaccaro, age 32, was acquitted in the Columbus Day, 1970 bombings. He also was identified as a leader in the insurgent Mafia "B Team". He was arrested later in the day of DiDio's death and was scheduled to go on trial for an illegal weapon charge. As a persistent felon, Vaccaro could be sentenced to life in prison.

Stanley Valenti, age 58, was the brother of deposed mob boss Frank J. Valenti. He ran a wholesale produce store at the Rochester Public Market. The brothers were among 58 men identified as mobsters who attended the infamous 1957 organized crime meeting in Appalachian. (34)

## Rosario Chirico Found Guilty of Loansharking

On **July 9, 1979**, a Monroe County Court found Rosario Chirico guilty on four counts of loan sharking. He faced a prison term of 5-15 years.

Rosario 'Ross' Chirico, in profile at front, is escorted by Monroe County sheriff deputy to jail after guilty verdicts.

**Chirico found guilty of loansharking**

**Schlesinger deputy quits**

**Democrat and Chronicle**
**July 10, 1979**

On **September 10, 1979**, defendant Stanley Valenti was granted a severance from his bombing trial due to ill health. **(57)**

He was originally indicted with 7 others on bomb related charges. The seven, said to be members of an insurgent Rochester Mafia group that fought for control of the rackets in 1978, were scheduled to go to trial on a variety of charges in U.S. District Court.

## Starkweather Testifies

The defendants were William Barton, 43; Anthony Chirico, 27; Rosario Chirico, 53; Dominic "Sonny" Celestino, 49; Francesco Frassetto Jr., 30; his wife Betti, 29; and Angelo Vaccaro, 60.

Mobster Rodney Starkweather was called to testify before the Monroe County Grand Jury on **October 31, 1979**.

Detailed in the article on the left, "Mobster Describes Bombing," he coolly told the jury how he and Dominic Celestino went to 1455 University Avenue to plant a bomb early in the morning on May 22, 1978. (35)

state

Rodney Starkweather, witness *said Celestino planted bomb*

### Mobster describes bombing

By BRIAN ROONEY

Rodney Starkweather coolly told a County Court jury yesterday how he and Dominic Celestino went to 1455 University Ave. to plant a time bomb early in the morning May 22, 1978.

"He took the package (bomb) around the corner of the building and returned without the package," Starkweather said.

Starkweather, 32, is the main prosecution witness against Dominic "Sonny" Celestino, accused of first-degree arson in the bombing of a gambling club at 1455 University Ave.

Starkweather, now a member of the federal Witness Protection Program, pleaded guilty in January to various charges that could get him up to 20 years in prison. As part of a deal with state and local prosecutors, he agreed to the guilty plea in exchange for his testimony and the promise of possible consideration in his sentence.

Because of Starkweather's appearance, everyone entering the court yesterday was searched with metal detectors.

On direct examination by Assistant District Attorney Donald J. Wisner, Starkweather told of his role in the May 22 bombing.

A large man with long brown hair and a beard, Starkweather spoke in a low voice and showed no emotion. Starkweather said he, Celestino and Frank Frassetto, who is indicted on federal charges, met the next day.

"We sat around and talked about the results of the bombing," Starkweather said. "Sonny made mention that now

*Turn to Page 2B*

**Democrat and Chronicle November 1, 1979**

## 32 Nabbed in Gambling Raid

### 32 nabbed in gambling raid

By GREGG MORRIS

Rochester police, in an early morning raid, arrested 32 people yesterday on promotion of gambling charges at five social clubs identified by police as gambling joints with organized crime connections.

Police last night were looking for 17 other suspects wanted on warrants charging them with second-degree promotion of gambling.

Sgt. Robert Wiesner, head of the vice squad's gambling unit, said the arrests were the result of a seven-month investigation.

Operating in five teams, 35 police officers confiscated about $8,000 in cash as well as cards, dice, records to keep track of the money and other "gambling paraphernalia connected to illegal gambling operations" in the clubs.

Weisner said the clubs were the ones two underworld factions fought to control more than 18 months ago. Salvatore "Sammy G" Gingello and Thomas Didio, reputed leaders of the two warring organized crime factions, were slain and numerous bombings rocked city neighborhoods during the fight.

After the arrests yesterday, fourteen persons pleaded innocent in Rochester City Court to charges of second-degree promotion of gambling.

They were released on bail ranging from $100 cash to $250 cash or $500 bail bond and are to reappear in court Dec. 20, according to the City Court clerk's office.

The eighteen remaining suspects were released on bail and are to be arraigned tomorrow in City Court.

Wiesner identified the five social clubs as: The Goodman Street Social Club Inc., 495 North Goodman St.; Hellenic Social Club, 188 North St.; Yahambis Social Club, 221 Franklin St.; Caserta Social and Political Club, also known as the 44 Club, 44 Lake Ave.; and Olymbos Inc., 308 Andrews St.

Police said about 10 gambling joints operate in the city.

The raids started about 3 a.m. Some patrons, ignoring police cars outside, sought entrance to the clubs even while police were inside making arrests, an officer said.

Wiesner said no patrons were arrested although some were interviewed.

Blackjack, craps and poker are the main operations in the clubs, Wiesner said.

Some clubs are open about 16 hours a day, seven days a week. An average blackjack game can bring in $150 to $200 an hour, Wiesner said.

Some of the clubs operate principally in the daytime while others make most of their money in late night and early morning operations. On some weekend nights as many as 60 or 70 people will be in the 44 Club, Wiesner said.

*Turn to Page 2B*

**Democrat and Chronicle November 25,**

Early morning on **November 24, 1979,** Rochester Police arrested 32 people on promotion of gambling charges at five different social clubs in Rochester. Each of them had been previously identified by police as gambling joints with organized crime connections (above).

# Reputed Mobsters Face Trial

The two rival factions of the Rochester Mafia, dubbed by police as the "A Team," the incumbents, and the insurgent "B Team," ruthlessly battled for control of the rackets.

Incidents in the war included a series of bombings, shootings and two murders, one of them the bombing death of mob "Underboss" Salvatore "Sammy G" Gingello.

Reputed mobsters face trial Tuesday

By BRIAN ROONEY

Defendants are, clockwise beginning at top, Anthony Chirico, Dominic 'Sonny' Celestino, William Barton, Rosario Chirico, Betti Frassetto, Francesco Frassetto, and Angelo Vaccaro.

**The defendants were, beginning at the top center, going clockwise, Anthony Chirico, Dominic 'Sonny' Celestino, William Barton, Rosario Chirico, Betti Frassetto, Francesco Frassetto, and Angelo Vaccaro.**

Bombs exploded and people were shot over a period of six months. Eventually a strike force of local and federal agents arrested those believed to be responsible for starting and waging the war. Some of the defendants had long been associated with nefarious doings in and around Rochester.

Billy Barton was a reputed strong-arm, once accused of being an enforcer in the Broome County vending machine rackets. Dominic "Sonny" Celestino also was one. Their day in court, possibly as much as six weeks in court, was coming for the seven reputed mobsters facing federal conspiracy, racketeering and weapons charges.

The seven, said to be members of an insurgent Rochester Mafia group that fought for control of the rackets in 1978, were scheduled to go to trial on a variety of charges in U.S. District Court. The defendants were William Barton, 43; Anthony Chirico, 27; Rosario Chirico, 53; Dominic "Sonny" Celestino, 49; Francesco Frassetto Jr., 30; his wife Betti, 29; and Angelo Vaccaro, 60. (Barton's status in the trial was uncertain. He underwent spinal surgery and a ruling was expected on whether or not he can stand trial.) **(36)**

## “B Team” Members Charged In 14 Count Indictment

In a fourteen-count indictment, most “B Team” members other than Betti Frassetto were charged with possession of destructive devices in violation of 26 U.S.C. §§ 5861(d), (f), and 5871 (1976), and with malicious damage to buildings in violation of 18 U.S.C. § 844(i) (1976); all defendants except Betti Frassetto were charged with conspiring to perform the above acts in violation of 18 U.S.C. § 371 (1976), and to conduct the affairs of an enterprise through a pattern of racketeering activity in violation of the Racketeer Influenced and Corrupt Organizations Act (RICO), 18 U.S.C. §§ 1962(c) and (d) (1976); and defendants Anthony Chirico and Betti and Frank Frassetto were charged with endeavoring to obstruct justice, in violation of 18 U.S.C. § 1503 (Supp. III 1979).

On **January 8, 1980**, the trial of “B Team”defendants commenced , before the Honorable Lloyd F. McMahon in Federal Court Rochester, N.Y. in the case of:

**647 F.2d 224**

**UNITED STATES of America, Appellee,**
**v.**
**William BARTON, Anthony Chirico, Rosario Chirico, Dominic**
**"Sonny" Celestino, Betti Frassetto, Frank Frassetto and Angelo Vaccaro,**
**Defendants-Appellants.**

On **January 30, 1980**, a jury reached a guilty verdict against all defendants for all counts of the indictment.

# All 7 Found Guilty in Mob War Trial

## All 7 found guilty in mob-war trial

By BRIAN ROONEY

Seven people accused in the 1978 mob war for control of the rackets were found guilty last night in Rochester by a U.S. District Court jury.

The verdict was delivered to tense and emotional defendants and their families who, minutes earlier, watched defendant Rosario Chirico collapse while awaiting the verdict.

Medical technicians were administering oxygen and other aid to Chirico in one courtroom at the very moment the jury delivered its verdict in another courtroom down the hall.

The proceedings were moved after Chirico was stricken.

Chirico was taken to the Park Ridge Hospital emergency room where he was being examined early today. A hospital official said Chirico "had apparently fainted."

The defendants, all found guilty on a variety of charges of conspiracy, weapons violations, racketeering and obstructing justice are Chirico, 53; William "Billy" Barton, 43; Anthony Chirico, 27; Dominic "Sonny" Celestino, 49; Francesco Frassetto Jr., 30; his wife Betti, 29; and Angelo Vaccaro, 63.

The charges carry penalties of up to 20 years in jail.

The defendants sat, for the most part, expressionless as the court clerk read the verdicts on the 14-count indictment. Family members and friends held each other and wept.

Judge Lloyd F. MacMahon revoked bail on the four present male defendants, who have been free since their indictment April 12. He issued a bench warrant for Barton, who has been at home throughout the trial, recovering from elective spinal surgery.

The judge allowed Mrs. Frassetto to remain on bail. He set sentencing for all seven on March 18.

In revoking bail, MacMahon commented that "The court has heard three weeks of evidence that these defendants behaved in a brutal, barbaric way." He said they were a danger to the community.

The lawyers, defendants and family members, who had remained cool throughout day-long deliberations yesterday, were in a state of shock by the time the verdict was delivered.

The jury sent out word at about 10:30 that it had reached a verdict. The lawyers and defendants gathered and Chirico's family comforted each other.

Chirico began to have trouble breathing and his lawyer, Alfred Kremer, moved to help [illegible] his tie and belt. Within a few moments Chirico slumped in his seat, losing color.

The courtroom was chaotic as spectators became more excited and U.S. marshals sent for an ambulance.

Family and lawyers helped Chirico to the floor and administered aid. His wife, Carolyn, and two daughters sought to help him as he lost color and consciousness.

The defendant Vaccaro, with a hand on Chirico's head, said "Stay with us Boss, stay with us."

Kremer stood with Mrs. Chirico, comforting her as ambulance attendants arrived and began to work on Chirico. A marshal brought word that the judge wanted to see Kremer, who waved the marshal away.

"We're indisposed," Kremer said with irritation in his voice. "I'll stand in contempt."

The findings against the defendants were as follows:

Barton: guilty of one count of conspiracy to make bombs and one count of racketeering in restraint of interstate

Please turn to page 13A

All seven defendants in the Mafia bombing trial were found guilty. They each faced sentences of up to 20 years in prison for each offense. Rosario Chirico collapsed after the verdict was read and he was was taken to Parkridge Hospital. **(37)**

# Judge Scolds Bombers

## Judge to bombers: 'a vicious conspiracy'

• Bill O'Brien's view (1B).

By NANCY MONAGHAN
D&C Staff Writer

One by one the six reputed Mafia figures walked out of the prisoners' holding room into U.S. District Court to face Judge Lloyd F. MacMahon.

Federal agents were squeezed into the front rows of the filled courtroom gallery. Four U.S. marshals ringed each defendant in the courtroom, then looked down at the floor when MacMahon spoke.

MacMahon glared at each defendant. "This was a vicious conspiracy," he said, "barbaric, cruel acts that terrorized the whole community."

All six men were convicted in January of a bombing conspiracy that resulted in the death of Mafia underboss Salvatore "Sammy G" Gingello and the destruction of several Mafia gambling parlors.

Yesterday they were sentenced to federal prison. The lightest term — 10 years — was handed to William "Billy" Barton. Francesco Frassetto Jr. and Dominic "Sonny" Celestino received the longest terms — 30 years. Rosario Chirico and Angelo Vaccaro received 25 years each. And Anthony Chirico, Rosario's son, was sentenced to 15 years.

Each man was asked if he wanted to say anything before sentence was passed. Each said no. When it was over their wives were allowed to visit with them for five minutes.

Frassetto's wife, Betti, convicted of obstruction of justice, was sentenced to two years but will remain free on bail pending appeal.

Mrs. Frassetto wept at the defense table, taking off her glasses to wipe tears from her face as she listened to MacMahon call her husband a "monster." Frassetto stared straight ahead and then walked quickly back to the holding room. He yanked open the door, and the flying door hit a marshal in the head.

The bombings began in late 1977 when the defendants tried to take control of organized crime from Rochester's Mafia leaders. The war accelerated when Gingello was killed by a remote control bomb on April 23, 1978, and ended when the insurgent faction's leader, Thomas DiDio, was machine-gunned to death July 6 in a Victor motel.

Please turn to page 3A

**Democrat and Chronicle March 12, 1980**

Judge Lloyd MacMahon scolded each of the 6 defendants individually, prior to sentencing them for their roles in a bombing campaign that killed "Sammy G" Gingello and terrorized countless others.

The bombing campaign was part of a Mafia war that raged in the Rochester area while insurgents were attempting to overthrow the established Mafia regime there. **(38)**

After a three-week trial, the defendants were convicted on all counts. Judge MacMahon sentenced them to prison terms ranging from two years to thirty years. The trial and convictions related to a series of bombings and attempted bombings in Rochester, New York, between December 1977 and June 1978, depicted as part of a struggle between rival underworld factions to gain control of gambling and other unlawful enterprises in the Rochester area.

The theory of the prosecution was that the defendants represented the insurgent faction who were seeking to unseat the incumbent faction, headed by Salvatore Gingello. Gingello, who was released from jail in February 1978, was eventually killed when a bomb exploded under his car on April 23, 1978.

## The Jail Sentences Given To The "B Team"

On **March 11, 1980**, Honorable Lloyd F. McMahon sentenced William Barton to 10 years imprisonment, Anthony Chirico to 15 years imprisonment; Rosario "Ross" Chirico to 25 years imprisonment, Dominic "Sonny" Celestino to 30 years imprisonment Frank Frassetto to 30 years imprisonment, Angelo Vaccaro to 25 years imprisonment and Betti Frassetto to 2 years imprisonment.

**Rosario Chirico**

**Dominic Celestino**

**Frank Frassetto**

**Angelo Vaccaro**

**Betti Frassetto**

**William Barton**

**Anthony Chirico**

All the "B Team" members began serving their sentences immediately except Betti Frassetto who remained free at that time pending her appeal. **(40)**

# *Chapter 5*
# The War is Revived
# (John Fiorino is Murdered)

## Frank Valenti To Be Paroled

Frank Valenti, the former Rochester crime “Boss,” who in 1980 had spent the previous seven years in prison, was scheduled to be released from the federal penitentiary in Atlanta on June 19, 1980. Valenti, who was 68 that year, was Rochester's crime “Boss” from about 1964 until he was deposed in 1972, was serving a 20-year prison term on a federal extortion conviction. He had been granted parole, federal officials say. What that meant for the Rochester underworld, if anything, remained to be seen, federal officials and mob watchers said.

Federal parole officials said they weren't expecting Valenti to go back to Rochester, but other information regarding Valenti's release was considered secret. Valenti bought land near Phoenix, Ariz., before he was sent to prison and at least part of his family was believed to be there. Valenti who was always described as being in poor health, spent his entire prison term in medical facilities, both in Springfield, Mo., and Atlanta.

Valenti and his younger brother, Costanze P. "Stanley," 54, were at the heart of the history of the Rochester underworld, going all the way back to Nov. 14, 1957. That's when state police rounded up 62 Mafia chiefs holding a summit meeting in the Southern Tier town of Apalachin. The two Valentis were among those arrested.

Stanley was believed to have been instrumental in the 1978 mob war to win back control of the rackets. He was indicted in April 1979 on federal charges of conspiracy and racketeering, then he was granted a delay of prosecution because of poor health. Federal officials hadn't attempted to bring Stanley to trial since the previous September, when his case was separated from seven others indicted in the mob war. He lived on a hilltop in Victor. (191)

Officials believe that Stanley was a central figure here before the Apalachin arrest but that his control slipped when he spent 16 months in jail rather than testify before a state investigating commission. It was about then that Frank came to town. Frank was convicted of election law violations and, as part of his probation, he was sent out of state for three years. He returned and, soon after, reigning crime boss Jake Russo disappeared. Valenti was soon telling people he was "the man to see" in Rochester.

Over time, Frank Valenti developed a cadre of close associates, all of whom became familiar names: Dominic Chirico, Thomas Didio, Dominic Celestino, Angelo Vaccaro, Ross Chirico, Vincent Massaro, Joseph Lanovara, Eugene DiFrancesco and Angelo Monachino. Federal investigators believe that in the early 1970s, Frank Valenti had a falling out with other, less close, crime leaders over the accounting of money. Frank Valenti, investigators said, was ordered to retire by Samuel Russotti, Rene Piccarreto and Salvatore Gingello. The shotgun killing of Dominic Chirico was a message to Valenti to quit.

He soon moved to Phoenix and, shortly thereafter, legal troubles landed him in jail. The war to regain control of the rackets was waged in spring 1978. Amidst a series of bombings, two men died and at least two others were shot. In January of 1980 a U.S. District Court jury convicted, among others, Ross Chirico and his son, Anthony, Angelo Vaccaro and Dominic Celestino. They were sent to prison for terms ranging from 15 to 30 years. Those convictions wiped out the old Valenti soldiers, but Assistant U.S. Attorney Gregory Baldwin, who prosecuted the case, testified in Washington that spring that "it was unlikely that these convictions have ended this violence." **(41)**

## Informant to aid New Mafia Probe

Federal and local officials planned to have a major grand jury investigation of organized crime with the help of their latest mafia informant Anthony Oliveri. Oliveri was arrested on March 13, 1979 for attempting to murder Angelo "Oskie" DeMarco. Oliveri became a government informant in early July of 1980. **(42)**

## Man Guilty of Causing Blast

The former director of a federally funded program for ex-offenders pleaded guilty on **October 15, 1980** in U.S. District Court to exploding the Irondequoit offices of Mark Kitchens Ltd.

Dean W. Haynesworth, who was secretly working with authorities, was scheduled to be in protective custody during his three year prison term.

# Man guilty of causing blast

The former director of a federally funded program for ex-offenders pleaded guilty yesterday in U.S. District Court to exploding the Irondequoit offices of Mark Kitchens Ltd.

Dean W. Haynesworth, who has been secretly cooperating with federal authorities, will be in protective custody during the three-year prison term Judge Harold P. Burke imposed yesterday.

Haynesworth, 52, was arraigned and sentenced yesterday in a 15-minute court appearance and whisked out of the courtroom by two U.S. marshals.

After two unsuccessful attempts to damage Mark Kitchens, 635 Shelford Road, Haynesworth, who was hired for the job, burned the building Sept. 28, 1978.

According to the criminal charge filed yesterday, Haynesworth was recruited to destroy the building by Vincent J. Rallo, a former insurance broker.

Mark Kitchens' co-owner, Kenneth J. Malta, then filed a false insurance claim with General Accident Insurance Co., between October 1978 and February 1979, according to the charge.

Malta's partner, Patrick Lippa, is not implicated in the scheme, sources said.

No charges have been filed against Rallo, Malta or a third man named in court, Frank Pacella, who was not identified further. The 18-month investigation is continuing.

Haynesworth also pleaded guilty yesterday to passing counterfeit $20 bills. According to that charge, Haynesworth talked to a man named Arnold E. McNeil, who is also known as Ali Hasan, about counterfeit money, and Haynesworth identified "Vince" as the supplier.

On July 14, 1979, Haynesworth talked to Rallo about delivering some counterfeit bills, the charge said.

The next month Rallo solicited Haynesworth for the arson job at Mark Kitchens "so the owners could collect the insurance proceeds," Haynesworth admitted in court.

Haynesworth is the former executive director of the 7th Step Foundation, an agency funded primarily by the Law Enforcement Assistance Administration of the U.S. Department of Justice. The agency works with inmates before they leave prison to help them stay clear of the law.

Before Haynesworth took over leadership of the Rochester chapter, he served prison terms for counterfeiting and forgery.

According to the charge, Rallo gave Haynesworth an undisclosed amount of money and a package of explosives in August 1978, to destroy Mark Kitchens. Rallo told Haynesworth to give the package to Pacella, who was to build a remote control device.

Then one Saturday morning Rallo arranged for Haynesworth to tour Mark Kitchens to examine the layout of the building. Sometime between Sept. 21 and Sept 28 Haynesworth poured an acidlike compound on furniture and carpeting inside the building, but "Rallo directed Haynesworth to return to the building and destroy it further by using gasoline," the charge said.

At 10:30 p.m. Sept. 28, Haynesworth drove Rallo's car to Mark Kitchens and opened the door with keys Rallo gave him, poured the gasoline about and ignited it, the charge said.

**October 16, 1980 Democrat and Chronicle**

According to Haynesworth, he was recruited to destroy the building by former insurance broker Vince J. Rallo. Rallo, a reputed Rochester Mob figure, had not been charged. **(43)**

## Man Shoots Self To Death at Downtown Social Club

Joseph A. DelGuercio shot himself inside a downtown social club and was pronounced dead at the scene.

He was inside the Yahambas Social Club at the time, shortly after 5 a.m. **November 17, 1980**, when the death occurred.

An autopsy determined that DelGuercio was intoxicated at the time. **(44)**

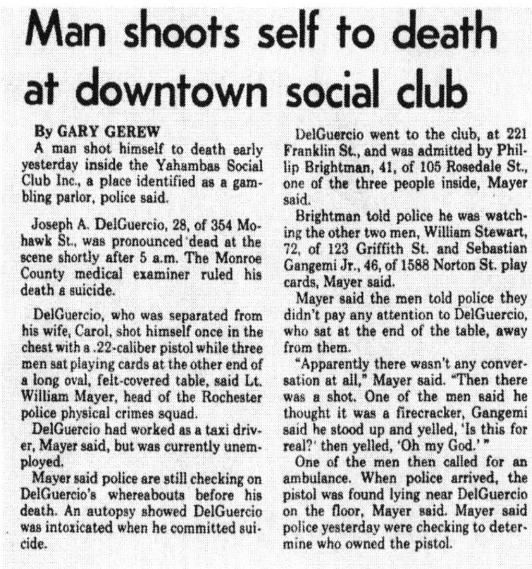

# Man shoots self to death at downtown social club

By GARY GEREW

A man shot himself to death early yesterday inside the Yahambas Social Club Inc., a place identified as a gambling parlor, police said.

Joseph A. DelGuercio, 28, of 354 Mohawk St., was pronounced dead at the scene shortly after 5 a.m. The Monroe County medical examiner ruled his death a suicide.

DelGuercio, who was separated from his wife, Carol, shot himself once in the chest with a .22-caliber pistol while three men sat playing cards at the other end of a long oval, felt-covered table, said Lt. William Mayer, head of the Rochester police physical crimes squad.

DelGuercio had worked as a taxi driver, Mayer said, but was currently unemployed.

Mayer said police are still checking on DelGuercio's whereabouts before his death. An autopsy showed DelGuercio was intoxicated when he committed suicide.

DelGuercio went to the club, at 221 Franklin St., and was admitted by Phillip Brightman, 41, of 105 Rosedale St., one of the three people inside, Mayer said.

Brightman told police he was watching the other two men, William Stewart, 72, of 123 Griffith St. and Sebastian Gangemi Jr., 46, of 1588 Norton St. play cards, Mayer said.

Mayer said the men told police they didn't pay any attention to DelGuercio, who sat at the end of the table, away from them.

"Apparently there wasn't any conversation at all," Mayer said. "Then there was a shot. One of the men said he thought it was a firecracker, Gangemi said he stood up and yelled, 'Is this for real?' then yelled, 'Oh my God.' "

One of the men then called for an ambulance. When police arrived, the pistol was found lying near DelGuercio on the floor, Mayer said. Mayer said police yesterday were checking to determine who owned the pistol.

**Democrat and Chronicle**
**November 18, 1980**

## Leonard Stebbins Surrenders

On **March 26, 1981**, reputed mobster Leonard Stebbins turned himself in to the FBI for a robbery that he and three others allegedly committed. He was immediately charged with bank burglary and bank larceny.

The four were accused of cutting a hole in the roof of the Avon Marine Midland bank and entering the bank early in the morning on September 13, 1978. **(45)**

### Reputed mobster surrenders, denies bank-theft counts

Early yesterday the Rochester police broadcast an order to pick up reputed mob figure Leonard Stebbins, and police in unmarked cars settled in to watch Stebbins' brother's home off Dewey Avenue at 3:05 a.m.

But they never found him there. At noon yesterday Stebbins surrendered to the FBI, and half an hour later he was taken to U.S. District Court. There, visiting Judge John T. Curtin opened a sealed indictment charging him and three others with bank burglary and bank larceny.

The four-count indictment, handed up by a federal grand jury that investigated for more than a year, accuses them of stealing $2,216.30.

As a condition of his release pending trial, Curtin ordered Stebbins to telephone the U.S. Marshal every Monday morning.

The four are accused of cutting a hole in the roof of the Avon Marine Midland bank and entering the bank early in the morning of Sept. 13, 1978.

One investigator said the four took plastic explosives inside to gain entrance to the night depository, but the explosives were never detonated because the burglars were interrupted.

Charlene Russo Miles, 24, of 421 Ridgeway Ave., and Stebbins, 39, of 46 Oneida St., pleaded not guilty to the charges.

Curtin released Miles on a $5,000 personal recognizance bond and Stebbins on a $25,000 personal recognizance bond.

A third defendant, Bruce Thomann, who is in custody in the federal penitentiary at Lewisburg, Pa., on other charges, asked Curtin for a court-appointed lawyer. Curtin entered a not guilty plea on his behalf.

The fourth defendant, Eugene LaRue, is in custody in federal prison in Wisconsin and will be arraigned later, Assistant District Attorney Rosemary Roberts said.

Thomann, 42, and LaRue, 36, both of Utica, are in prison for burglarizing a bank in New Hampshire in 1978. Warrants for their arrest were issued nationwide after the Hampton National Bank of Seabrook, N.H. was broken into.

The two were captured by the FBI in Rochester. They had been staying at Miles' home for about a week when they were arrested for the New Hampshire burglary on Sept. 19, 1978, six days after the Avon burglary.

Stebbins, Miles, Thomann and LaRue are accused of conspiracy to commit bank larceny and bank burglary. Stebbins is accused alone in one count of the indictment of possession of $600 of the proceeds of the larceny.

Stebbins was not arrested at the time of the burglary, and yesterday Roberts refused to disclose how investigators connected the $600 to the money taken from the bank. She also refused to disclose who "interrupted" the burglars and thwarted the explosion of the night depository.

The next court date for the four is April 13, when Roberts will ask that the case be placed on the trial calendar.

**Democrat and Chronicle**
**3-27-81**

## Vincent J. Rallo Becomes Government Informant

### Informant who knows 'everything'

By NANCY MONAGHAN
D&C Staff Writer

The federal Organized Crime Strike Force has a new informant, and he apparently has cracked open a new treasure chest for federal agents: underworld corruption in several local labor unions.

Vincent J. Rallo, a Rochester insurance man, pleaded guilty two weeks ago to two arsons and has become the 15th Rochester-area resident known to have entered the federal Witness Protection Program since its inception in 1970.

*Turn to INFORMANT, Page 2A*

A Rochester insurance man, Vincent J. Rallo, had become the Federal Organized Crime Strike Force's new informant.

He pleaded guilty earlier in March of 1981 to two arsons. He was the 15th Rochester resident to enter into the Federal Witness Protection Program.

Rallo was expected to provide information about several organized crime arsons and loan sharking activities. He was also supposed to have had valuable information about Mafia infiltration into labor unions. According to one source, "He knew everything."

Ironically, Rallo's son Joseph was already in the Witness Protection Program, he entered about a week prior to his father. Joseph Rallo was believed to have had information about incidents that took place in 1978 at the height of the mob wars.

### INFORMANT

*From Page 1A*

Rallo's cooperation is a major break for the Strike Force, which for several months has been conducting a grand jury investigation of organized crime in Rochester. He is the second underworld figure known to have "flipped" since the investigation began.

"There will be trouble over this one," an underworld source said yesterday.

In addition to his knowledge of Mafia infiltration into labor unions — "he knows everything," one source said — Rallo will give valuable testimony about a string of organized crime arsons and loansharking activities.

Rallo, 61, whose last known address was 5 LaCroix Court, Irondequoit, has reportedly left town with a new identity, as Anthony F. Oliveri did last spring when he turned informant for the Strike Force. It could not be learned yesterday whether Rallo has already testified before the federal grand jury or if federal agents are still debriefing him.

Special Assistant U.S. Attorney Donald J. Wisner, contacted by telephone yesterday at his home, refused to answer questions about Rallo's cooperation. He did confirm that Rallo pleaded guilty to two arsons, including the 1978 explosion that destroyed Mark Kitchens, an Irondequoit kitchen remodeling firm.

In October, Dean W. Haynesworth, the former

Vincent J. Rallo.

director of a federally funded program for ex-offenders, pleaded guilty to the same fire. According to court papers filed at that time, Haynesworth was recruited by Rallo to destroy the building for the insurance.

In 1961, Rallo won the Republican nomination for 18th Ward supervisor but was defeated in the general election.

In 1977, Rallo was convicted, along with Eugene DeFrancesco, a reputed Mafia figure, of federal conspiracy and racketeering charges involving a Mafia-controlled arson-for-hire ring. Four other defendants — Rene Piccarreto, the reputed organized crime boss, Richard Marino, a reputed underboss, Anthony C. Arena, and Joseph Nalore, the former Rochester Fire Chief — were acquitted.

In 1976, Rallo was convicted of third-degree grand larceny in connection with the financial collapse of a housing project the Rochester Barbers Union Local 246 sponsored in Greece in the early 1970s. He was accused of stealing from the union's hospitalization fund.

In January 1980, he filed for bankruptcy, listing debts totaling $301,502.88 and assets of $405.

Rallo has been identified as a known associate of several highly placed organized crime figures, including Carmelo "Charlie the Ox" Indovino, who said he was a plumber, and who was a frequent visitor to the construction site of the Barbers Union's $3.2 million project in Greece.

The focus of the federal grand jury's probe has been the established organized crime leaders, the group that became known as the "A Team" during the 1978 Mafia war for control of the rackets.

During that war, the A Team's underboss, Salvatore "Sammy G" Gingello, and the B Team's boss, Thomas DiDio, were slain. Last year, six of DiDio's associates were convicted of racketeering and weapons charges, and are serving prison terms in federal penitentiaries around the country.

# Joey Tiraborelli On Trial For Assault

## Witnesses describe 'sucker' punch

By JODY McPHILLIPS
D&C Staff Writer

Reputed Mafia figure Joseph Tiraborelli went looking for a man he thought helped reposess his truck, asked him to step outside, then threw a "sucker" punch that nearly severed the man's tongue, witnesses testified yesterday as Tiraborelli's assault trial opened.

Tiraborelli is accused of assaulting Neil Silvarole just before noon on March 31 at Genesee Ford Truck Sales, 1280 Jefferson Road. Tiraborelli, 37, dressed in a cream-colored open-necked sweater, brown slacks and cowboy boots, spoke just once during the 2½-hour session in Henrietta Town Court.

As Assistant District Attorney Douglas Stoddard squabbled with defense lawyer Charles West Jr. over a procedural matter during a recess, Stoddard snapped, "Why are you being such a ----- about this, Charley?"

Tiraborelli started from his seat and said, "Hey, you watch your language. There are ladies present."

"Are you going to hit me, too?" Stoddard bristled.

"Why don't you just conduct yourself the way you're supposed to?" Tiraborelli replied.

The prosecution claims Tiraborelli punched Silvarole because he believed Silvarole worked for Northeast Repossession Inc. and located Tiraborelli's truck for repossession.

Tiraborelli's truck was repossessed about 5 a.m. March 30 by Kathleen Probst, who owns the firm at 160 S. Plymouth Ave. She testified Silvarole did not work for the firm at that time and was not present when the truck was repossessed.

Silvarole, a self-employed trucker, has worked for the firm as a "spotter" or locator of vehicles to be repossessed from time to time since then, she said.

Gary Waye, used-truck manager at Genesee Ford, testified he was in his office the morning of March 31 when Tiraborelli came in and asked for Silvarole.

"I was on the phone when Neil went out with him," Waye said. "Next, I heard a lot of hollering and screaming. Joe said he'd get even with Neil.

"Neil was shouting he wanted to know who Joe was. Next thing I heard was a big thump on the side of the trailer."

Wayne Willmes, a Genesee Ford truck salesman, testified he was also in the office and went to a window to look when he heard shouting outside.

Seconds later he saw Tiraborelli punch Silvarole once in the face, Willmes said.

Later that day Silvarole was treated at Strong Memorial Hospital. Dr. Neil Robert Schachter testified at the non-jury trial that Silvarole required seven stitches on his tongue, which was cut clear through.

Silvarole said he didn't know who Tiraborelli was when he talked to him March 31.

"He asked if I was looking for him. I said no. He said, 'I'm Joe Tiraborelli' and then he sucker-punched me," Silvarole said.

Testimony will continue tomorrow at 10 a.m. before Town Justice Michael Iaculli.

**November 6, 1981 Democrat and Chronicle**

Joseph F. Tiraborelli
... in court yesterday

**Joseph F. Tiraborelli**

Reputed Mafia figure Joseph Tiraborelli, the step-son of "Red" Russotti, the "Boss" of the Rochester Mafia, was accused of assaulting a man whom he thought helped repossess his truck.

Tiraborelli asked the man, identified as Neil Silvarole, to step outside, then he sucker punched him, nearly severing his tongue. Silvarole required seven stitches on his tongue. **(46)**

## Rochester Mob Figure Is Shot Dead

Mob figure shot dead

today

FBI captures 2 of top 10

Police arrest one supect after Irondequoit slaying; search goes on for 2nd man

U.N. rebuffs Israel

A demand on Cody

Investigators stand over the body of John Fiorino, who was shot dead in front of the Blue Gardenia restaurant last night.

**Democrat and Chronicle December 18, 1981**

**On December 17, 1981, Rochester Mafia "Capo" and Teamsters Local #398 Vice-President John Fiorino was shot dead as he entered the Blue Gardenia Restarant in Irondeqoit, N.Y.**

### The Murder of John Fiorino

Thomas M. Torpey, and Thomas E. Taylor, were accused of plotting the murder of John Fiorino in an effort to take control of Rochester's rackets. Taylor said the mob didn't deserve to run the rackets in Rochester and that he and Torpey wanted to take control. "I helped them take this town," Torpey said. "Why should I pay? They're just a bunch of punks. They're like that all over the country.

Torpey had to make weekly payments, or "juice," of $700 to the mob, whose members ran their own string of gambling parlors. But Torpey upset mob bosses including Fiorino when he began missing those payments during the late spring and early summer of 1981. He confided in Thomas Taylor and Louis DiGiuilio that he was "having trouble with a certain bunch of guys," DiGiuilio testified. Taylor and DiGiuilio agreed that Torpey shouldn't have to pay.

In the fall, Torpey met reputed local crime bosses Samuel "Red" Russotti and Rene Piccarreto at his joint. The three were seated in the back room at a round table haggling over the weekly gambling payments. Taylor sat behind Torpey. DiGiuilio testified that he walked in the room and overheard part of the conversation. "You got something going on in this town, and I want a piece of it," Russotti said to Torpey. "Business is bad," Torpey said. "I got nothing going on." After the meeting, DiGiuilio testified, it was agreed that "the juice" would be cut to $350 a week.

DiGiuilio further testified that Torpey started missing payments again in December and that Fiorino had stopped by the club just days before his death. He was wearing a long coat.

DiGiuilio recalled asking Fiorino, "John, what brings you here?" "Torpey ain't paying," Fiorino replied. "I'm here to close this place down."

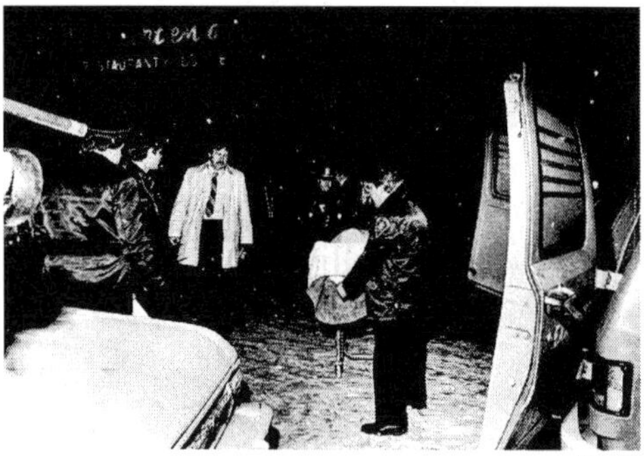

FILE PHOTO

Medical examiner removes the body of John Fiorino from outside the Blue Gardenia in 1981. Torpey served a prison term until 2008 for his role in the killing.

**The Medical Examiner removes the body of John Fiorino from outside the Blue Gardenia.**

Torpey then showed up, and told Fiorino that he was tired of making the weekly payments. "You're causing trouble in this town," Fiorino said. "I want to avoid another war. I'll give you the $350 a week. Just say you'll pay," Fiorino insisted. "You ain't closing my place down," Torpey said harshly. "And I ain't paying either." Before he left, Fiorino told Torpey, "You know Tom, you're no superman, you can bleed and die just like everyone else."

Louis DiGiuilio testified that on **December 14, 1981**, he was on his way to Thomas Taylor's apartment in the Green Leaf Meadows complex in Greece when he stopped at a gasoline station at the corner of Lake Avenue and Stutson Street to buy gas and cigarettes. By chance, Taylor and Torpey drove into the station in Taylor's brown 1979 Thunderbird. "Hey, Louie," they said. "How ya doing? Sully's in town." DiGiuilio testified he'd first met the small, muscular Sullivan a year before at Taylor's house. He next saw him during the summer of 1981 at a cookout Taylor held near Hamlin Beach.

On **December 15, 1981**, DiGiuilio met Torpey and Taylor at Taylor's apartment. DiGiuilio said they told him to go to the Marriott Inn on West Ridge Road in Greece to meet Sullivan who would be staying on the seventh floor under a fake name.Torpey and Taylor were to show up later. DiGiuilio testified that he arrived at Sullivan's room at 6:45p.m. When the hit man answered the door, he was holding a large hunting knife inside a sheaf. On the bed was a pump-action sawed-off shotgun, an automatic handgun and a silencer.

Sullivan asked DiGiuilio, "What do you got for me?" DiGiuilio replied, "There's two guys, one's an “Underboss,” one's a “Captain," Fiorino had been identified by law enforcement officials as a "Captain" in Rochester's organized Crime Family. After half an hour's conversation, they came up with a sketchy plan. DiGiuilio and Sullivan would drive around to various bars, hoping to run across Fiorino and Richard Marino. "I'd point them out to Joe and he was going to blast them," DiGiuilio testified. Torpey and Taylor were to follow in Taylor's car, which they'd use as a "crash car" if they saw DiGiuilio and Sullivan were being chased by a police car, Torpey and Taylor were to crash into it.

Later, when Sullivan was on trial, defense lawyers ridiculed DiGiuilio’s story, pointing out Torpey was hiding out from police in December of 1981. Why would Taylor and Torpey risk crashing into a police car in Taylor's car in the area of a gangland murder? they asked. But DiGiuilio didn't waver in his testimony. He said that on the night of **December 15, 1981** the four drove in two cars to search for Fiorino and Marino. Sullivan was driving his 1977 peach-colored Cadillac and Taylor was driving his Thunderbird.

They had drinks at Jason's restaurant on Hudson Avenue, the former Blue Gardenia Restaurant in the Empire Plaza and a bar on East Ridge Road, all in Irondequoit. But they couldn't find either of the men they were planning to kill.

They decided to drive to Tommy's restaurant on East Avenue. On the way they spotted a familiar truck parked in front of a gambling club on St. Paul Street. It belonged to Joseph "Joe the Hop" Rossi, Fiorino's mob associate and close friend. DiGiulio testified he went inside and told Rossi that Taylor was at Tommy's and wanted to talk to him. At the bar, Taylor said to Rossi, "Why don't you give John (Fiorino) a call? Tell him to come out and have a couple of drinks." Sullivan and Torpey waited outside in the car. Rossi made the call, but Fiorino never showed.

On **December 17, 1981**, DiGiuilio picked Sullivan up at the Marriott and helped him carry his suitcases down to the Cadillac after he checked out. The two met Torpey and Taylor at Trebor's Restaurant on State Street, where DiGiuilio said they ate lunch, drank wine and cocktails, and snorted cocaine. The group left Trebor's at about 3:30 p.m. and planned to meet again two hours later at Jason's, where they would try to lure Fiorino to kill him.

On the night of the murder, Taylor said he was having trouble getting Fiorino to Jason's but that he would be at the Blue Gardenia about 7. By 5:30, DiGiuilio and Sullivan were waiting in the parking lot at Jason's. Torpey and Taylor arrived-shortly afterward. A short time later John Fiorino arrived. "Fiorino pulled up in a green Lincoln Continental and started walking toward the entrance of the restaurant. It was about 6:45.

"That him?" Sullivan asked DiGiuilio. "I can't be sure" answered DiGiuilio. "Is it him or isn't it?" persisted Sullivan. "Yeah, it's him," DiGiuilio replied while nodding his head. Then Sullivan, concealing a sawed-off shotgun underneath his coat, stepped out of the car and walked toward Fiorino. "I heard the shots," DiGiuilio testified. "I looked. I saw John drop." Sullivan started walking back toward the Cadillac. He hesitated for a moment, turned and walked back toward Fiorino's body. He stood over the body and deliberately fired another blast into Fiorino's head. Sullivan told DiGiuilio to keep the car's lights turned off, drive slowly out of the plaza and stay calm.

## The Getaway

They drove toward the plaza's entrance, rather than its exit. At that instant, Irondequoit Police Officer Michael DiGiovanni, patrolling on Empire Boulevard, passed the Cadillac in the entrance as it was turning east onto Empire Boulevard. The officer turned his car around and gave chase. The traffic light at the nearby intersection of Empire Boulevard and Helendale Road was red, but Sullivan told DiGiuilio to ignore it and keep on going. They ran the light and their car barreled into another car. The Cadillac spun out on the icy road, jumped a curb and landed in a snow bank on the south side of the road.

As DiGiovanni was driving up, Sullivan got out and started firing shotgun blasts at the patrol car. The officer ducked down on the seat of the car. "I could feel the glass spraying over my head," DiGiovanni said. The officer crawled out and returned fire. Sullivan tossed DiGiuilio a handgun and the two ran behind a building and separated. That night police followed tracks in the snow to a lot behind nearby Pardee Elementary School on Helendale Road, where they captured DiGiuilio, who was lying face down in the snow. Sullivan escaped.

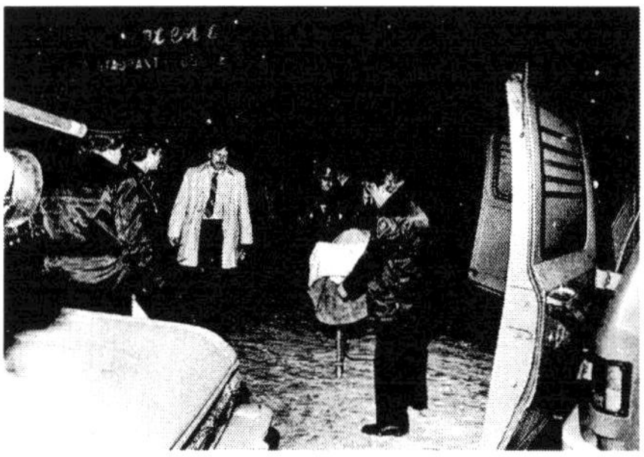

FILE PHOTO

Medical examiner removes the body of John Fiorino from outside the Blue Gardenia in 1981. Torpey served a prison term until 2008 for his role in the killing.

**John Fiorino's body at the crime scene.**

# Teamster, Mob "Captain," Informant and Family Man

**John "Johnny Flowers" Fiorino** was Vice-President of Teamsters Local #398 in Rochester, New York. He was murdered on December 17, 1981, outside of the Blue Gardenia Restaurant in Irondequoit, New York by Joseph "Mad Dog" Sullivan, on the orders of "C Team" leaders Thomas Torpey and Thomas Taylor.

Democrat and Chronicle/Dave Coon

Investigators stand over the body of John Fiorino, who was shot dead in front of the Blue Gardenia restaurant last night.

At the time of his death, The FBI considered John Fiorino to have been a "made" member and "Captain" of the Rochester Mafia Crime Family. **(171)** He had also recently become an informant and had began cooperating with the US Organized Crime Strike Force. **(172)**

John Fiorino was also a family man who lived in the suburbs. He was described by his daughters as a great dad who never talked about crime, ever, in front of them.

They said their father had a good sense of humor, took pride in taking care of his car and his lawn and was also a good cook. **(173)**

'They never say he was a family man'

Daughters of John Fiorino remember him as a great dad who didn't talk about crime

By Jody McPhillips
Democrat and Chronicle

John Fiorino's daughters weren't among the hundreds of people who packed the courtroom during the eight days of Joseph John Sullivan's trial for Fiorino's murder.

"I just wanted to stay away from there," said Nancy Fiorino, 19. Nancy sat at the kitchen table of her family's suburban home and smoothed the cover of a family photo album. "I didn't think I could control my emotions," she said.

"I don't know who killed my father, but whoever did, I think should be punished."

Earlier, Fiorino's mother Mimi Fiorino said, "People should know what kind of man John was."

Fiorino's daughters agree. They say they're proud of the name Fiorino, because of the man their father was.

"The newspapers only say he was a mobster," Nancy said. "They never say he had a job, that he worked his way up in the Teamsters," Marie, 21, added. "They never say he was a family man."

Sullivan is on trial for killing Fiorino, vice president of Teamsters Local 398, in front of the Blue Gardenia Restaurant Dec. 17. Police have called Fiorino a lieutenant in Rochester's Mafia, serving under reputed underboss Richard J. Marino.

Nancy last saw her father alive at 4 p.m. the day he died, at her maternal grandmother's house. They talked for a half-hour.

SULLIVAN TRIAL, 3B

The last thing he said to her was, "Call me later, honey. I'll be home."

According to testimony in Sullivan's trial last week, Fiorino never got that call from his daughter because reputed underworld insurgent Thomas E. Taylor called him first.

Fiorino, home and settled for the night at 6 p.m., got dressed again and went out to meet Taylor at the Blue Gardenia. Fiorino was shot to death as he moved toward the restaurant's door.

Prosecutors say Sullivan had never seen Fiorino before Dec. 17. They say Taylor and Thomas E. Torpey wanted Fiorino and Marino killed so they could take over mob operations in Rochester.

Police informant Louis A. DiGiulio, who had been Fiorino's friend, testified last week that he pointed Fiorino out to Sullivan moments before the shooting.

Nancy remembers that December night when she heard the news. Marie had just returned from Christmas shopping to the family home at 78 Venice Circle, Irondequoit, when a family friend told her.

Marie called Nancy to tell her their father had been killed. "I was shocked. I dropped the phone. I couldn't believe it," Nancy remembered.

Their father never talked to them about anything related to organized crime or even to his job, they said. They didn't know many of his friends. "He never brought them home," Nancy said.

"I don't believe he was involved in all the things people said he was," Marie said. "He never talked about it in front of us."

In the weeks leading up to the shooting, he hadn't seemed worried about himself or about their safety, they said. But Fiorino, who did not normally carry a gun, had a silver handgun in his boot the night he died.

Police have theorized he may have armed himself because he feared violence from organized crime figures.

Fiorino's daughters watched on the television screen in their own house and saw the nightmarish image of a man they loved, killed on a snowy night by a shotgun blast.

"I saw people get killed all the time on television," Nancy said. "Then all of a sudden it was my own father."

"Why do they keep showing those pictures?" Marie asked. "Don't they ever think what it does to his family?" Nine months after her father died, she is visibly upset.

Nancy Fiorino and late father, John.

Nancy, 19, left, and Marie Fiorino, 21, the daughters of slaying victim John Fiorino.

Fiorino loved his family, his daughters said. "He liked to stay home at night and play with his baby daughter (Jeannie)," Marie said. Jeannie, 4, is her half-sister.

Last December, Nancy and Marie were living with Fiorino, his second wife, Lois, and their little sister. Since the slaying, they have moved into a shared apartment.

"At least Nancy and I knew him," Marie said. "Jeannie will never get to see the kind of guy he was . . . I can see if he was some kind of bum who was never home, but he was a family man. It's just unfair."

His daughters say Fiorino had a good sense of humor, took pride in keeping his cars and lawn in top shape, and was an excellent cook. "He took a lot of pride in eating what he cooked, too," said family friend Chris Ruoff, who has known the Fiorinos for about four years.

Ruoff worked with Fiorino, and said Fiorino gave him some "good breaks" when he was starting out as a truck driver. "He was a big guy, solid, six-two or six-three," Ruoff said.

"He had this big booming voice; he was the kind of guy who couldn't ever whisper. Just by the way he talked, you respected him. But you wouldn't be afraid of him.

TURN TO PAGE 8B

# *Chapter 6*
# The "C Team"
# A New Enemy in the Mob War

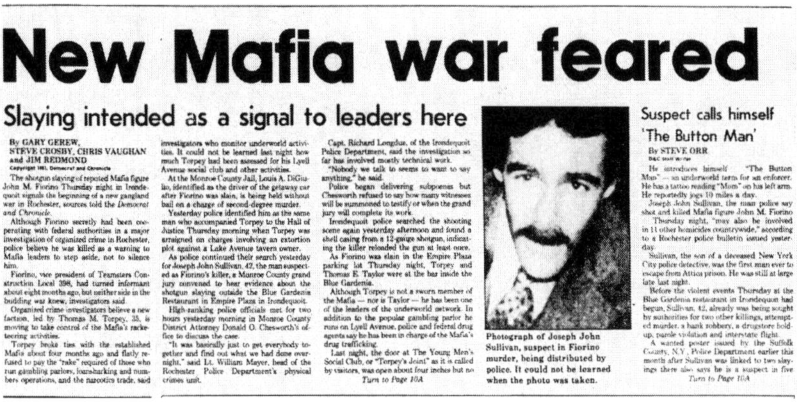

## New Mafia war feared

### Slaying intended as a signal to leaders here

By GARY GEREW, STEVE CROSBY, CHRIS VAUGHAN and JIM REDMOND
Copyright 1981, Democrat and Chronicle

The shotgun slaying of reputed Mafia figure John M. Fiorino Thursday night in Irondequoit signals the beginning of a new gangland war in Rochester, sources told the *Democrat and Chronicle*.

Although Fiorino secretly had been cooperating with federal authorities in a major investigation of organized crime in Rochester, police believe he was killed as a warning to Mafia leaders to step aside, not to silence him.

Fiorino, vice president of Teamsters Construction Local 398, had turned informant about eight months ago, but neither side in the budding war knew, investigators said.

Organized crime investigators believe a new faction, led by Thomas M. Torpey, 35, is moving to take control of the Mafia's racketeering activities.

Torpey broke ties with the established Mafia about four months ago and flatly refused to pay the "take" required of those who run gambling parlors, loansharking and numbers operations, and the narcotics trade, said investigators who monitor underworld activities. It could not be learned last night how much Torpey had been assessed for his Lyell Avenue social club and other activities.

At the Monroe County Jail, Louis A. DiGiulio, identified as the driver of the getaway car after Fiorino was slain, is being held without bail on a charge of second-degree murder.

Yesterday police identified him as the same man who accompanied Torpey to the Hall of Justice Thursday morning when Torpey was arraigned on charges involving an extortion plot against a Lake Avenue tavern owner.

As police continued their search yesterday for Joseph John Sullivan, 42, the man suspected as Fiorino's killer, a Monroe County grand jury convened to hear evidence about the shotgun slaying outside the Blue Gardenia Restaurant in Empire Plaza in Irondequoit.

High-ranking police officials met for two hours yesterday morning in Monroe County District Attorney Donald O. Chesworth's office to discuss the case.

"It was basically just to get everybody together and find out what we had done overnight," said Lt. William Mayer, head of the Rochester Police Department's physical crimes unit.

Capt. Richard Longdue, of the Irondequoit Police Department, said the investigation so far has involved mostly technical work.

"Nobody we talk to seems to want to say anything," he said.

Police began delivering subpoenas but Chesworth refused to say how many witnesses will be summoned to testify or when the grand jury will complete its work.

Irondequoit police searched the shooting scene again yesterday afternoon and found a shell casing from a 12-gauge shotgun, indicating the killer reloaded the gun at least once.

As Fiorino was slain in the Empire Plaza parking lot Thursday night, Torpey and Thomas E. Taylor were at the bar inside the Blue Gardenia.

Although Torpey is not a sworn member of the Mafia — nor is Taylor — he has been one of the leaders of the underworld network. In addition to the popular gambling parlor he runs on Lyell Avenue, police and federal drug agents say he has been in charge of the Mafia's drug trafficking.

Last night, the door at The Young Men's Social Club, or "Torpey's Joint" as it is called by visitors, was open about four inches but no

Turn to Page 10A

**Photograph of Joseph John Sullivan, suspect in Fiorino murder, being distributed by police. It could not be learned when the photo was taken.**

### Suspect calls himself 'The Button Man'

By STEVE ORR
D&C Staff Writer

He introduces himself "The Button Man" — an underworld term for an enforcer. He has a tattoo reading "Mom" on his left arm. He reportedly jogs 10 miles a day.

Joseph John Sullivan, the man police say shot and killed Mafia figure John M. Fiorino Thursday night, "may also be involved in 11 other homicides countrywide," according to a Rochester police bulletin issued yesterday.

Sullivan, the son of a deceased New York City police detective, was the first man ever to escape from Attica prison. He was still at large late last night.

Before the violent events Thursday at the Blue Gardenia restaurant in Irondequoit had begun, Sullivan, 42, already was being sought by authorities for two other killings, attempted murder, a bank robbery, a drugstore holdup, parole violation and interstate flight.

A wanted poster issued by the Suffolk County, N.Y., Police Department earlier this month after Sullivan was linked to two slayings there also says he is a suspect in five

Turn to Page 10A

**December 19, 1981 Democrat and Chronicle**

Despite the fact that John Fiorino was cooperating with federal authorities in a major investigation into organized crime, it was believed that he was killed as a message to the "A Team" to back off, and not as a result of him becoming an informant.

A new faction led by Thomas Taylor and Thomas Torpey, the "C Team," were now trying to take over control of the Rochester Mafia's racketeering activities. Torpey broke ties with the established Mafia several months beforehand when he flatly refused to continue paying his weekly "juice" payments. Those payments were required by the Mafia of all who ran gambling parlors or numbers operations. There were no exceptions. "Juice" payments were the Mafia's primary source of income.

The profit derived from gambling operations was so great that there was no end to mobsters who were willing to kill each other to gain control of that money. **(48)**

## Mistrial Declared In Stebbins Arson Case

A mistrial was declared on **February 3, 1982**, in the attempted arson and criminal possession of a dangerous weapon case of Arthur Stebbins. The case was in connection with a bombing of a Dewey Avenue Barber Shop.

After 24 hours of deliberations, the State Supreme Court Jury declared a deadlock, resulting in the judge declaring a mistrial. Stebbins was originally indicted along with his brother Leonard Stebbins, who had been identified as an organized crime figure. The case would be tried again. **(49)**

## Fire at the Young Man's Social Club Believed to Be an Accident

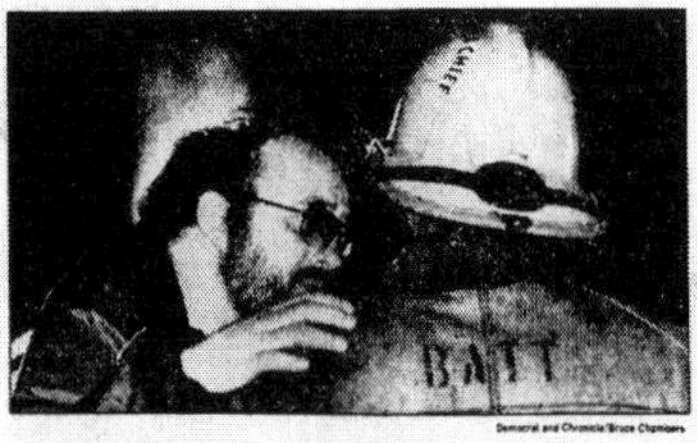


Thomas Torpey talks with a battalion chief during fire at Torpey's club

**Club fire believed an accident**

By JIM REDMOND and CHRIS VAUGHAN
D&C Staff Writers

Rochester fire investigators are no longer calling suspicious the two-alarm fire that late Friday extensively damaged a reputed gambling parlor on Lyell Avenue and three apartments above it.

The fire in the two-story brick building at 251-253 Lyell Ave. rekindled into a second two-alarm fire shortly before 7 a.m. yesterday.

Seven tenants living in the three second-floor apartments were able to escape unharmed Friday night. No injuries were reported from either fire.

The fire's cause remains undetermined, fire investigator Edward Klingenberger said, "but we're leaning toward accidental rather than suspicious."

Klingenberger refused to definitely rule out arson as the cause, but said, "We don't think it was intentionally set."

Fire officials yesterday said the fire appeared to start in the Young Men's Social Club in the building's first floor.

Reputed organized crime figure Thomas Torpey operated the club, which police said is a gambling parlor.

The fire, which was first reported at 11:45 p.m. Friday, appeared to have started near the front of the boarded up storefront at 251 Lyell Ave., Fire Chief Leonard Huether said.

The fire probably began in a couch or chair, Klingenberger said. The fire destroyed the furniture, he added.

The fire spread up the west wall and into the ceiling before tenant Geraldine Vary, who was watching television with her children, smelled smoke and alerted neighbors.

The fire burned for almost two hours before being declared under control the first time.

Shortly after midnight, Huether ordered all of his men out of the burning building when officials began to worry that the roof and two walls were about to collapse.

But deep-seated burning continued in a partition after firefighters left the scene early yesterday, officials said. The burning eventually spread upward along the west side of the building and into the ceiling between the first- and second-floors.

Firefighters were called back to the building at 6:55 a.m. and called for a second-alarm 14 minutes later. The fire was declared under control for the second time at 7:41 a.m. but firefighters remained at the scene until about 2 p.m.

*Turn to Page 4B*

**Above, Thomas Torpey (left) talks to a fireman.**
**February 7, 1982 Democrat and Chronicle**

The fire at the Young Man's Social Club, located at 251-253 Lyell Avenue on **February 5, 1982**, was no longer being called "suspicious." Investigators now believed that the fire was the result of an accident, although the cause was still undetermined.

The Young Man's Social Club was a known gambling parlor run by Thomas Torpey, former body guard and chauffeur to Rochester Mafia "Underboss" Sammy Gingello.

Firefighters thought they had the blaze under control that evening but were called back to the scene the following morning at 6:55 a.m. for a second two alarm fire. That fire was under control less than an hour later. **(50)**

# "Mad Dog" Sullivan Is Captured

'Mad Dog' Sullivan, the son of a detective and a suspect in 11 killings statewide, was captured Tuesday , **February 23, 1982** by FBI agents outside a suburban Rochester motel and charged with bank robbery, authorities said.

Sullivan captured at motel

FBI agents nab suspect in Mafia 'contract' killing

By Gary Gerew
Democrat and Chronicle

A morning phone tip and a rush by 10 armed FBI agents yesterday ended the two-month search for Joseph John Sullivan, a suspect in a December gangland slaying in Irondequoit.

Sullivan is being held in the Monroe County Jail on a federal bank robbery charge.

Sullivan, whom police believe shot reputed Mafia figure and Teamsters union official John M. Fiorino, was captured about 10:20 a.m. in the parking lot of the Denonville Inn.

The motel, at 1750 Empire Blvd., Penfield, is about [illegible] miles from the parking lot in front of the Blue Gardenia Restaurant on Empire Boulevard in Irondequoit where Fiorino was killed by a shotgun blast on Dec. 17.

"It's incredible he would be found that close by," one police officer said. "The last place I thought he would be was anywhere near Rochester."

Police said they had received information before that Sullivan was in the Rochester area but were never able to confirm it.

"Information we had said that he was in and out of Rochester regularly," said Special Agent Philip Smith of the FBI, "but this was the first chance we had to get him." Smith refused to say what precise information led to yesterday's arrest, except that the information indicated Sullivan was in the Webster area.

FBI agents had been staked out around

TURN TO PAGE 3A

'THE BUTTON MAN' 3A
AT THE FEDERAL BUILDING 3A

Joseph John Sullivan, left, suspect in shooting of Mafia figure here in December, is put into a car by FBI agents after his arraignment at federal building yesterday.

The arrests at the inn

'I wish this hadn't happened here'

By Gary Gerew
Democrat and Chronicle

It was about 1:30 p.m. Monday when a young woman asked for a room at the Denonville Inn and signed the registration card for Room 3.

She signed her name as "Terry Palmieri" and gave an Islip, Long Island, address.

She said she and a friend would be staying the night and paid [illegible] in advance for the room at the inn at 1750 Empire Blvd.

She would not be seen with that friend until their arrest until the next day.

About 30 minutes after she checked in, Palmieri came into the Penfield inn's lounge accompanied by a man, who has not been identified. They each ordered a drink while sitting at the bar.

The man asked for directions to the Lake Ontario State Parkway and to Greenleaf Road, the bartender, who asked that his name not be used, said. "The woman didn't even finish her drink," the bartender said. "She had a Heineken's beer and he had a Dewar's White Label with a splash. She left half a bottle of beer on the bar." The bartender said the couple left a 30-cent tip after paying $2.70 for the drinks.

That evening, the bartender and the motel's owner, Paul Meyers went to play darts. "We got in shortly before midnight and I saw the (unidentified) guy again standing at the bar," the bartender said. "He didn't say anything to me, but he nodded towards me."

TURN TO PAGE 3A

Theresa Palmieri is taken from the federal building after arraignment.

BACKGROUND

On Dec. 17 at about 7 p.m., reputed Mafia leader John M. Fiorino was fatally shot outside the Blue Gardenia restaurant in Irondequoit's Empire Plaza. Police called his death "a contract killing," and warned of a new gangland war here.

Two men fled the restaurant's parking lot in a 1976 Cadillac, and an Irondequoit police officer gave chase. When the getaway car jumped a curb, shots were exchanged between the policeman and one of the men in the car. The driver was arrested after a brief chase, and the passenger escaped.

Louis A. DiGiulio, 25, of Rochester, was arrested at the scene. Police said the man who escaped was Joseph John Sullivan, 42, of Long Island, the self-styled "Button Man," an underworld enforcer.

**February 24, 1982**
**Democrat and Chronicle**

Joseph John Sullivan, 42, whose nickname was 'Mad Dog,' was arrested without incident about 10 a.m. in front of the Denonville Inn in Penfield, N.Y., as he was about to enter his car with his girlfriend, Theresa Palmieri, 25.

The car contained a .38-caliber revolver and an AR-15 automatic rifle in the back seat, Special Agent Philip Smith said. He said a bulletproof vest was also found in the car. Smith said Sullivan, who also called himself the 'Button Man,' an organized crime term for a hit man, offered no resistance.

Sullivan was charged only with the Dec. 14, 1981, robbery of a Marine Midland Bank in Utica, N.Y., and with unlawful flight, the FBI said. Sullivan pleaded innocent before U.S. Magistrate Stephen Joy, who set bail at $500,000.

FBI agents staked out the motel when the bureau received a tip that Sullivan was staying there, Smith said. Sullivan was captured by 10 agents as he checked out.

Mr. Sullivan was a suspect in a number of homicides, approximately 11, Smith said. Among the homicides in which he was a suspect was the December 17, 1981, gangland-style slaying of John Fiorino, Vice President and Business Agent of Teamsters Local #398. Lee Lasker, Assistant Director of the FBI's New York office, said Sullivan was wanted for a double homicide in Selden, N.Y., on Dec. 8, 1981 He was also a suspect in a killing Jan. 21, 1982 in Manhattan.

FBI spokesman Joseph Brannigan said Sullivan was the son of a New York City detective, Jeremiah Sullivan, who died in 1961. Brannigan also said Ms. Palmieri was the sister-in-law of fugitive Stephen Catalanotte, 32, who was wanted for a jewel robbery at the time.

Ten years prior, Sullivan escaped from the Attica Correctional Facility where he was serving a 20 to 30 year term for second-degree manslaughter stemming from a holdup in New York City. Sullivan, believed to be the only person ever to escape the maximum-security facility, was recaptured in New York City six weeks later. (51)

INN
Sullivan arrested
at Denonville Inn
1750 Empire Blvd.
The Denonville Inn on Empire Boulevard in Penfield where FBI agents captured
Joseph John Sullivan, a suspect in the December shotgun-slaying of John Fiorino
Owner wishes arrests hadn't happened


**"Mad Dog" Sullivan was arrested at The Denonville Inn (above) in Penfield, N.Y., February 24, 1982 Democrat and Chronicle**

# DiDio's Wife Slain in Miami Home

**DiDio's widow slain in Miami home**

By Chris Vaughan
Democrat and Chronicle

Carol DiDio, wife of slain Rochester Mafia figure Thomas DiDio, was fatally shot yesterday inside her Miami home by an unknown assailant, Miami police said.

Mrs. DiDio, 42, was found by her boyfriend, Robert Daboul, 52, about 11:45 a.m. when Daboul returned to their house after a grocery shopping trip. She had been shot several times, apparently with a handgun, police said.

Her husband, Thomas DiDio, met a similar fate in a Victor hotel room July 6, 1978. He was cut down in a spray of machine gun fire in what police termed a mob-related killing. DiDio was one of the leaders of a Mafia faction seeking control of Rochester area organized crime, police said. His killer was never found.

Special assistant U.S. attorney Donald J. Wisner said yesterday that while a federal grand jury investigation of Mafia activities in Rochester involves Thomas DiDio's death, "Carol DiDio was not an important witness in the investigation."

Wisner refused to say if Mrs. DiDio had been interviewed by the grand jury or if she was going to be questioned.

Mrs. DiDio was estranged from her husband when he was killed, but had visited him the evening before he was shot to death in the Exit 45 Motel, 683 Pittsford-Victor Road, Victor. A car registered in her name was found parked outside the hotel room her husband died in. DiDio had used the car that night, police said.

Miami police had no suspects but were investigating the crime last night, Detective Randy Baker said. Baker said police did not know how long Mrs. DiDio had lived with Daboul at 915 N.E. 89th Terrace, a modest middle-class neighborhood. She moved to Miami from Rochester 14 months ago, said Sgt. Richard Phelps.

Phelps said police would not divulge details of the investigation last night. He would not say if anyone else was in the concrete block structure when Mrs. DiDio was shot, where she was shot, how many bullets hit her or exactly how long Daboul was away from the house.

**March 10, 1982**
**Democrat and Chronicle**

Carol DiDio, wife of slain Rochester Mafia figure Thomas DiDio, was fatally shot on **March 9, 1982**, inside her Miami home by an unknown assailant, Miami police said. Mrs. DiDio, 42, was found by her boyfriend, Robert Daboul, 52, when Daboul returned to their modest house in a middle-income neighborhood after a grocery shopping trip. She had been shot several times, apparently with a handgun, police said.

Her husband, Thomas DiDio, met a similar fate in a Victor hotel room July 6, 1978. He was cut down in a spray of machine gun fire in what police termed a mob-related killing. DiDio was a leader of a Mafia faction seeking control of Rochester area organized crime, police said. His killer was never found.

Special Assistant U.S. Attorney Donald J. Wisner said at the time, "that while a Federal Grand Jury investigation of mafia activities in Rochester involved Thomas DiDio's death, Carol DiDio was not an important witness in the investigation." Wisner refused to say if Mrs. DiDio had been interviewed by the Grand Jury or if she was going to be questioned.

**Carol Didio (bottom left) at her husband Thomas Didio's funeral in July of 1978.**

Miami police had no immediate suspects but they were investigating the crime scene , Detective Randy Baker said at the time. Baker said police did not know how long Mrs. DiDio had lived with Daboul at 915 N.E. 89th Terrace.

Mrs. DiDio was estranged from her husband when he was killed but had visited him the evening before he was shot to death in the Exit 45 Motel, 683 Pittsford-Victor Road, Victor. **(52)**

# Three Reputed Mobsters Charged In Assault

Thomas Taylor, Thomas Pelusio and Michael Pelusio were arraigned on **March 13, 1982** on charges of assault stemming from a beating at a Lake Avenue bar. The Caserta Political and Social Club located at 44 Lake Avenue in Rochester, a known mafia gambling establishment run by the "A Team," was the scene of the beating.

Taylor and the Pelusio brothers belonged to an insurgent faction of the Rochester Mafia labeled the "C Team" by police. **(53)**

**Grand jury to hear of assault**

3 reputed mob figures charged in beating

By Jim Redmond
Democrat and Chronicle

The assault case against three reputed organized crime figures accused of beating a man inside a Lake Avenue gambling parlor Friday night is expected to be presented to a grand jury tomorrow.

Thomas E. Taylor, 41, Thomas A. Pelusio, 35, and Michael Pelusio, 27, were arraigned in City Court yesterday on second-degree assault charges in the beating, felony offenses.

Samuel Alaimo, 34, of 39 Fifth St., was beaten minutes after the three men and two others who weren't charged went into the Caserta Political and Social Club, 44 Lake Ave., shortly before 7 p.m., Rochester police said.

Alaimo was beaten on the face, head and back with a broom handle and then kicked in the chest and throat. He was treated at Genesee Hospital.

Taylor and the Pelusios were under police surveillance when they went into the club, but police outside didn't see the attack, said police Capt. Thomas Conroy. Local organized crime figures have been under surveillance periodically since the Dec. 17 shotgun slaying of reputed mobster John Fiorino.

Police identified the club, commonly known as the "44 Club," as a known gambling parlor controlled by mob figures and have identified Alaimo as an associate of area organized crime figures. Officials have a found a motive behind the attack but refused to disclose it.

"It's going into the facts of the case," said Assistant Monroe County District Attorney Melchor Castro. "It's going beyond what I'm permitted to tell you."

Thomas Pelusio, of 96 Laurelton Road, and Michael Pelusio, of 418 Lake Ave., were freed yesterday after posting the $1,000 bail each.

Monroe County Court Judge Andrew Celli set bail for Taylor at $10,000, which was posted after arraignment.

City Court judges weren't permitted to set bail for Taylor because he has been convicted of two previous felonies, Castro said. In 1961, Taylor was convicted of second-degree assault for attacking a Greece police officer. In 1964, he was convicted of attempted extortion, for which he served eight years in prison.

**March 14, 1982 Democrat and Chronicle**

# Fire Damages Yahambas Social Club Linked to Mob

Jim Laragy Democrat and Chronicle

Firefighters take a breather and a television cameraman records the scene yesterday morning after a fire was extinguished at a social club that's linked to mobsters. The fire started near an inside wall. Investigators are trying to determine the cause.

**Fire damages social club linked to mob**

FROM PAGE 1B

The first blow of the 1978 underworld war in Rochester that resulted in the deaths of Sammy Gingello and Thomas DiDio was a Molotov cocktail thrown through a window of the Yahamba's Club on Jan. 2, 1978.

Sources said the club is tied to the established underworld leaders. Early last month police stopped Samuel Alaimo, a reputed underworld figure, outside the club and found about $30,000 in his possession.

Alaimo was recently beaten up inside another club associated with organized crime. People accused of beating Alaimo have been identified as belonging to a group which, according to sources, are attempting to break free of the established underworld leadership.

One of the leaders of the insurgent group is Thomas Torpey, according to sources. A club police said Torpey operated at 251 Lyell Ave. was destroyed by a fire Feb. 5.

Investigators said the fire at the Young Men's Social Club may have started accidentally in a couch, but no official cause has been determined.

Investigators said they talked with a man who often cleaned the club and who said he may have been smoking a cigarette while on the couch, but wasn't certain.

Torpey, sources said, hasn't yet opened another club.

**March 23, 1982**
**Democrat and Chronicle**

On **March 22, 1982**, the Yahambas Club, a social club, on Franklin Street was the second building associated with organized crime to suffer extensive damage due to fire in recent weeks.

The Yahambas was a known gambling parlor associated with Rochester's organized crime family.

The building had been the scene of several gambling arrests in the past. The Club was operated by Anthony Alongi, who was also the last person known to have been inside the building. **(54)**

# Nicholas Mastrodonato Is Murdered

## Man linked to local mob shot to death in coin store

### Nicholas Mastrodonato slain, but motive remains a mystery

**By Gary Gerew**
Democrat and Chronicle

Several police agencies, including the FBI, are investigating the slaying yesterday afternoon of Nicholas Mastrodonato, who police identified as an organized crime figure.

Mastrodonato, 33, died at Park Ridge Hospital about 30 minutes after he was shot several times about 3 p.m. as he worked at a gold- and silver-buying store in Gates.

Gates Police Chief Thomas Roche said robbery hasn't been eliminated as a motive, but he said Mastrodonato's killer apparently began firing as he entered the store, Mr. Gold's Coin Shop at 481 Spencerport Road.

Police put together this description of Mastrodonato's killer: A stocky man between 20 and 35 who wore sunglasses, a blue jacket, blue pants and a blue baseball cap. The man had bushy, sandy-colored hair that stuck out around the sides and back of the baseball cap.

Roche said ballistics tests won't be completed until today, but it's believed Mastrodonato was shot with a .45-caliber pistol, based on shell casings found in the store.

"It appears the person went there specifically to shoot a firearm," Roche said. Roche said investigators are still trying to complete an inventory of the store, but he said there was money, including $20 bills, left in the cash register.

"The cabinets in the store weren't cleaned out either," Roche said. "If the motive was robbery, it appears the shooting happened before anything was taken."

An autopsy will be performed today. Roche said Mastrodonato was apparently shot at least once in the head, but there may have been as many as nine shots fired.

Roche said there had been no reports of robberies at stores near the coin shop in the past year.

Because of Mastrodonato's association with organized crime figures, police are also considering that may be a motive for his death. Mastrodonato, police sources said, was linked to an insurgent group within local organized crime lead by Thomas Torpey and Thomas Taylor.

"He (Mastrodonato) was involved with them, but he wasn't a sworn member of the Mafia," said one law enforcement official. "He was on the fringe."

Some law enforcement officials believe the insurgent group was involved in last December's slaying of John Fiorino in Irondequoit.

Capt. Thomas Conroy, head of the Rochester Police Department's special criminal investigation unit, said he and several officers from his unit were assisting the Gates police investigation, as were investigators from the Monroe County Sheriff's Department and other organized crime investigators from other police departments.

Roche said there isn't any evidence that yesterday's killing was related to organized

TURN TO PAGE 3A

**May 26, 1982 Democrat and Chronicle**

Several police agencies including the FBI were involved in investigating the **May 25, 1982** shooting death of Nicholas Mastrodonato. He was shot several times and died while working at his coin shop in Gates.

Robbery had not been ruled out as a motive although police say that the killer entered the store firing shots at the victim and nothing appeared to be missing.

Mastrodonato had ties to an insurgent mafia faction labeled the "C Team" led by Thomas Torpey and Thomas Taylor that police believed were responsible for the murder of John Fiorino. (55)

# DiGiulio Ends His Silence Torpey and Taylor Arrested for the Murder of John Fiorino

## DiGiulio ends his silence

### Informant blames pair for breaking promises

**By Dede Murphy**
Democrat and Chronicle

They promised to "take care of him," Louis DiGiulio claims, but he couldn't get them to pay his legal fees or even send him $50 for spending money in the Monroe County Jail.

The refusal by Thomas M. Torpey and Thomas E. Taylor to aid DiGiulio cost them his silence.

On Sunday, the day before his trial for the Dec. 17 murder of John M. Fiorino began, DiGiulio, angry and betrayed, decided he wanted to send Torpey and Taylor to prison.

"I was left hanging," he told Monroe County Court Judge Eugene W. Bergin yesterday, explaining why he had decided to cooperate with authorities.

DiGiulio's sudden decision to testify against Torpey and Taylor closed a net on the two reputed organized crime insurgents that a task force of law enforcement officials had been weaving since Fiorino was shot to death outside the Blue Gardenia restaurant in Irondequoit.

A few minutes before midnight Monday,

TURN TO PAGE 3A

'I was left hanging. . . . I was there to drive the car. I didn't think I was actually killing anybody. I knew I was involved in a conspiracy. . . . I want to turn state's evidence'

**— Louis DiGiulio, who decided to turn informant.**

## Torpey, Taylor arrested

**By Gary Gerew and Jim Redmond**
Democrat and Chronicle

The statement of a participant in last year's killing of Mafia figure John M. Fiorino not only led to the arrests of Thomas M. Torpey and Thomas E. Taylor on murder charges early yesterday, police say, but it has crippled the insurgent organized crime faction they reputedly head.

"I think it's knocked the main blocks out," one investigator said. "I think any time you deal with a Torpey or Taylor you're dealing with muscle. You're talking about the strongarms of the mob."

As Louis DiGiulio's defection unfolded Monday, the organized crime task force of local, state and federal authorities investigating Fiorino's death stepped up its surveillance of crime figures. The same task force is also investigating last month's slaying of Nicholas Mastrodonato in Gates, sources said yesterday.

Although Mastrodonato, 33, was an associate of Torpey and Taylor, he was not under close police surveillance, as others have been since Fiorino's death.

Mastrodonato was gunned down May 25 in his coin and precious metals shop, and authorities believe he may have been killed as a retaliatory signal from established organized crime figures to the insurgents to back off.

The split in Rochester's organized crime family began when one faction, reputedly led by Torpey and Taylor, refused to pay Mafia leaders the traditional operating fees to run their gambling establishments. They then tried to urge others to do the same.

Fiorino's slaying Dec. 17 outside the Blue Gardenia restaurant in Irondequoit was seen as the insurgents' warning that they meant business.

Yesterday, officials said the investigation of Fiorino's death is continuing. Torpey, Taylor, DiGiulio, and Joseph John Sullivan, who police said fired the fatal shots at Fiorino, are all in custody. Torpey and Taylor are in the Monroe County Jail; Sullivan is in Syracuse awaiting trial on bank robbery charges; and DiGiulio was taken to an

TURN TO PAGE 2A

**Democrat and Chronicle June 9, 1982**

On **June 8, 1982,** Thomas Torpey and Thomas Taylor were arrested for ordering the murder of John Fiorino.

The arrest was the direct result of Louis DiGiulio, a participant in the Fiorino murder ratting out his co-conspirators. DiGiulio broke his silence after Torpey and Taylor refused to "take care of" him while he was in jail. DiGiulio was the driver of the getaway car that Joseph Sullivan was in when he murdered reputed mob figure John Fiorino. DiGiulio said he could not even get Torpey or Taylor to send him $50 for spending money while he was incarcerated.

"I was left hanging...I was there to drive the car. I didn't think I was actually killing anybody. I knew I was involved in a conspiracy....I want to turn state's evidence." Those are the words of Louis DiGiulio, the latest mob associate to turn informant. **(56)**

For more than five months while awaiting trial, DiGiuilio refused to cooperate with authorities. But on **June 6, 1982**, on the eve of his second-degree murder trial, DiGiuilio broke his silence and turned police informant, implicating Torpey and Taylor in the Fiorino murder. Torpey and Taylor were arrested a few days later after DiGiuilio agreed to testify against them and Sullivan.

DiGiuilio's deal also required testimony against Torpey and Taylor. DiGiuilio gave four days of testimony in Monroe County Court, testimony the defense called "the gospel according to Louie." Felix V. Lapine, Torpey's lawyer, and John F. Speranza, who represented Taylor, labeled DiGiuilio a conniving liar, saying he made up the story for the lighter sentence.

As Torpey and Taylor watched intently, sometimes taking notes, Lapine and Speranza grilled DiGiuilio, impassive behind dark-tinted glasses. In his testimony, DiGiuilio spoke of growing tension and animosity between rival organized crime factions in 1981. On one side was Taylor and his friend Torpey, who ran a lucrative gambling club on Lyell Avenue known as Torpey's joint. On the other were the long-established members of the Rochester underworld, including Fiorino.

The street-tough DiGiuilio, a convicted burglar and thief, said he met Torpey about 12 years prior in the 44 Club, a gambling parlor on Lake Avenue. DiGiuilio also provided key testimony in the murder trial of Sullivan, who was convicted in 1982 of firing the shotgun blast that killed Fiorino on Dec. 17, 1981. Without question, DiGiuilio has benefited by testifying for the prosecution. He and Sullivan were initially charged with second-degree murder in the Fiorino killing. DiGiuilio was supposed to be tried first, in June 1982. But on the eve of his trial, he agreed to cooperate with the District Attorney's office. His testimony was crucial in obtaining Sullivan's murder conviction in September.

In exchange for his cooperation, DiGiuilio was allowed to plead guilty to a lesser charge of conspiracy to commit murder. For that, prosecutors recommended a five- to 10-year sentence in a federal prison, rather than a state facility. He had been looking at a maximum sentence of life in prison for a second-degree murder conviction. (57)

## Sullivan Murder Trial Begins August 31, 1982

# Sullivan: 'I'm no hit man'

*Police call him a cold-blooded contract killer, one of the most dangerous and ruthless men in America. Dubbed "Mad Dog" by the media, a nickname he despises, Joseph John Sullivan is accused of killing local Teamsters union official John Fiorino outside an Irondequoit restaurant Dec. 17.*

*The only man ever to escape from inside the 30-foot walls of Attica prison, Sullivan is a suspect in a dozen executions, police say. Sullivan says that's unjust — that law enforcement agencies have added to his notoriety in an attempt to build their own record of convictions.*

*Sullivan is now being held without bail in the Monroe County Jail, where he's kept in a cell away from other jail inmates.*

*On Aug. 31 his trial in County Court on murder charges stemming from the Fiorino slaying will begin.*

*Yesterday, Sullivan granted a request from* Democrat and Chronicle *courts reporter Jody McPhillips for an interview.*

## In interview, accused killer laughs at 'Mad Dog' image

**By Jody McPhillips**

Joseph John Sullivan doesn't deny he has killed, but he says he didn't kill Rochester Teamsters official John Fiorino.

"I'm no hit man," he said.

Sullivan smoked Camel cigarette after cigarette yesterday during a two-hour interview with the *Democrat and Chronicle*. He talked about his past, which police say may involve as many as a dozen homicides. Sullivan has never been convicted of murder, but has served time for manslaughter.

What does it feel like to kill somebody? "Nothing. I don't think about it," he says, his gray gaze level and steady.

"I've done maybe 10 percent of what they say I've done," he said.

"I didn't kill no Mary Poppins. Look at the histories. Another few seconds, it would have been me lying there."

Wearing a worn Navy sweatshirt, Sullivan talked in a small cell in the Monroe County Jail.

His muscular physique is that of a man 15 years younger than his 43 years, but his forehead is deeply lined.

Sullivan admits he was in Rochester the night Fiorino was killed.

He says he loaned Louis DiGiulio, arrested minutes after the shooting, his peach-colored Cadillac that night.

But he says he wasn't the man who gunned Fiorino down in the parking lot of the Blue Gardenia Restaurant.

"Sure, I was here, but I was at the Marriott" Airport Motel in Greece when Fiorino was shot, Sullivan said. It is the first published interview with Sullivan since his arrest on murder charges Feb. 23.

Sullivan said he was in Rochester that December night for the same reason he was here five months before that: to see Thomas E. Taylor, his friend from their days of playing together on the Attica prison football team 10 years ago.

He said he met DiGiulio and Thomas M. Torpey "once or twice" through Taylor, but that he didn't know either well.

"I was visiting. I like it up here. I shared a bungalow or whatever last summer with my wife and kids and him and his family on — what's that lake around here? — Lake Ontario.

"I mean, we're talking barbecues for the kids, not any Apalachin meeting," referring to a Mafia meeting held in a small Southern Tier town in November, 1957.

Sullivan said he couldn't remember the name of the lakeside town but said the two families stayed for several weeks.

TURN TO PAGE 6A

**August 18, 1982 Democrat and Chronicle**

Accused killer Joseph Sullivan granted a request for an interview to Jody McPhillips, a Democrat and Chronicle court reporter. Sullivan was the only man in history to ever escape the maximum security prison at Attica, N.Y. He was awaiting trial for the murder of John Fiorino, which began on August 31, 1982.

Sullivan did not deny that he had killed, but he claimed that he did not kill John Fiorino and he said that he was no hit man, despite the fact that he referred to himself as the "button man," a Mafia term meaning "hit man." (58)

# Gerald F. Pelusio Is Murdered

Gerald F. Pelusio was gunned down in front of a town house in Irondequoit on **August 27, 1982**. Gerald was the brother of Thomas and Michael Pelusio, both of whom were linked to organized crime. (60)

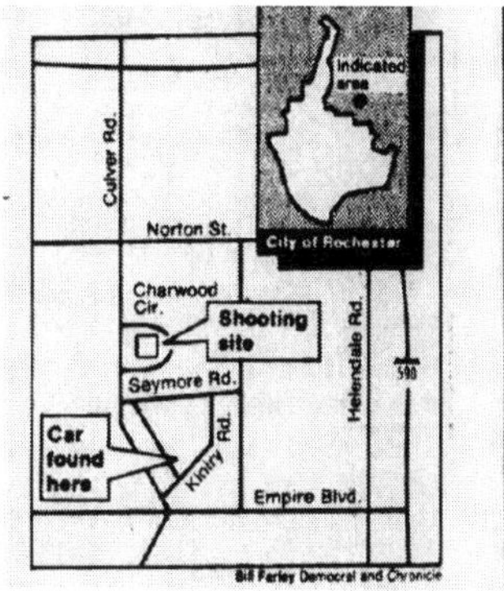


**Location of Pelusio murder.**

Police believed that Gerald Pelusio's murder was a case of mistaken identity and that the real target was Gerald's brother Thomas. Apparently the two brothers looked alike.

Thomas was suspected of leading the insurgent faction of the Rochester Mafia dubbed the "C Team" after the imprisonment of Thomas Torpey and Thomas Taylor. (59)

## Gang retaliation feared after Perinton man gunned down

FROM PAGE 1A

ion of weapons, and will be arraigned this morning in City Court.

Conroy would not say whether the men were being questioned in connection with the window shooting, but "It's a very logical connection."

In the slaying earlier yesterday, Pelusio was shot three times — twice in the back and once in the arm — with a large caliber weapon, most likely a handgun, said Irondequoit Police Chief William H. Frey.

He was pronounced dead at Rochester General Hospital at noon. An autopsy is scheduled for today.

Police last night had no suspects in the slaying.

A 1973 green Chevrolet Impala matching witnesses' descriptions of the getaway car used in the shooting was discovered at Deerfield and Gilbert drives, a few blocks away by a Rochester police officer about 3:30 p.m., Frey said.

Pelusio was shot dead about 11:15 a.m. as he and two men were walking to the front door of the townhouse at 44 Charwood Circle in Irondequoit, Frey said.

The townhouse is owned by Paul D. Comfort, who police have linked with an insurgent group of organized crime figures.

Pelusio was with an unidentified man and Comfort's brother, Robert, who also has been linked with the insurgent faction, authorities said.

A man in a green car drove up and fired an undetermined number of shots out the passenger window from about 30 feet away, witnesses told police.

Police would not speculate if Pelusio, who was considered by police as having minor connections to organized crime, was the intended victim.

Pelusio fell face down in a bed of yellow and violet flowers on the left side of the concrete steps leading to the front door, Frey said. The gunman sped away, witnesses told police.

The Rochester police department's K-9 unit searched the crime scene yesterday for evidence, but no weapon was found, Frey said.

Law enforcement officials from the Rochester Police Department's Organized Crime Task Force and physical crimes unit were meeting last night with Irondequoit police detectives. The FBI and investigators from the Monroe County Sheriff's Department, the state police and the Monroe County District Attorney's office also have been called into the investigation.

Both Comfort brothers were questioned for several hours yesterday at the Irondequoit Police Department on Titus Avenue. Police also took statements from 15 people who said they had witnessed the shooting.

Police sources say they fear the shooting will prompt retaliatory action from the insurgent faction because Michael and Thomas Pelusio are known to be allied with Thomas Taylor and Thomas Torpey, authorities said.

Taylor and Torpey have been held in the Monroe County Jail since March on second-degree murder charges in connection with the Dec. 17 shotgun slaying of union leader John M. Fiorino outside the Blue Gardenia restaurant in Irondequoit.

Fiorino was underboss for the established mob, authorities said.

The insurgent faction wants to run gambling and drug operations now controlled by the establised mob led by Rene Piccaretto and Samuel "Red" Russotti, police say.

The Fiorino slaying is believed to have been a warning to the established underworld not to interfere with the new faction, police have said.

Michael Pelusio of 418 Lake Avenue and Thomas Pelusio of 96 Laurelton Road were arrested along with Taylor in March in connection with the beating of a man inside a Rochester social club. Both Pelusio brothers pleaded not guilty to second-degree assault charges.

Paul Comfort has been convicted on eight gambling charges from 1963 through 1971, but he never served time in jail. He was convicted in 1975 of robbery and grand larceny and was sentenced to up to seven years in Attica prison, but an appeals court overturned the convictions in 1978.

In 1972, Robert Comfort served two and a half years in prison after being convicted of second-degree burglary in connection with the theft of $4 million in jewels and securities from the Hotel Pierre in New York City.

## Former page says charges were false

FROM PAGE 1A

plained that a man was spitting in their hair.

Williams, who left the page service in January, acknowledged previously he failed a lie detector test given by the FBI, but said at the time he was standing by his story.

After Williams made his charges earlier this summer, both the Justice Department and the ethics committee launched investigations.

The Justice Department reportedly has finished its investigation and the Washington Post has reported FBI agents have been unable to obtain evidence that would warrant a criminal prosecution.

The allegations of misconduct prompted creation of a special page commission by House Speaker Thomas P. O'Neill.

That panel recommended earlier this month that pages be at least 16; that they live in central, supervised housing on Capitol Hill, and that their terms be limited to one school semester. Under the present system, pages must find their own housing, their terms in Washington vary, and Senate pages may be as young as 14.

**August 28, 1982 Democrat and Chronicle**

## Pelusio Brothers Retaliate
## "A Team" Gambling Parlor Windows Shot Out By "C Team" After Pelusio Murder

The building on Fernwood Avenue (below) had been used "on and off" as a gambling establishment since the 1930s. In 1978, the former gambling parlor at 1266 Clifford Ave., known then as the Clifford Novelty Shop, was damaged when a bomb exploded in the basement beneath a first floor office. "A Team" Mafia "Boss" Samuel Russotti controlled operations at the Clifford Avenue parlor. Police believed the parlor was bombed by a group of mobsters, known then as the "B Team," who were trying to take over the empire.

After the bombing, those who patronized the Clifford Avenue establishment became regular clientele at the Fernwood Avenue parlor.

**7 Fernwood Avenue in Rochester, New York. This building was the site of illegal gambling operations in the 1980's. The front windows were shot out on August 27, 1982 by Thomas and Michael Pelusio after their brother Gerald was murdered earlier the same day.**

In December 1979, several individuals were arrested on gambling charges during a police raid at Fernwood Avenue. Two undercover policemen had been staked out in the parlor for about nine months before the raid. Those arrested were charged with second-degree promoting gambling but none had been convicted.

The most recent warring between the two sides of the local underworld began with the slaying of Fiorino in front of the former Blue Gardenia Restaurant in Irondequoit, police said. Fiorino was a "Captain" for the "A Team" led by Samuel Russotti and Rene Piccarreto.

The current dispute between the two sides began when the insurgent faction led by Taylor and Torpey became involved in narcotics, police said.

The established mob was linked to illegal gambling operations and never had been involved in drug operations on a large scale. Police said the warring continued in May of 1982 when Nicholas Mastrodonato was shot dead in a Gates coin shop. Mastrodonato was also linked to the Taylor and Torpey faction.

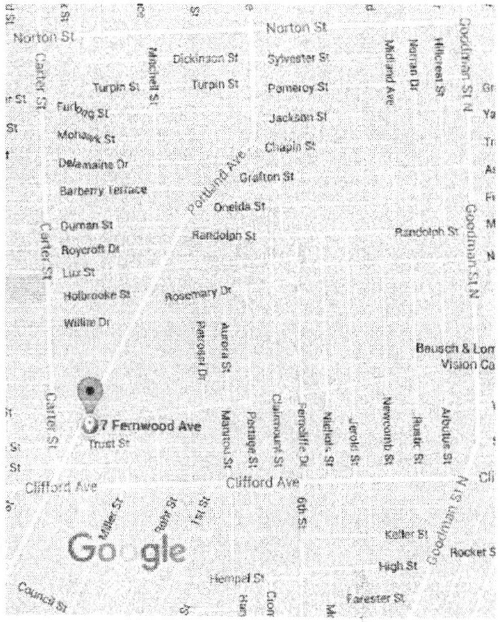

**The dot above is the location of the gambling establishment that was shot-gunned after Gerald Pelusio's murder. 7 Fernwood Avenue is near the corner of Clifford Avenue and Carter Street in the city of Rochester, New York.**

Police had questioned more than 200 people in connection with the Pelusio slaying. Irondequoit police headed the investigation with help from the city Police Department's Organized Crime Task Force, the Monroe County Sheriff's Department the Monroe County district attorney's office, the state police and the FBI. (61)

# Thomas Pelusio Leads Mob Faction

## Police Say Slain Man's Brother is Chief of Insurgent Group

Thomas Pelusio, whose brother was gunned down August 27, 1982, in Irondequoit, had been the leader of an insurgent group of organized crime figures since June 8, 1992 when Thomas M. Torpey and Thomas E. Taylor were arrested on murder charges, a high-ranking police source said. Pelusio, 35, of 96 Laurelton Road, was chief of an organized crime faction that was warring with the established Rochester underworld led by reputed mobsters Samuel "Red" Russotti and Rene Piccarreto, the police source said. Police believed Pelusio's brother, Gerald, 33, was the mistaken victim of a gangland slaying when he was shot four times in the back Aug. 27, 1982 in front of a town house in Irondequoit.

Pelusio and his brother were look-alikes, and police believed Thomas Pelusio was the intended target of a hit ordered by the established mob. Thomas Pelusio became the insurgent faction's leader when Thomas Torpey and Thomas Taylor were jailed in connection with the Dec. 17, 1981 shotgun slaying of union leader John Fiorino. Pelusio also took over the operation of a suspected gambling establishment on St Paul Street, once controlled by Torpey, when Torpey and Taylor were arrested, the police source said.

But police surveillance of the St Paul Street parlor disclosed that business had slumped considerably since Pelusio took over. Thomas Pelusio was also involved in his family's business, Rochester Linoleum and Carpet Center, police say.

Repeated attempts to contact Pelusio by the Democrat and Chronicle were unsuccessful. After Pelusio's brother was killed, Rochester police feared retaliation from the insurgent faction. Patrolmen were ordered to pay close attention to all suspected gambling parlors operated by the established mob.

The night of the Pelusio slaying a shotgun blast was fired through the front plate glass window of a suspected gambling parlor at 7 Fernwood Ave. operated by the established mob. Later Pelusio and his brother, Michael, and Raymond Samson, who is said to be a mob "strong-arm," were arrested on Laurelton Road on weapons charges. Police found a 12-gauge pump-action shotgun in the back seat of their car. The suspected gambling parlor on Fernwood Avenue was unoccupied at the time of the window shooting. That led police at first to suspect the shotgun blast was meant as a warning from the Pelusio faction to the established mob, but police since have discounted that theory. They believe the shot was fired "out of pure frustration" over the mistaken slaying of Gerald Pelusio, the police source said.

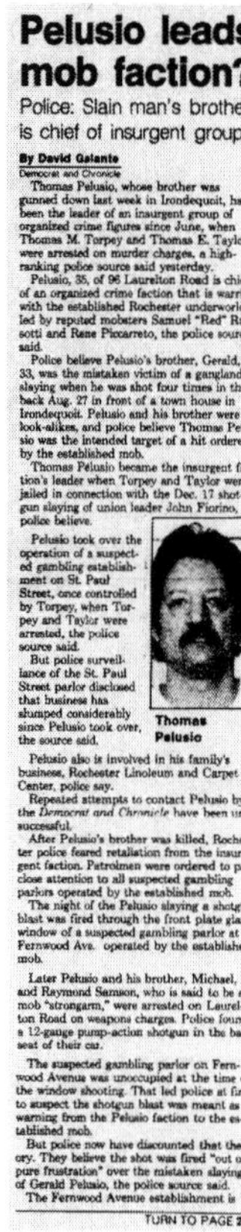

**Pelusio leads mob faction?**

Police: Slain man's brother is chief of insurgent group

By David Galante
Democrat and Chronicle

Thomas Pelusio, whose brother was gunned down last week in Irondequoit, has been the leader of an insurgent group of organized crime figures since June, when Thomas M. Torpey and Thomas E. Taylor were arrested on murder charges, a high-ranking police source said yesterday.

Pelusio, 35, of 96 Laurelton Road is chief of an organized crime faction that is warring with the established Rochester underworld led by reputed mobsters Samuel "Red" Russotti and Rene Piccarreto, the police source said.

Police believe Pelusio's brother, Gerald, 33, was the mistaken victim of a gangland slaying when he was shot four times in the back Aug. 27 in front of a town house in Irondequoit. Pelusio and his brother were look-alikes, and police believe Thomas Pelusio was the intended target of a hit ordered by the established mob.

Thomas Pelusio became the insurgent faction's leader when Torpey and Taylor were jailed in connection with the Dec. 17 shotgun slaying of union leader John Fiorino, police believe.

Pelusio took over the operation of a suspected gambling establishment on St. Paul Street, once controlled by Torpey, when Torpey and Taylor were arrested, the police source said.

But police surveillance of the St. Paul Street parlor disclosed that business has slumped considerably since Pelusio took over, the source said.

Thomas Pelusio

Pelusio also is involved in his family's business, Rochester Linoleum and Carpet Center, police say.

Repeated attempts to contact Pelusio by the *Democrat and Chronicle* have been unsuccessful.

After Pelusio's brother was killed, Rochester police feared retaliation from the insurgent faction. Patrolmen were ordered to pay close attention to all suspected gambling parlors operated by the established mob.

The night of the Pelusio slaying a shotgun blast was fired through the front plate glass window of a suspected gambling parlor at 7 Fernwood Ave. operated by the established mob.

Later Pelusio and his brother, Michael, and Raymond Samson, who is said to be a mob "strongarm," were arrested on Laurelton Road on weapons charges. Police found a 12-gauge pump-action shotgun in the back seat of their car.

The suspected gambling parlor on Fernwood Avenue was unoccupied at the time of the window shooting. That led police at first to suspect the shotgun blast was meant as a warning from the Pelusio faction to the established mob.

But police now have discounted that theory. They believe the shot was fired "out of pure frustration" over the mistaken slaying of Gerald Pelusio, the police source said.

The Fernwood Avenue establishment is

TURN TO PAGE 2B

**Sep. 4, 1982 Democrat and Chronicle**

The shooting at the Fernwood Avenue establishment could have been a warning for the insurgent faction to back down. "In both cases the motive appeared to be consistent," the police source said. Police said that they had no suspects in the Pelusio slaying, but they believe the same man was responsible for the Mastrodonato killing because of similarities in the shootings and descriptions of the gunman. Both victims were hit by bullets fired from a .45-caliber revolver, and in both cases the suspected get-away car was found abandoned nearby. The dark green Chevrolet Impala police believe was used in the Pelusio slaying was found on Deerfield Drive.

## Sullivan Murder Trial Opens

Joseph Sullivan's trial for the murder of reputed mobster John Fiorino opened on **September 9, 1982.**

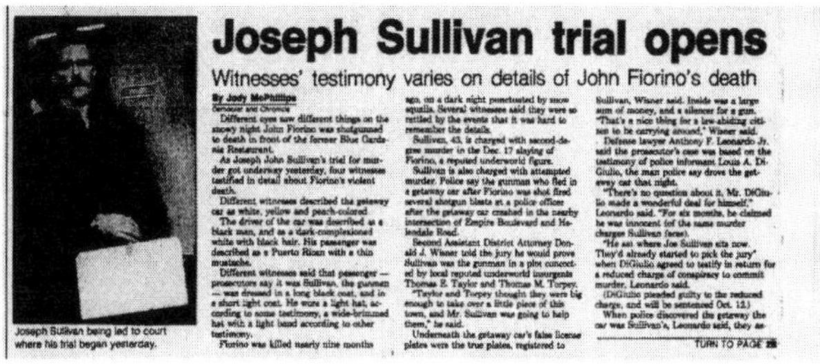

**Joseph Sullivan trial opens**

Witnesses' testimony varies on details of John Fiorino's death

By Jody McPhillips
Democrat and Chronicle

Different eyes saw different things on the snowy night John Fiorino was shotgunned to death in front of the former Blue Gardenia Restaurant.

As Joseph John Sullivan's trial for murder got underway yesterday, four witnesses testified in detail about Fiorino's violent death.

Different witnesses described the getaway car as white, yellow and peach-colored.

The driver of the car was described as a black man, and as a dark-complexioned white with black hair. His passenger was described as a Puerto Rican with a thin mustache.

Different witnesses said that passenger — prosecutors say it was Sullivan, the gunman — was dressed in a long black coat, and in a short light coat. He wore a light hat, according to some testimony, a wide-brimmed hat with a light band according to other testimony.

Fiorino was killed nearly nine months ago, on a dark night punctuated by snow squalls. Several witnesses said they were so rattled by the events that it was hard to remember the details.

Sullivan, 43, is charged with second-degree murder in the Dec. 17 slaying of Fiorino, a reputed underworld figure.

Sullivan is also charged with attempted murder. Police say the gunman who fled in a getaway car after Fiorino was shot fired several shotgun blasts at a police officer after the getaway car crashed in the nearby intersection of Empire Boulevard and Helendale Road.

Second Assistant District Attorney Donald J. Wisner told the jury he would prove Sullivan was the gunman in a plot concocted by local reputed underworld insurgents Thomas E. Taylor and Thomas M. Torpey.

"Taylor and Torpey thought they were big enough to take over a little piece of this town, and Mr. Sullivan was going to help them," he said.

Underneath the getaway car's false license plates were the true plates, registered to Sullivan, Wisner said. Inside was a large sum of money, and a silencer for a gun. "That's a nice thing for a law-abiding citizen to be carrying around," Wisner said.

Defense lawyer Anthony F. Leonardo Jr. said the prosecutor's case was based on the testimony of police informant Louis A. DiGiulio, the man police say drove the getaway car that night.

"There's no question about it, Mr. DiGiulio made a wonderful deal for himself," Leonardo said. "For six months, he claimed he was innocent (of the same murder charges Sullivan faces).

"He sat where Joe Sullivan sits now. They'd already started to pick the jury" when DiGiulio agreed to testify in return for a reduced charge of conspiracy to commit murder, Leonardo said.

(DiGiulio pleaded guilty to the reduced charge, and will be sentenced Oct. 12.)

When police discovered the getaway the car was Sullivan's, Leonardo said, they as-

TURN TO PAGE 2B

Joseph Sullivan being led to court where his trial began yesterday.

**September 10, 1982 Democrat and Chronicle**

Two weeks later, on **September 23, 1982**, Joseph Sullivan was found guilty of second degree murder for the shooting death of John Fiorino.

He was acquitted of attempted murder for allegedly shooting at Rochester Police Officer Michael DiGiovanni. Sullivan was scheduled to be sentenced on **October 7, 1982**. He faced a sentence of 25 years to life. **(62)**

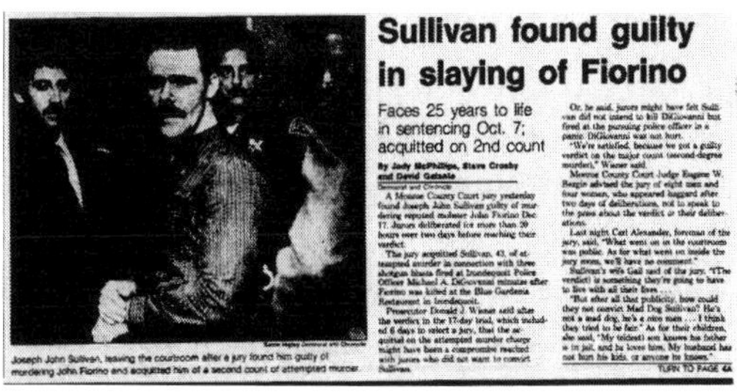

**Sullivan found guilty in slaying of Fiorino**

Faces 25 years to life in sentencing Oct. 7; acquitted on 2nd count

By Jody McPhillips, Steve Crosby and David Galante
Democrat and Chronicle

A Monroe County Court jury yesterday found Joseph John Sullivan guilty of murdering reputed mobster John Fiorino Dec. 17. Jurors deliberated for more than 20 hours over two days before reaching their verdict.

The jury acquitted Sullivan, 43, of attempted murder in connection with three shotgun blasts fired at Irondequoit Police Officer Michael A. DiGiovanni minutes after Fiorino was killed at the Blue Gardenia Restaurant in Irondequoit.

Prosecutor Donald J. Wisner said after the verdict in the 17-day trial, which included 6 days to select a jury, that the acquittal on the attempted murder charge might have been a compromise reached with jurors who did not want to convict Sullivan.

Or, he said, jurors might have felt Sullivan did not intend to kill DiGiovanni but fired at the pursuing police officer in a panic. DiGiovanni was not hurt.

"We're satisfied, because we got a guilty verdict on the major count (second-degree murder)," Wisner said.

Monroe County Court Judge Eugene W. Bergin advised the jury of eight men and four women, who appeared haggard after two days of deliberations, not to speak to the press about the verdict or their deliberations.

Last night Carl Alexander, foreman of the jury, said, "What went on in the courtroom was public. As for what went on inside the jury room, we'll have no comment."

Sullivan's wife Gail said of the jury, "(The verdict) is something they're going to have to live with all their lives . . .

"But after all that publicity, how could they not convict Mad Dog Sullivan? He's not a mad dog, he's a nice man . . . I think they tried to be fair." As for their children, she said, "My (eldest) son knows his father is in jail, and he loves him. My husband has not hurt his kids, or anyone he knows."

TURN TO PAGE 4A

Joseph John Sullivan, leaving the courtroom after a jury found him guilty of murdering John Fiorino and acquitted him of a second count of attempted murder.

**Sept. 24, 1982 Democrat and Chronicle**

## 3 mob figures indicted on weapons charges

### Thomas Pelusio arraigned here; two others being held in Boston

**By Jody McPhillips**
Democrat and Chronicle

A federal grand jury in Rochester has indicted three reputed underworld figures on weapons charges stemming from an incident Aug. 27.

Arraigned yesterday in Rochester on those federal charges was Thomas A. Pelusio, 36, of 96 Laurelton Road. Thomas Pelusio pleaded not guilty to federal charges of unlawful possession of a 12-gauge shotgun and ammunition at his arraignment in U.S. District Court, the day after the grand jury indictments were made public.

He was released on $5,000 bail.

His brother Michael Pelusio, 28, of 540 Lake Ave., and Raymond Samson, 47, of 732 Broad St., will be arraigned on the same federal charges in Rochester next week. They were arrested in Boston Saturday on the same charges and are in federal custody there in lieu of $100,000 bail.

All three men had been arraigned on similar state weapons charges in Monroe County Court in connection with the same incident and were out on bail at the time of their federal indictments.

If convicted on the federal charges, they could face up to five years in jail and a $5,000 fine, or both.

Police say all three men have ties to an insurgent faction in the Rochester underworld formerly led by Thomas E. Taylor and Thomas M. Torpey. Taylor and Torpey are in Monroe County jail, awaiting trial on charges of killing reputed Mafia figure John Fiorino last December.

Last Aug. 27, a third Pelusio brother, Gerald, of 25 Heatherwood Road, Perinton, was slain by a gunman in front of a townhouse at 44 Charwood Circle, Irondequoit.

Police theorize Gerald Pelusio, whose ties to organized crime are said to be minor, was killed by mistake and that the true target was his look-alike brother Thomas.

The slaying of Gerald Pelusio is thought to have been in retaliation for a "confrontation" a month earlier between Thomas Pelusio, Michael Pelusio and Rene Piccarretto, reputed leader of the established Mafia that the Taylor-Torpey faction was challenging.

Hours after Gerald Pelusio was slain, police stopped a 1976 tan and white Buick on Laurelton Road after the car's lights were turned off as police approached.

Police had been investigating shots that were fired through the front window of 7 Fernwood Ave. at 7 p.m. that night, apparently in retribution for Gerald Pelusio's slaying. The building, which was not occupied at the time, was a suspected gambling operation controlled by the established underworld, police said.

Inside the car were the two Pelusio brothers and Samson, a convicted felon who also has ties to the insurgent faction.

Police found a loaded Mossberg 12-gauge pump-action shotgun on the back seat. It is illegal for convicted felons to own weapons.

**October 20, 1982 Democrat and Chronicle**

On **October 19, 1982**, a six-count indictment was filed against Michael A. Pelusio, Thomas A. Pelusio and Raymond Sampson, charging each in two counts of unlawful receipt of a firearm and unlawful receipt of ammunition in violation of 18 U.S.C. Secs. 922(h)(1), 924(a) and 2.1.

Sampson's case was severed by the district court prior to trial. Motions by Michael and Thomas to suppress evidence of the seizure of the firearm and ammunition as violative of their Fourth Amendment rights were denied by Judge Telesca after an extended evidentiary hearing.

Michael A. Pelusio (Michael) and Thomas A. Pelusio (Thomas) were both found guilty. Both filed an Appeal, from a judgment of the Western District of New York, entered after a jury trial before Judge Michael A. Telesca, convicting them of unlawful receipt of firearms and ammunition transported in interstate commerce, 18 U.S.C. Secs. 922(h)(1), 924(a) and 2.

Michael was convicted of one count charging receipt of a gun (Count I) and another charging receipt of ammunition (Count IV), while under felony indictment and while having previously been convicted of a felony.

Thomas was likewise convicted on two counts (II and V), charging unlawful receipt of the gun and ammunition while under indictment for a felony. The Court affirmed their convictions of unlawful receipt of the gun (Counts I and II), and reversed their convictions of unlawful receipt of the ammunition (Counts IV and V). **(63)**

# *Chapter 7*
# "A Team" Indictments
# (Marotta is Shot Twice)

## Federal Jury Indicts 10

On **November 8, 1982** Dick Marino, Teamsters Local #398 Business Agent, and 9 other men were indicted in United States vs. Russotti, et al., 82 Cr.156 for racketeering and murder.

Russotti was the "Boss" of the Rochester Family LCN and Dick Marino was his "Underboss." Also Rene Piccarreto was the Families' "Consigliore."

The first count of the indictment alleged that among other acts Russotti, Marino and Piccarreto along with the other defendants, had conspired to murder Vincent "Jimmy the Hammer" Massaro in November 1973 and Thomas Didio in July 1978.(64)

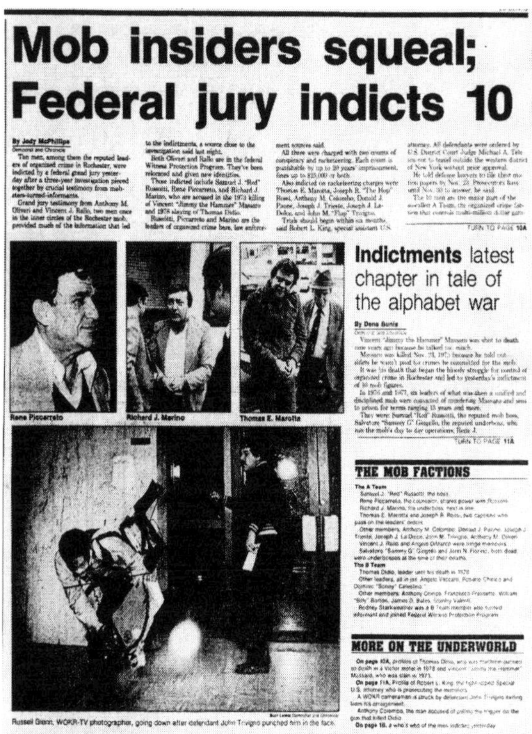

**Mob insiders squeal; Federal jury indicts 10**

By Jody McPhillips
Democrat and Chronicle

Ten men, among them the reputed leaders of organized crime in Rochester, were indicted by a federal grand jury yesterday after a three-year investigation pieced together by crucial testimony from mobsters-turned-informants.

Grand jury testimony from Anthony M. Oliveri and Vincent J. Rallo, two men once in the inner circles of the Rochester mob, provided much of the information that led to the indictments, a source close to the investigation said last night.

Both Oliveri and Rallo are in the federal Witness Protection Program. They've been relocated and given new identities.

Those indicted include Samuel J. "Red" Russotti, Rene Piccarreto, and Richard J. Marino, who are accused in the 1973 killing of Vincent "Jimmy the Hammer" Massaro and 1978 slaying of Thomas Didio.

Russotti, Piccarreto and Marino are the leaders of organized crime here, law enforcement sources said.

All three were charged with two counts of conspiracy and racketeering. Each count is punishable by up to 20 years' imprisonment, fines up to $25,000 or both.

Also indicted on racketeering charges were Thomas E. Marotta, Joseph R. "The Hop" Rossi, Anthony M. Colombo, Donald J. Paone, Joseph J. Trieste, Joseph J. LaDolce, and John M. "Flap" Trivigno.

Trials should begin within six months, said Robert L. King, special assistant U.S. attorney. All defendants were ordered by U.S. District Court Judge Michael A. Telesca not to travel outside the western district of New York without prior approval.

He told defense lawyers to file their motion papers by Nov. 23. Prosecutors have until Nov. 30 to answer, he said.

The 10 men are the major part of the so-called A Team, the organized crime faction that controls multi-million dollar [illegible]

TURN TO PAGE 10A

Rene Piccarreto — Richard J. Marino — Thomas E. Marotta

**Indictments latest chapter in tale of the alphabet war**

By Dena Bunis
Democrat and Chronicle

Vincent "Jimmy the Hammer" Massaro was shot to death nine years ago because he talked too much.

Massaro was killed Nov. 23, 1973 because he told outsiders he wasn't paid for crimes he committed for the mob.

It was his death that began the bloody struggle for control of organized crime in Rochester and led to yesterday's indictment of 10 mob figures.

In 1976 and 1977, six leaders of what was then a unified and disciplined mob were convicted of murdering Massaro and sent to prison for terms ranging 15 years and more.

They were: Samuel "Red" Russotti, the reputed mob boss, Salvatore "Sammy G" Gingello, the reputed underboss, who ran the mob's day to day operations, Rene J.

TURN TO PAGE 11A

**THE MOB FACTIONS**

**The A Team**

Samuel J. "Red" Russotti, the boss.

Rene Piccarreto, the counselor, shares power with Russotti.

Richard J. Marino, the underboss, next in line.

Thomas E. Marotta and Joseph R. Rossi, two captains who pass on the leaders' orders.

Other members: Anthony M. Colombo, Donald J. Paone, Joseph J. Trieste, Joseph J. LaDolce, John M. Trivigno, Anthony M. Oliveri.

Vincent J. Rallo and Angelo DiMarco were fringe members.

Salvatore "Sammy G" Gingello and John N. Fiorino, both dead, were underbosses at the time of their deaths.

**The B Team**

Thomas Didio, leader until his death in 1978.

Other leaders, all in jail: Angelo Vaccaro, Rosario Chirico and Dominic "Sonny" Celestino.

Other members: Anthony Chirico, Francesco Frassetto, William "Billy" Barton, James D. Bates, Stanley Valenti.

Rodney Starkweather was a B Team member who turned informant and joined Federal Witness Protection Program.

**MORE ON THE UNDERWORLD**

**On page 10A,** profiles of Thomas Didio, who was machine-gunned to death in a Victor motel in 1978 and Vincent "Jimmy the Hammer" Massaro, who was slain in 1973.

**On page 11A,** Profile of Robert L. King, the tight-lipped Special U.S. attorney who is prosecuting the mobsters.

A WOKR cameraman is struck by defendant John Trivigno exiting from his arraignment.

Anthony Colombo, the man accused of pulling the trigger on the gun that killed Didio.

**On page 1B,** a who's who of the men indicted yesterday.

Russell Glenn, WOKR-TV photographer, going down after defendant John Trivigno punched him in the face.

**Above, mobster John Travigno allegedly punched the cameraman.**

The murder of Vincent Massaro was chronicled in the book titled "The Hammer Conspiracies" written by Frank A. Aloi in 1982. At least three others indicted were **Local #398** members including future **Local #398** President John Travigno. (192)

## Of The Ten Men Were Indicted For Murder and Conspiracy, Many Had Ties To Teamsters Local #398

| | Ten Men Indicted | Tie to Teamsters **Local #398** |
|---|---|---|
|  | Russotti (Rochester LCN Boss) | At least 25 men under his command in the Rochester mob were employed some where within **Local #398.** |
|  | Rene Piccareto (LCN Consigliore) | |
|  | Thomas Marotta (LCN Captain) | Trieste, LaDolce and Travigno (all **Local #398** members) worked under Thomas Marotta |
|  | Richard Marino ( LCN UnderBoss) | Dick was a Business Agent and Trustee for **Local #398.** |
|  | Joseph R. Rossi | |
|  | Anthony M. Columbo | Steward of **Local #398** |
|  | Donald J. Paone | Donald Paone's daughter would become the future Secretary for **Local #398** |
|  | Joseph J. Trieste | Joseph's Brother George was the Sec.-Treas. of **Local #398** his wife became the Local's Fund Manager and Rec.-Sec. |
|  | Joseph J. LaDolce | Was once a union steward. He was kicked out of **Local #398** for being a Mafia Member. |
|  | John Travigno | **Local #398** President. |

## Mobsters tied to 2 unions, police say

### Teamsters Local 398, Laborers Local 435 are infiltrated, he testifies

By David Galante
Democrat and Chronicle

RUSSOTTI FREE ON $200,000 BAIL 4B

At least two Rochester labor unions have been infiltrated by local organized crime figures, among them six men who were indicted Tuesday by a federal grand jury on racketeering charges, authorities say.

For almost two decades, the Rochester underworld has used its power to provide patronage union jobs — in some cases lucrative, "no show" positions — to mob leaders, loyal associates and relatives, law enforcement officials say.

Membership in these labor unions allows reputed mobsters to show legitimate income while they actually are "involved in sports bookmaking, various gambling and other organized crime businesses," says Sgt. John Grande, head of the Rochester Police Department's Intelligence Squad.

Recently, Grande and several other law enforcement officials and union leaders from around the state testified at public hearings before the state Commission of Investigations in New York City.

At Gov. Hugh Carey's request, the commission is conducting a year-long investigation of suspected ties between the construction industry and organized crime, says Thomas Staffa, the commission's chief counsel.

Although Grande stresses that the "overwhelming majority of labor unions in Rochester are legitimate," he identified in testimony and in a recent interview two unions infiltrated by the powers of organized crime as the International Brotherhood of Teamsters Local 398 and the Laborers International Union of North America Local 435.

Six of the 10 men indicted Tuesday on charges of murder, conspiracy, arson and obstructing justice currently hold or have held top-level positions in locals 398 and 435, authorities say.

Officials from both unions refused to be interviewed over the past few weeks, and national Teamsters officials would not discuss specifics.

Despite what police say are links between members of the Teamsters and the mob, a local council of union officials apparently has no power to investigate Local 398.

"We do not have control over the election of stewards. That is controlled

TURN TO PAGE 2B

**November 11, 1982 Democrat and Chronicle**

# Mobsters Infiltrate 2 Unions, Teamsters Local 398 and Laborers Local 435

At least two Rochester labor unions were infiltrated by organized crime for almost two decades, the Rochester law enforcement officials said. Despite the obvious links between the unions and organized crime, the Joint Council, which oversaw all three Rochester Teamsters Locals, had no power to investigate Local #398.

According to Thomas J. Kenny, Teamsters Joint Council #17 Secretary-Treasurer, "there had been no need to discuss mob infiltration; there was nothing I could have done about it."

## Organized crime tied to 2 local unions, cop says

FROM PAGE 1B

by the members," said Thomas Kenny, a business representative for Local 791 and a member of Joint Council 17, affiliated with the Teamsters.

The Joint Council oversees three Rochester unions — Locals 118, 398 and 791 — which have seven delegates to the joint council. It is the step above the locals in union hierarchy, although it falls below regional and international groups.

Kenny says there has been no need to discuss mob infiltration with the council. "There's nothing I can do about it."

Many local Teamsters are upset about allegations that reputed mob figures hold union positions, Kenny says.

"I think some of us are pretty clean, and (now) everyone looks at us with evil eyes."

On Tuesday, a federal grand jury's three-year probe into local organized crime activities culminated with the arrests of 10 reputed members of the Rochester underworld, including the local mob's upper echelon.

One of the men indicted Tuesday on racketeering charges, Joseph Trieste of Rochester, is the business agent of Local 435. Another, Richard Marino of Irondequoit — the reputed "underboss" of the Rochester mob — was elected in 1973 as the first full-time director of the Allied Building Trades Council, which represents 18 AFL-CIO local trade unions.

Marino, 43, was suspended from that position in July 1975, when he and five others were indicted in the 1973 slaying of reputed mobster Vincent "Jimmy the Hammer" Massaro.

Marino and the others were sentenced to 25 years to life in a state prison after they were convicted of murder in the Massaro slaying. But the convictions were overturned and Marino was released in 1978 when Monroe County sheriff's investigators admitted that key evidence used in the Massaro trials was fabricated.

The indictments handed up Tuesday by a federal grand jury once again charge Marino in the Massaro slaying.

Also indicted in the slaying are Samuel J. "Red" Russotti, the reputed "boss" of the Rochester mob, and Rene J. Piccarreto, the reputed "consiglieri" — an advisor who shares power with the boss.

Russotti has never been a member of a labor union, police say, but Piccarreto was once a member of a local painters' union.

After Marino was released from prison, he assumed a "no show" job as a steward in Local 398, Grande says.

At the hearings, Grande presented to the commission police surveillance records made between September and December of 1978 of 57 sightings of Marino doing something other than construction or union work when he was supposedly on the job.

The commission documented evidence that Marino was on the payroll of a road construction company on the days the sightings were made, Staffa said.

"The no show job is by far the most lucrative," Grande said, but there are other types of positions awarded to organized crime members, associates and relatives.

For example, the current business agent of Local 398 is Marino's brother-in-law, Angelo Misuraca, who is not a member of the Rochester mob, Grande testified.

Misuraca became the union's business agent in December, when his predecessor, John Fiorino, was shotgunned to death in front of the former Blue Gardenia restaurant in Irondequoit, Grande testified.

Fiorino was underboss of the established local mob, police say, and his death was ordered by an insurgent faction of organized crime figures who were trying to gain control of the established mob's operations.

A "working steward" and a "worker" are two other positions commonly awarded by organized crime members, Grande says.

Those who assume these positions may or may not work a full day as a legitimate steward or worker, he says. The difference is many are given these positions only because they are loyal associates or relatives of mob leaders.

An example is Piccarreto's son, Loren, a steward in Local 435, Grande testified.

Three of the men indicted Tuesday on various racketeering charges also are union stewards. They are: Anthony M. Colombo of Rochester, a steward in Local 435; Joseph J. LaDolce of Rochester, a steward in Local 398; and John M. "Flap" Trivigno of Rochester, also a steward in Local 398.

Another job given to underworld figures is what Grande calls a "parts chaser." He says parts chasers report to construction sites and are given trucks and assignments, which usually take about 30 minutes to an hour a day.

These parts chasers generally spend most of their days in gambling-related activities, he says, particularly sports bookmaking.

Police Sgt. John Grande

Grande believes tougher state laws are needed to fight mob infiltration of labor unions.

Under current laws, these activities are technical violations of state labor laws and misdemeanors under the penal code, said Monroe County District Attorney Donald O. Chesworth.

It wouldn't be productive, Grande says, to assign officers to investigate labor law violations in unions when the best possible results would be arrests on misdemeanors.

Grande believes many of the violations should be changed to felonies, and he is hoping the state Commission of Investigations' probe will lead to tougher laws.

Staffa says the commission will report its findings to Governor-elect Mario Cuomo and the state Legislature when the inquiry is completed in mid-1983. The commission could recommend tougher legislation involving labor law violations, he says.

Organized crime members also assume positions in labor unions to supplement other sources of revenue, Grande says.

"If (Fiorino) was making $500 clear, declarable as the business agent, we know that Mr. Fiorino was paid $50 a day, seven days a week as an operator of a gambling establishment," Grande testified.

"As far as organized crime is concerned it's extremely lucrative," Grande says. "The unions don't get anything from this, they lose. The legitimate members are often deprived of jobs, and they have to stand in unemployment lines because someone else is handed a job."

**November 11, 1982**
**Democrat and Chronicle**

Unfortunately, that was a very true statement. Each Teamster Local Union acted independently from the others. Each local conducted its own elections, and each local had its own set of rules or by-laws.

Absent of formal charges originating within the respective Local Union, the Joint Council had no jurisdiction. Also any criminal accusations against union officials were also well outside the jurisdiction of local governing bodies. (65)

# New Club Is Suspected Gambling Front Police Say

New club is suspected gambling front, police sa

By Jim Redmond
Democrat and Chronicle

Rochester police are investigating a recently opened social club on Jay Street for possible links to organized crime.

Police suspect the club, The Young Men's Club Inc. at 431 Jay St., is a front for illegal gambling, sources said. They have recorded the license numbers of cars parked outside the club on several occasions during the past month, sources said.

"Some of the cars have been seen outside a gambling parlor on St. Paul St.," said one police officer.

Known members of organized crime have

The building at 429-433 Jay St. is owned by 431 Jay St. Inc., according to tax records in the Monroe County clerk's office. Rita Piccarreto, wife of reputed organized crime leader Rene Piccarreto Sr., is listed on the property's deed as president of 431 Jay St. Inc., records show.

Rene Piccarreto was indicted earlier this month on federal conspiracy and racketeering charges. He has pleaded innocent to the charges and is free on $200,000 bond while awaiting trial.

Piccarreto is not a member of the club, but his son, Loren, belongs, members and police said.

The club had been dormant for the past nine or 10 years until it was revived about a month ago, club members said.

"A few guys got together and we wanted to form our own private club," Russo said.

People join private social clubs because "you want to be with your own people — friends and relatives," Russo said.

The club plans to sponsor a softball team and bowling team at the request of younger members.

The club has between 50 and 60 members who pay $10 each month in dues and attend monthly meetings.

Elections for officers are scheduled for the club's monthly meeting on the first Thursday of December.

The club is looking for new members, Russo said.

"The more we get the better it is," Russo said. "The more members we have, the less dues we pay."

The club in the past has made donations to area charities when it has had extra money, members said. "We've donated quite a bit in the past," Russo said. "I can't tell you how much off-hand."

The club facilities the second-floor of th two-story building o between 6 and 7 p.m daily. Eventually, clu members would like be able to keep the club open 24 hours a day.

The club itself is "plush," Stebbins sai Kitchen facilities are available to provide meals for members.

"We don't serve liquor," Russo said. "W have it, but we don't serve it. If a member brings a bottle, he do nates it to the members."

The club doesn't h any paid employees. "Everyone's a donation," Russo said.

**November 28, 1982 Democrat and Chronicle**

In late **November of 1982**, Rochester Police were investigating a  new social club that opened in Rochester at 431 Jay Street called The Young Man's Social Club. It was suspected of being a front for gambling operations, with links to organized crime.

The building was owned by Rita Piccarreto, Rene Piccarreto's wife.  Rene Piccarreto had been the #2 ranked Mafiosa in the City of Rochester for over 20 years. Rita was not a member of the "social club" but her son Loren was.  Police sources said that Loren was also a member of the Rochester Mafia Crime Family." **(66)**

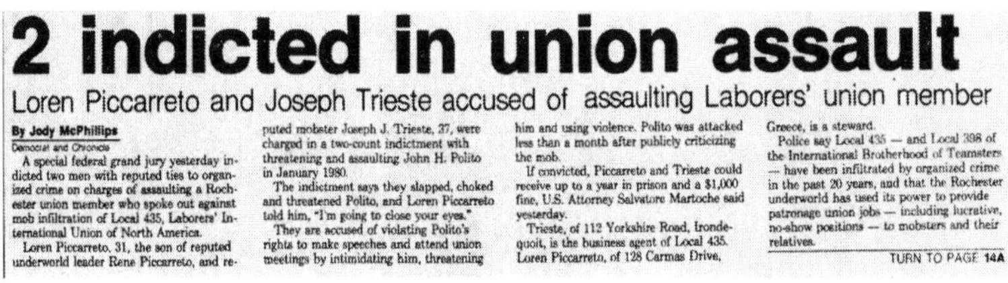

2 indicted in union assault

Loren Piccarreto and Joseph Trieste accused of assaulting Laborers' union member

By Jody McPhillips
Democrat and Chronicle

A special federal grand jury yesterday indicted two men with reputed ties to organized crime on charges of assaulting a Rochester union member who spoke out against mob infiltration of Local 435, Laborers' International Union of North America.

Loren Piccarreto, 31, the son of reputed underworld leader Rene Piccarreto, and reputed mobster Joseph J. Trieste, 37, were charged in a two-count indictment with threatening and assaulting John H. Polito in January 1980.

The indictment says they slapped, choked and threatened Polito, and Loren Piccarreto told him, "I'm going to close your eyes."

They are accused of violating Polito's rights to make speeches and attend union meetings by intimidating him, threatening him and using violence. Polito was attacked less than a month after publicly criticizing the mob.

If convicted, Piccarreto and Trieste could receive up to a year in prison and a $1,000 fine, U.S. Attorney Salvatore Martoche said yesterday.

Trieste, of 112 Yorkshire Road, Irondequoit, is the business agent of Local 435. Loren Piccarreto, of 128 Carmas Drive, Greece, is a steward.

Police say Local 435 — and Local 398 of the International Brotherhood of Teamsters — have been infiltrated by organized crime in the past 20 years, and that the Rochester underworld has used its power to provide patronage union jobs — including lucrative, no-show positions — to mobsters and their relatives.

TURN TO PAGE 14A

**December 16, 1982 Democrat and Chronicle**

## 2 Indicted In Union Assault

On **December 15, 1982,** a special Federal Grand Jury indicted two men with organized crime ties on charges of assaulting a Rochester union member who spoke out against mafia infiltration of Local 435, Laborers' International Union of North America.

## Union Official Joseph Trieste Denies Charge

Loren Piccarreto, son of underworld leader Rene Piccarreto, and mobster Joseph J. Trieste were charged with two counts of threatening and assaulting John H. Polito in January 1980. The indictment stated that the defendants choked, slapped and threatened Polito to prevent him from speaking out at a union meeting.

Joseph Trieste pleaded not guilty at his hearing. (67)

### Union official denies charge

Accused of threatening another local member for 'mob infiltration' talk

**By Jody McPhillips**
Democrat and Chronicle

Joseph J. Trieste, hands clasped behind his back, stood silently before U.S. District Court Judge Michael A. Telesca yesterday as his defense lawyer, Charles T. Noce, told the judge Trieste pleaded not guilty.

Trieste, 37, ignored reporters and television cameramen at his arraignment on charges of violating the rights of a fellow member of Local 435, Laborers International Union of North America, by slapping and threatening him.

Telesca set a $10,000 personal recognizance bond, which he said could be secured by Trieste's signature. He told Noce to file any pretrial motions by Jan. 5, and told federal prosecutors they had until Jan. 19 to respond.

Trieste, of 112 Yorkshire Road, was indicted last Wednesday with Loren Piccarreto, 31, of 128 Carmas Drive, Greece. Piccarreto pleaded not guilty to the charges last Friday. The misdemeanor carries a maximum penalty of a year in prison, a $1,000 fine or both.

They are accused of threatening John H. Polito, then a member of Local 435, after he made a speech Dec. 28, 1979, to other union members, protesting against the infiltration of the union by organized crime.

According to the indictment, Polito told Local 435 members at a union meeting that "the mob is infiltrating" the local and that inexperienced members who didn't "know anything about conditions, or safety, or team work, or tunnel work in general" were being considered for jobs as tunnel stewards.

The indictment says Polito was slapped, choked and threatened to prevent him from speaking out against the mob, a violation of his rights under federal labor law.

Piccarreto is a steward with Local 435 and Trieste is a business agent.

Piccarreto is the son of reputed Rochester mob leader Rene Piccarreto, one of 10 reputed mobsters indicted Nov. 8 on federal conspiracy and racketeering charges. Trieste was also named in the Nov. 8 indictment.

**December 21, 1982**
**Democrat and Chronicle**

## Torpey Guilty on Four Charges

### Torpey guilty on four charges

Convicted in extortion attempt to take over Lake Avenue bar

**By Gary Gerew**
Democrat and Chronicle

Reputed underworld figure Thomas M. Torpey was convicted of four charges last night in connection with an extortion attempt involving a Lake Avenue bar in 1981.

He was found not guilty of related charges of assault and criminal possession of a weapon.

Torpey gave no reaction as the verdict was read shortly after 9:15 p.m. His lawyer, Felix Lapine, said he expected a guilty verdict on some charge.

"We pretty much knew it was coming this afternoon," Lapine said.

Lapine said he didn't understand how the jury, which deliberated for about 17 hours over two days, reached a split verdict on the seven-count indictment against Torpey.

"I don't know how they came up with the verdict and find it somewhat repugnant," he said. "It's basically impossible for a man like Mr. Torpey to get a fair trial in this town given the type of publicity and rumors associated with his name," Lapine said.

TURN TO PAGE **6A**

**March 11, 1983 Democrat and Chronicle**

Thomas Torpey, reputed Mafia strongarm was found guilty on **March 10, 1983** on four charges in relation to his attempted takeover by extortion of a Lake Avenue bar. Torpey's lawyer said at the time, " It's basically impossible for a man like Mr. Torpey to get a fair trial in this town." (68)

# 2 Mobsters on Trial for Assault

## Piccarreto says he saw co-defendant raise hand at Polito

**By Gary Gerew**
Democrat and Chronicle

Testimony ended yesterday in the trial of two reputed mobsters accused of threatening union member John H. Polito with one of the two defendants saying the other raised his hand toward Polito.

Asked if he saw co-defendant Joseph J. Trieste slap Polito, Loren Piccarreto said he saw Trieste and Polito apparently arguing and did see Trieste raise his hand.

"John swore at Joey as I walked up to him," Piccarreto said. "It looked like he was slapping him."

But when Piccarreto was asked if he saw Trieste actually slap Polito, Piccarreto said, "I don't recall."

Piccarreto, 32, and Trieste, 38, are accused of slapping, choking and threatening Polito before a Jan. 25, 1980, meeting of Local 435 of the Laborers International Union of North America.

They are charged with violating Polito's rights as a union member under federal labor law. The misdemeanor charge carries a maximum penalty of a year in federal prison, a $1,000 fine or both.

Piccarreto took the stand in his own defense yesterday and Thursday, but Trieste's

TURN TO PAGE 3B

**March 19, 1983**
**Democrat and Chronicle**

Testimony ended in the assault trial for two Rochester mobsters on **March 18, 1983**.

Loren Piccarreto and Joseph Trieste were accused of slapping and choking a union man at a union meeting because he spoke out against mafia infiltration of the union.

# Rochester Mobster Thomas Marotta Is Shot Six Times

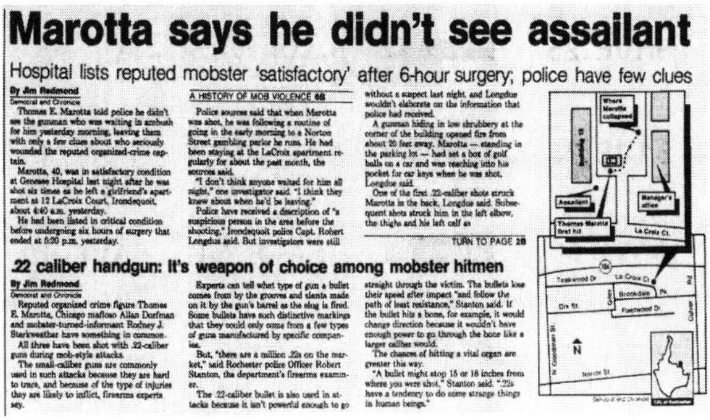

# Marotta says he didn't see assailant

## Hospital lists reputed mobster 'satisfactory' after 6-hour surgery; police have few clues

**By Jim Redmond**
Democrat and Chronicle

Thomas E. Marotta told police he didn't see the gunman who was waiting in ambush for him yesterday morning, leaving them with only a few clues about who seriously wounded the reputed organized-crime captain.

Marotta, 40, was in satisfactory condition at Genesee Hospital last night after he was shot six times as he left a girlfriend's apartment at 12 LaCroix Court, Irondequoit, about 4:40 a.m. yesterday.

He had been listed in critical condition before undergoing six hours of surgery that ended at 5:20 p.m. yesterday.

A HISTORY OF MOB VIOLENCE 68

Police sources said that when Marotta was shot, he was following a routine of going in the early morning to a Norton Street gambling parlor he runs. He had been staying at the LaCroix apartment regularly for about the past month, the sources said.

"I don't think anyone waited for him all night," one investigator said. "I think they knew about when he'd be leaving."

Police have received a description of "a suspicious person in the area before the shooting," Irondequoit police Capt. Robert Longdue said. But investigators were still without a suspect last night, and Longdue wouldn't elaborate on the information that police had received.

A gunman hiding in low shrubbery at the corner of the building opened fire from about 20 feet away. Marotta — standing in the parking lot — had set a box of golf balls on a car and was reaching into his pocket for car keys when he was shot, Longdue said.

One of the first .22-caliber shots struck Marotta in the back, Longdue said. Subsequent shots struck him in the left elbow, the thighs and his left calf as

TURN TO PAGE 2B

## .22 caliber handgun: It's weapon of choice among mobster hitmen

**By Jim Redmond**
Democrat and Chronicle

Reputed organized crime figure Thomas E. Marotta, Chicago mafioso Allan Dorfman and mobster-turned-informant Rodney J. Starkweather have something in common.

All three have been shot with .22-caliber guns during mob-style attacks.

The small-caliber guns are commonly used in such attacks because they are hard to trace, and because of the type of injuries they are likely to inflict, firearms experts say.

Experts can tell what type of gun a bullet comes from by the grooves and slants made on it by the gun's barrel as the slug is fired. Some bullets have such distinctive markings that they could only come from a few types of guns manufactured by specific companies.

But, "there are a million .22s on the market," said Rochester police Officer Robert Stanton, the department's firearms examiner.

The .22-caliber bullet is also used in attacks because it isn't powerful enough to go straight through the victim. The bullets lose their speed after impact "and follow the path of least resistance," Stanton said. If the bullet hits a bone, for example, it would change direction because it wouldn't have enough power to go through the bone like a larger caliber would.

The chances of hitting a vital organ are greater this way.

"A bullet might stop 15 or 18 inches from where you were shot," Stanton said. ".22s have a tendency to do some strange things in human beings."

**April 13, 1983 Democrat and Chronicle**

Rochester Mafia "Capo" Thomas Marotta was shot six times on **April 12, 1983** by a .22 caliber handgun. Marotta, who survived the attack, was shot at 4:40 a.m. after he left his girlfriend's apartment on La Croix Circle in Irondequoit, New York.

Thomas Marotta ran a gambling parlor on Norton Street at the time. Police suspected that that Marotta was shot while following his regular routine of going in for an early to visit to that gambling parlor. **(174)**

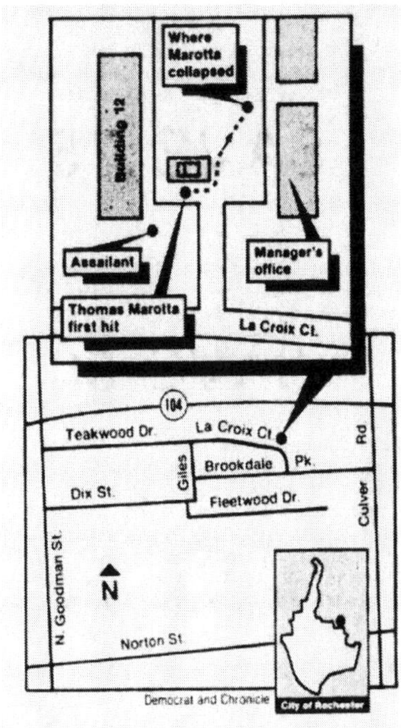


**Location of Marotta shooting.**

## Brucato charged with lying to grand jury

### Salesman is accused in sale of an auto

By Jody McPhillips
Democrat and Chronicle

Used-car salesman Robert R. Brucato, 42, was released on his own recognizance yesterday after his arraignment in U.S. District Court on charges of twice lying to a federal grand jury about a car used in an attempted gangland murder.

Reputed mobsters Richard J. Marino and Vincent J. Rallo were named as co-conspirators in the three-count indictment unsealed yesterday. A special federal grand jury handed up the indictment Tuesday.

Marino was indicted Nov. 9 with nine other men on federal racketeering and conspiracy charges. Rallo, who turned informant in 1981, is in the federal Witness Protection Program.

Brucato is also charged with obstructing justice by fabricating evidence with the help of the other two.

Brucato, of 123 Spanish Trail, Greece, was arrested at 3:15 p.m. yesterday at his business, B.B. Motors, at 3950 W. Ridge Road, Greece. He pleaded not guilty at his arraignment.

According to the indictment, Brucato told grand jurors on March 22, 1979, that he sold a 1973 Ford LTD on Feb. 5, 1979, to a "Michael Lockhart." On Oct. 15, 1980, he told grand jurors Lockhart signed registration forms for the car.

On March 13, 1979, reputed mobsters Anthony M. Colombo and Anthony F. Oliveri were arrested in the LTD after a high-speed police chase. Police spotted the car parked on Firestone Drive, near the home of Angelo "Oskie" DeMarco.

But "Lockhart", the man Brucato described to police on March 15, 1979, was fictitious and Brucato knew it, prosecutors charge. Between March 13, 1979 and March 31, 1981, Brucato, Marino and Rallo "did corruptly plan and agree to give false testimony" that "Lockhart" bought the car and filled out registration forms.

The obstruction charge carries a maximum penalty of five years in a federal penitentiary, a $5,000 fine or both. The two perjury charges carry maximum penalties of five years, a $10,000 fine or both.

The DeMarco incident, described in yesterday's indictment as "the attempt to murder Angelo 'Oskie' DeMarco on March 13, 1979," is one of numerous criminal activities alleged in the complex Nov. 9 indictment charging Marino and others.

**Democrat and Chronicle**
**April 28, 1983**

# Brucato Charged With Lying to Grand Jury

Used-car salesman Robert R. Brucato, 42, was released on his own recognizance after his arraignment in U.S. District Court on charges of twice lying to a federal grand jury about a car used in an attempted gangland murder.

Reputed mobsters Richard J. Marino and Vincent J. Rallo were named as co-conspirators in the three-count indictment unsealed on **April 27, 1983**. A special federal grand jury handed up the indictment. Marino also was previously indicted on Nov. 9, 1982 with nine other men for federal racketeering and conspiracy charges.

# Brucato Charged With Obstructing Justice

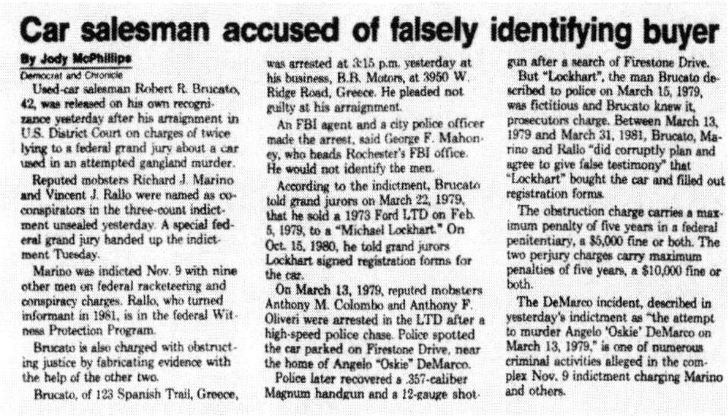

**Car salesman accused of falsely identifying buyer**

**By Jody McPhillips**
Democrat and Chronicle

Used-car salesman Robert R. Brucato, 42, was released on his own recognizance yesterday after his arraignment in U.S. District Court on charges of twice lying to a federal grand jury about a car used in an attempted gangland murder.

Reputed mobsters Richard J. Marino and Vincent J. Rallo were named as co-conspirators in the three-count indictment unsealed yesterday. A special federal grand jury handed up the indictment Tuesday.

Marino was indicted Nov. 9 with nine other men on federal racketeering and conspiracy charges. Rallo, who turned informant in 1981, is in the federal Witness Protection Program.

Brucato is also charged with obstructing justice by fabricating evidence with the help of the other two.

Brucato, of 123 Spanish Trail, Greece, was arrested at 3:15 p.m. yesterday at his business, B.B. Motors, at 3950 W. Ridge Road, Greece. He pleaded not guilty at his arraignment.

An FBI agent and a city police officer made the arrest, said George F. Mahoney, who heads Rochester's FBI office. He would not identify the men.

According to the indictment, Brucato told grand jurors on March 22, 1979, that he sold a 1973 Ford LTD on Feb. 5, 1979, to a "Michael Lockhart." On Oct. 15, 1980, he told grand jurors Lockhart signed registration forms for the car.

On March 13, 1979, reputed mobsters Anthony M. Colombo and Anthony F. Oliveri were arrested in the LTD after a high-speed police chase. Police spotted the car parked on Firestone Drive, near the home of Angelo "Oskie" DeMarco.

Police later recovered a .357-caliber Magnum handgun and a 12-gauge shotgun after a search of Firestone Drive.

But "Lockhart", the man Brucato described to police on March 15, 1979, was fictitious and Brucato knew it, prosecutors charge. Between March 13, 1979 and March 31, 1981, Brucato, Marino and Rallo "did corruptly plan and agree to give false testimony" that "Lockhart" bought the car and filled out registration forms.

The obstruction charge carries a maximum penalty of five years in a federal penitentiary, a $5,000 fine or both. The two perjury charges carry maximum penalties of five years, a $10,000 fine or both.

The DeMarco incident, described in yesterday's indictment as "the attempt to murder Angelo 'Oskie' DeMarco on March 13, 1979," is one of numerous criminal activities alleged in the complex Nov. 9 indictment charging Marino and others.

**Democrat and Chronicle**
**April 28, 1983**

On **April 27, 1983** Robert Brucato was also charged with obstructing justice by fabricating evidence with the help of the other two men. Brucato, of 123 Spanish Trail, Greece, was arrested at his business, B.B. Motors, at 3950 W. Ridge Road, Greece. He pleaded not guilty at his arraignment

According to the indictment, Brucato told grand jurors on March 22, 1979, that he sold a 1973 Ford LTD on Feb. 5, 1979, to a "Michael Lockhart." On Oct. 15, 1980, he told grand jurors Lockhart signed registration forms for the car. But "Lockhart", the man Brucato described to police on March 15, 1979, was fictitious and Brucato knew it, prosecutors charge.

The car was used in an attempted "hit" on Angelo "Oskie" DiMarco who was scheduled to testify about his involvement in mob activities. On March 13, 1979, reputed mobsters Anthony M. Colombo and Anthony F. Oliveri were arrested in the LTD after a high-speed police chase. Police had spotted them parked on Firestone Drive, near the home of Angelo "Oskie" DiMarco.

Between March 13, 1979 and March 31, 1981, Brucato, Marino and Rallo "did corruptly plan and agree to give false testimony" that "Lockhart" bought the car and filled out registration forms. The obstruction charge carries a maximum penalty of five years in a federal penitentiary, a $5,000 fine or both. The two perjury charges carry maximum penalties of five years, a $10,000 fine or both. **(69)**

# Shooting at the Young Man's Social Club

## Clues sought in shooting at mob-linked social club

Rochester police are searching for clues in a shooting incident early yesterday on Jay Street, at a suspected gambling parlor operated by reputed local organized crime figures.

Police say two shots were fired through second-floor windows of The Young Men's Social Club, 431 Jay St. shortly after 5 a.m. There were no injuries reported.

One club member, however, identified as reputed Rochester mobster Leonard Stebbins, told detectives he was almost hit by the shots.

Police had been dispatched to the parlor about 2 a.m. after receiving a report of a man standing in a nearby yard holding a gun wrapped in a blanket. Police searched the area but found no one and left.

The Young Men's Social Club, police say, is one of six gambling establishments operated by the Rochester mob.

Yesterday was the second time in two months that shots were fired through the windows of an establishment linked to organized crime.

On April 17, six bullet holes were discovered in the front window of a suspected gambling parlor at 7 Fernwood Ave. Police say the establishment is operated by the reputed head of local organized crime, Samuel Russotti. Russotti is awaiting trial on federal racketeering charges.

The Fernwood Avenue building also was hit with a shotgun blast last Aug. 27, the day Gerald Pelusio was slain in Irondequoit. Police sources have said Pelusio's slaying by an unidentified assailant may be the cause of the current violence.

The club on Jay Street had been dormant for about nine years before its operations were resumed in October 1982, police said. The building itself at 429-433 Jay St. is owned by 431 Jay St. Inc. Police say the president of the corporation is Rita Piccarreto, wife of Rene Piccarreto, reputed to be the mob's second in command. He is also facing racketeering charges.

**May 28, 1983 Democrat and Chronicle**

Rochester Police responded to a shooting at the Young Man's Social Club on **May 27, 1983**. The Club located at 431 Jay Street was a suspected gambling parlor run by the Rochester Mafia. One club member identified as reputed mobster Leonard Stebbins, told detectives he was almost hit by the shots. The building is owned by Rita Piccarreto, wife of Rochester Mafia leader Rene Piccarreto. **(70)**

D&C Photo by John G. Walter

**Young Man's Social Club located at 431 Jay Street**

# Dino Tortatice is Murdered

## Slain gang leader's ambition may have led mob to order his death

### Tortatice was known as a tough guy

**By David Galante**
Democrat and Chronicle

Dino Tortatice had a reputation of being a tough guy.

He frequented bars on Rochester's northeast side and was a street brawler since his early teens, high-ranking law enforcement sources said yesterday.

He led a gang of 10 to 15 young men who would shake down bar owners for money and threaten people who stepped in their way, sources said.

Some called them a "junior mob."

Though just 24 and a small-time operator compared to Rochester's established mob figures, Tortatice was determined to have his own niche in the local underworld, sources said.

His determination, however, meant treading into criminal activity normally hands-off to all but the area's long-standing organized crime family.

Dino Tortatice

That determination left Tortatice dead Tuesday night.

He was gunned down about 8:45 p.m. while drinking a can of beer outside his mother's house on Norran Drive in the northern part of the city, said Rochester Deputy Police Chief Terrence Rickard.

An assassin emptied an automatic weapon and fled in a stolen car, which was later found abandoned nearby, police said.

Tortatice died less than an hour later at Rochester General Hospital. An autopsy lists the cause of death as gunshot wounds to the chest and stomach, a spokesman for

TURN TO PAGE 2B

### Police suspect organized crime behind shooting

**By David Galante**
Democrat and Chronicle

The slaying of Dino Tortatice Tuesday night is believed to be the third contract killing in two years ordered by the Rochester underworld as a warning to a rival organized crime faction, high-ranking law enforcement officials said yesterday.

Homicide detectives say they are investigating similarities in the slayings of Tortacice, 24, Nicholas Mastrodonato and Gerald Pelusio.

All three were associated with an insurgent faction of organized crime figures that has been warring with Rochster's established organized crime family, sources said.

All three homicides are unsolved. But some law enforcement officials are embracing the theory that the same gunman is responsible for all three slayings because:

- In all three, a lone gunmen has driven up to the scene in a stolen car that later was found abandoned a few minutes away.
- All three getaway cars were older model Fords, which suggests a thief may be familiar with how to hot wire these cars.
- At least two of the getaway cars were stolen from the same apartment complex in Greece, police sources said.
- The weapon is believed to have been a .45-caliber automatic handgun.

Mastrodonato, an insurgent faction ally, was shot to death May 25, 1982. A gunman strode into Mr. Gold's Coin Shop, 481 Spencerport Road, Gates, where Mastrodonato worked, and fired several gun shots.

On Aug. 27, 1982, Gerald Pelusio, 33, was gunned down in front of a townhouse in Irondequoit. Gerald and his brother, Thomas Pelusio, were look-alikes, and police believe Gerald was the mistaken target of bullets meant for Thomas.

**August 4, 1983 Democrat and Chronicle**

On **August 2, 1983**, Dino Tortatice 24, was gunned down outside of his mother's home on Norran Drive in the northern part of Rochester, N.Y. Tortatice had a reputation for being a "tough guy." He led a gang of 10 to 15 young men, who would shake down bar owners for money and threaten others that got in their way. "Some called them a junior mob." **(195)**

Police speculated, that kind of ambition is what led to his death. An assassin unloaded an automatic weapon on Tortatice as he sat outside his mother's home drinking a beer. Dino Tortatice died less as an hour later. He was the third recent homicide victim, associated with an insurgent faction of the Rochester Mafia. Police at the time were investigating similarities in the Mastrodonato and Pelusio murders. **(175)**

# Marotta Gunned Down Again

Marotta gunned down again

Reputed mobster seriously wounded in second attempt on life in 7 months

RAIN

TODAY

At-home drug test is coming

**Nov. 11, 1983 Democrat and Chronicle**

On **November 10, 1983** , reputed organized crime "Captain" Thomas E. Marotta was shot for the second time in less than a year. Police at the time thought that the shooting was in retaliation for the August 2, 1983 murder of Dino Tortatice.

Police also thought that the Tortatice killing may have been retribution for an attempt on Marotta's life the previous April. Toni Tortatice said her brother, Dino, 24, was killed after estab-

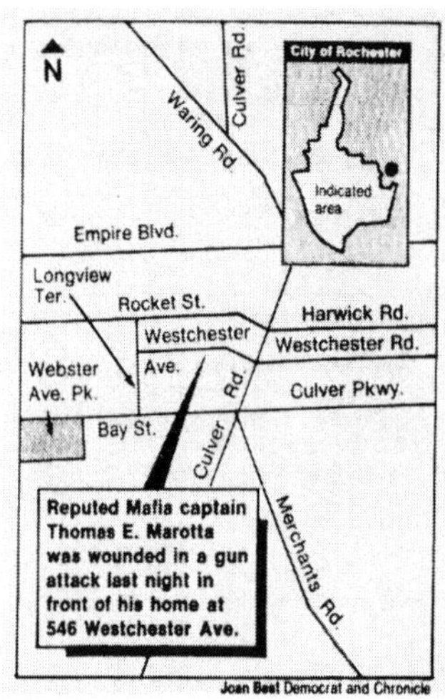


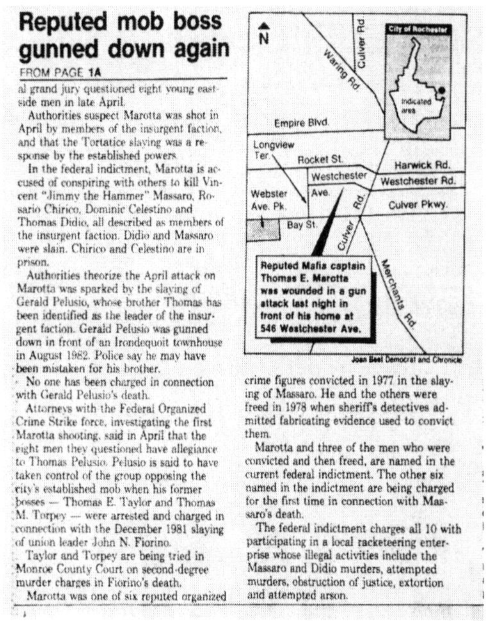

## Reputed mob boss gunned down again

FROM PAGE 1A

al grand jury questioned eight young east-side men in late April.

Authorities suspect Marotta was shot in April by members of the insurgent faction, and that the Tortatice slaying was a response by the established powers.

In the federal indictment, Marotta is accused of conspiring with others to kill Vincent "Jimmy the Hammer" Massaro, Rosario Chirico, Dominic Celestino and Thomas Didio, all described as members of the insurgent faction. Didio and Massaro were slain. Chirico and Celestino are in prison.

Authorities theorize the April attack on Marotta was sparked by the slaying of Gerald Pelusio, whose brother Thomas has been identified as the leader of the insurgent faction. Gerald Pelusio was gunned down in front of an Irondequoit townhouse in August 1982. Police say he may have been mistaken for his brother.

No one has been charged in connection with Gerald Pelusio's death.

Attorneys with the Federal Organized Crime Strike force, investigating the first Marotta shooting, said in April that the eight men they questioned have allegiance to Thomas Pelusio. Pelusio is said to have taken control of the group opposing the city's established mob when his former bosses — Thomas E. Taylor and Thomas M. Torpey — were arrested and charged in connection with the December 1981 slaying of union leader John N. Fiorino.

Taylor and Torpey are being tried in Monroe County Court on second-degree murder charges in Fiorino's death.

Marotta was one of six reputed organized crime figures convicted in 1977 in the slaying of Massaro. He and the others were freed in 1978 when sheriff's detectives admitted fabricating evidence used to convict them.

Marotta and three of the men who were convicted and then freed, are named in the current federal indictment. The other six named in the indictment are being charged for the first time in connection with Massaro's death.

The federal indictment charges all 10 with participating in a local racketeering enterprise whose illegal activities include the Massaro and Didio murders, attempted murders, obstruction of justice, extortion and attempted arson.



lished mob leaders read in newspaper articles that he and a group of friends had been extensively questioned by police in the first Marotta shooting. She was afraid of retaliation on her younger brother.

Toni vividly remembered watching her older brother, Dino, gunned down the previous August in front of their parents' Norran Drive home. She feared her younger brother, Rocco, could also die as violent attacks were exchanged by rival local mob factions. Both brothers grew up tough and street-wise, Toni Tortatice said, but neither had been involved with organized crime. **(176)**

# Men Questioned After Marotta Shooting

**Friends of slain gang leader arrested in area after Marotta shooting**

Charged with possesion of dagger half an hour after assassination try

**By David Galante**
Democrat and Chronicle

Two friends of slain gang leader Dino Tortatice were arrested yesterday shortly after Thursday's attempt on the life of reputed Rochester underworld leader Thomas E. Marotta, police said.

Irondequoit police Capt. Robert Longdue, who is heading the Marotta investigation, would not comment on the arrests, but high-ranking law enforcement authorities said the two were questioned about the incident.

The pair were arrested on weapons charges by Irondequoit police about 30 minutes after Marotta was shot in the driveway of his house at 546 Westchester Ave., Irondequoit, at about 11:45 p.m. Thursday.

Arrested were Frederick Kelch, 20, of 238 Milford St., and Timothy Hartwigh, 27, of 47 Child St., police said. They were charged with criminal possession of a dangerous weapon — a dagger — after being picked up near Marotta's house.

Kelch and Hartwigh are to appear at a later date in Irondequoit Town Court to answer the weapons charges.

Marotta, 41, who is said by local

TURN TO PAGE 4B

Tortatice's sister afraid of retaliation on younger brother

**By Steve Crosby**
Democrat and Chronicle

Toni Tortatice vividly remembers watching her older brother, Dino, gunned down last August in front of their parents' Norran Drive home.

Now she fears her younger brother, Rocco, may also die as violent attacks are exchanged by rival local mob factions. Both brothers grew up tough and street-wise, Tortatice said yesterday, but neither has been involved with organized crime.

"We weren't brought up that way," she said, sitting with her two children in the kitchen of her Norton Street apartment. "We're scared of drugs and we're scared of guns."

Police said they suspect that the shooting Thursday night of reputed organized crime captain Thomas E. Marotta was in retaliation for the Aug. 2 murder of Dino Tortatice. And in the see-sawing struggle for mob control, police think the Tortatice killing may have been retribution for an attempt on Marotta's life last April.

Tortatice said her brother, Dino, 24, was killed after established mob leaders read in newspaper articles

TURN TO PAGE 4B

Dino Tortatice

**Democrat and Chronicle November 12, 1983**

Two men were arrested near the house of reputed underworld leader Thomas Marotta, 546 Westchester Ave., Irondequoit. The men questioned after the Marotta shooting were arrested on weapons charges by Irondequoit police 30 minutes after Marotta was shot in the driveway of his house at 11:45 p.m. Frederick Kelch, 238 Milford St., and Timothy Hartwigh, 27, of 47 Child St. were scheduled to appear at a later date in Irondequoit Court to answer the weapons charge, they were charged with criminal possession of a dangerous weapon (dagger) after being caught near Marotta's house. Marotta, 41, was said by local authorities to be fourth in command of the Rochester Organized Crime Family.

Marotta was in fair condition the day after the shooting, at Genesee Hospital, a hospital spokeswoman said. He was struck at least three times in the chest in an ambush attack by an unidentified assailant who emptied a small-caliber handgun, missing several times, Longdue said. It was the second attempt on Marotta's life in seven months. On April 12, Marotta was shot six times by a gunman in the parking lot of an apartment building at La Croix Court in Irondequoit.

No one had been charged in either shooting, but Irondequoit police and members of the countywide Organized Crime Task Force say they were investigating similarities in the shootings. Some organized crime investigators theorize the latest Marotta shooting was in retaliation for the Aug. 2, 1983 slaying of gang leader Dino Tortatice, 24, of Norran Drive. The Tortatice shooting, investigators have said, was suspected to have been in retaliation for the first attempt on Marotta's life. "It's been a seesaw battle," one detective said.

The gunman stepped out from behind Marotta's house and fired from about eight feet away as Marotta was getting into a late-model Oldsmobile. The gunman then ran behind the house in a northeasterly direction toward the intersection of Whittington and Harwick roads, hopping two or three backyard fences. It's not clear whether a getaway vehicle was involved. Marotta's wife, Mary, told police she watched her husband fall, then saw the gunman flee. The only description she could provide of the assailant was that he was about six feet tall.

It would later be discovered that a "hitman" for the "A Team" of the Rochester Mafia, Dominic Taddeo, was the person who murdered Dino Tortatice right outside of his house on August 2, 1983. "Red" Russoti, the "Boss" of the "A Team", ordered the extermination of all "C Team" members involved in the Fiorino murder. John Fiorino was Teamsters **Local #398** Vice-President. Oddly enough, it would later be discovered that Dominic Taddeo was also responsible for the Marotta shootings as well. He would eventually admit to them all. He was the "A Team's" "one man house cleaner." (71)

Police say Tortatice led a gang of about a dozen Irondequoit and eastside Rochester men, including Kelch and Hartwigh, who tried to run a small-time racketeering operation. None has been charged or convicted of racketeering. Tortatice and the others were questioned by a federal grand jury in Rochester investigating the first Marotta shooting and local racketeering. The results of the investigation were not made public. Gang members interviewed in Democrat and Chronicle articles after the first attack on Marotta, pointed out the ambush-style and the "amateurish" manner of the shootings.

The shooting of Marotta, came a year and a day after Marotta and nine others were indicted by a federal grand jury in Rochester on racketeering charges. The 10 were still awaiting trial at the time. Investigators said the Tortatice gang was the third succession of an insurgent faction of mobsters warring with Rochester's established organized Crime Family for control of local rackets. The insurgents were first led by reputed mobsters Thomas A. Taylor and Thomas M. Torpey who were then on trial in Monroe County Court, in connection with the December 1981 shotgun slaying of union leader and mob "Underboss," John N. Fiorino.

After Torpey and Taylor were arrested, control of the insurgents was passed to Thomas Pelusio of Perinton, police say. He was serving a five-year prison term on a federal weapons conviction. On Aug. 27, 1982, Pelusio's brother, Gerald, was gunned down in front of a townhouse in Irondequoit. Police had suspected the first Marotta shooting was in response to the Pelusio slaying.

All suspects denied any involvement. One said he even considered Marotta his friend. Investigators suspect Marotta had been the target of assassination attempts because he may have been the most accessible of the reputed local underworld leaders and was believed to command the local rackets.

Marotta had been identified as a "Captain" in the Rochester underworld. His reputed superiors "Boss" Samuel "Red" Russotti, "Counselor" Rene Piccarreto and "Underboss" Richard Marino were said to be semi-retired. But Marotta had remained visible, leaving his house nightly to tend to business at one of the mob's after-hours gambling establishments, police said.

"In both (shootings) the gunman was quite familiar with his (Marotta's) routine," said an investigator who asked not to be identified. Other similarities in the two attacks police were studying included the use of a small-caliber weapons both times. (72)

# *Chapter 8*
# The Trials

## Torpey and Taylor's Murder Trial

Thomas E. Taylor

**Policeman tells of his close call on night Fiorino slain**

By David Galante
Democrat and Chronicle

Irondequoit police Officer Michael DiGiovanni remembers the snowy night two years ago when mobster John N. Fiorino was murdered and how DiGiovanni's own life was in danger, he testified yesterday in Monroe County Court.

DiGiovanni was on routine patrol on Empire Boulevard on Dec. 17, 1981 when he spotted a light-colored Cadillac with its lights off skid on the slippery pavement and land in a snowbank at the intersection of Helendale Road.

DiGiovanni, who was testifying in the murder trial of reputed gangland figures Thomas M. Torpey and Thomas E. Taylor, said he drove up to the intersection.

A man with a brown wide-brim hat got out of the Cadillac, crouched and aimed a shotgun at the officer from about 20 feet away, he testified.

Responding to questioning from prosecutor Melchor E. Castro, DiGiovanni said he ducked down in his patrol car.

"I started to hear shotgun blasts and I could feel the glass spraying over my head," he said. "The shots were rapid — one right after another."

Professional killer Joseph John "Mad Dog" Sullivan last year was convicted of murdering Fiorino in front of the Blue Gardenia Restaurant in Irondequoit and firing those shots at DiGiovanni from the getaway

TURN TO PAGE 7B

Thomas Torpey

**November 16, 1983 Democrat and Chronicle**

Irondequoit Police Officer Michael DiGiovanni testified at Torpey and Taylor's murder trial on **November 15, 1983**. DiGiovanni was on routine patrol the night of the Fiorino slaying and responded to the shooting. DiGiovanni testified that Louis DiGuilio was driving the getaway car and that Joseph Sullivan leveled a shotgun in his direction and fired several shots in rapid succession spraying glass from his patrol car everywhere.

DiGiovanni and his partner caught Louis DiGuilio at the scene after a foot chase in the snow. Joseph Sullivan, the shooter, escaped. **(73)**

**Lawyer claims judge's ruling blocked Sullivan from clearing Torpey**

Court refuses to grant immunity to convicted hit man, who then refuses to testify

Joe Watson Democrat and Chronicle
Joseph John Sullivan in County Court yesterday

By David Galante
Democrat and Chronicle

A judge's refusal to grant immunity to convicted murderer Joseph John Sullivan prevented him from giving testimony that would clear Thomas M. Torpey in the shotgun slaying of John N. Fiorino, a defense lawyer argued yesterday.

"Mad Dog" Sullivan, who was convicted for the 1981 killing of Fiorino in Irondequoit, was called by the prosecution to testify yesterday in the second-degree murder trial of Torpey and Thomas E. Taylor.

Torpey and Taylor are accused of scheming with Sullivan to murder Fiorino, a Rochester Teamsters official and reputed organized crime figure, in an attempt to gain control of local racketeering.

But Sullivan, saying he had "no options left," invoked his Fifth Amendment right against self-incrimination and refused to answer any questions about the Fiorino murder during a 15-minute appearance in Monroe County Court.

"Mr. Sullivan says ... he's between a rock and a hard place and he ain't going to change his mind," said Sullivan's lawyer, Anthony F. Leonardo Jr. of Rochester.

Judge Donald J. Mark denied a request by Torpey's lawyer, Felix V. Lapine, to grant Sullivan immunity from prosecution related to any of his testimony so that he would be required by law to answer the questions.

Lapine said he and Taylor's lawyer, John F. Speranza, talked with Sullivan Wednesday night in the Monroe County Jail.

In requesting immunity for Sullivan, Lapine argued, "Mr. Sullivan would have ... evidence to show Mr. Torpey is innocent. He would testify that my client had nothing to do with the murder of John Fiorino."

If granted immunity, a witness can't invoke the Fifth Amendment right. A person with immunity who refuses to testify can be sent to jail.

The muscular Sullivan, 44, appeared in handcuffs and jail clothes before the jury was brought in for the day. On the witness stand, he was flanked by two sheriff's deputies and Leonardo.

Leonardo said Sullivan wouldn't answer questions about his role in the Fiorino slaying because appeals are pending.

"Did you on Dec. 17, 1981, shoot John Fiorino?" prosecutor Melchor E. Castro asked Sullivan.

"Mr. Sullivan is invoking his Fifth Amendment right," said Leonardo.

"I got no options left," Sullivan said in a heavy New York accent, "so this is my reason for taking the Fifth."

Lapine asked Sullivan whether he appeared as a prosecution witness voluntarily or whether he appeared on a court order.

"Let's put it this way," Sullivan said. "I didn't get an invitation."

Castro said Sullivan was served with a subpoena to testify.

Security was beefed up as Sullivan was brought to Rochester from the Clinton Correctional Facility in Dannemora, Clinton County.

TURN TO PAGE 4B

**December 2, 1983 Democrat and Chronicle**

The Court refused to grant immunity to convicted killer Joseph Sullivan allowing him to testify in the Torpey and Taylor murder trial. He was called to testify by the prosecution. Sullivan claimed that he had no choice but to invoke his right to the 5th

Amendment and failed to testify because his testimony may have been self incriminating. Thomas Torpey's Lawyer, Felix Lapine claimed that Sullivan could have provided testimony proving that Torpey was innocent. Sullivan's Lawyer Anthony Leonardo Jr. stated that Sullivan will not answer any questions related to the Fiorino murder because appeals were pending in that case. (74)

## Fiorino's Widow Takes the Witness Stand

The widow of murdered Teamsters Local #398 Vice-President, John Fiorino, took the witness stand and testified at the trial of Thomas Torpey and Thomas Taylor. Torpey and Taylor were accused of hiring hitman Joseph Sullivan to murder Fiorino.

Lida Fiorino testified on **December 8, 1983**, that her husband John received a phone call about 6p.m. on the night he died. He then told her that he was going to the Blue Gardenia Restaurant to meet "The Eagle." "The Eagle" was Thomas Taylor's nickname.

### Fiorino's widow, on stand, recalls last hour she spent with husband

**By David Galante**
Democrat and Chronicle

The widow of slain Teamsters official John N. Fiorino took the witness stand yesterday in the murder trial of Thomas M. Torpey and Thomas E. Taylor, recalling the last hour she spent with her husband.

Lida Fiorino testified briefly, not looking at the two men accused of plotting her husband's death. Fiorino was the vice president and paid business agent of Teamsters Local 398.

Mrs. Fiorino told the Monroe County Court jury of 11 women and one man that on Dec. 17, 1981, her husband, dressed in a business suit, came home from work about 5:30 p.m.

"We talked for a few minutes," she said. "He changed his clothes. Then he went to lie down on the couch."

Mrs. Fiorino and her husband had planned a quiet evening together at their home on Venice Circle in Irondequoit, she said.

Mrs. Fiorino said her husband made a telephone call about 6 p.m. "It was just a friendly conversation," she said. Her husband then received a couple of calls and talked on the phone until about 6:15 p.m., she said.

Mrs. Fiorino testified that her husband left their house about 6:25, telling her he was going to the Blue Gardenia Restaurant.

The prosecution says Fiorino, a reputed

**Thomas Torpey**

**Thomas Taylor**

organized-crime figure, then drove to the Blue Gardenia, where he was shot and killed about 6:45 p.m. in the parking lot near the restaurant's front entrance by a professional hit man wielding a sawed-off shotgun.

The trigger man, Joseph John Sullivan of New York City, was convicted last year of second-degree murder in connection with the Fiorino slaying.

Torpey and Taylor are accused of hiring Sullivan to kill Fiorino as a signal to mob leaders that a new circle of organized-crime figures was moving in on the Rochester rackets.

Also yesterday, a prosecution witness apparently took prosecutor Melchor E. Castro by surprise when he changed the testimony he gave during Sullivan's trial.

TURN TO PAGE 2B

**December 9, 1983 Democrat and Chronicle**

Lida Fiorino testified that her husband left the house at about 6:25p.m. Twenty minutes later, at 6:45, Fiorino was shot dead in the parking lot of the Blue Gardenia. (75)

# Mistrial for Torpey, Taylor

## Jury hopelessly deadlocked; DA Relin to seek new trial, possibly outside county

**By David Galante**
Democrat and Chronicle

A mistrial was declared last night in the murder trial of reputed organized-crime figures Thomas M. Torpey and Thomas E. Taylor after jurors were unable to reach a verdict in six days of deliberation.

Monroe County Court Judge Donald J. Mark declared the mistrial at the request of defense lawyers at 10:30 p.m., after the jury of 11 women and one man reported that it was hopelessly deadlocked.

Thomas Torpey in court before mistrial declared.

Monroe County District Attorney Howard R. Relin said he would seek a new trial, possibly outside Monroe County, on charges that Torpey, 36, and Taylor, 44, masterminded the Dec. 17, 1981, slaying of Rochester Teamsters official John N. Fiorino.

A change of venue is possible because of publicity surrounding the case, Relin said.

Nine jurors voted for a conviction, while three voted for an acquittal, said one juror who asked not to be identified.

"It was frustrating to me," the juror said. "I just didn't feel the prosecution presented an adequate case."

"I'm ready to go any time, any place if they want to try it again," said Taylor, who remains free on $200,000 bail. "I still feel we should have been acquitted."

The 3½-month-long trial was the longest and most costly — about $250,000 — in Monroe County Court history.

Steve Boerner Democrat and Chronicle

Thomas Taylor and his wife, Marie, leaving the courtroom. 'I still feel we should have been acquitted,' he said.

**TORPEY AND TAYLOR** remain charged with second-degree murder. They are accused of hiring convicted triggerman Joseph John "Mad Dog" Sullivan to kill Fiorino, identified as a member of Rochester's organized-crime family, in a scheme to gain control of underworld rackets.

"I'm ecstatic," said Torpey's wife, Donna Torpey. "Not guilty would have been much better because my husband is not guilty. Look at the evidence — there wasn't any."

Torpey remains in custody on $200,000 bail. Mark denied an application by Torpey's lawyer, Felix V. Lapine, to reduce the bail.

TURN TO PAGE 3A

**January 3, 1984 Democrat and Chronicle**

The Torpey-Taylor murder trial was Monroe County's longest and costliest trial in its history. It ended in a mistrial, jurors being hopelessly deadlocked. Judge Donald J. Mark declared a mistrial on **January 2, 1983**, when jurors could not reach a verdict after six days of deliberation. The trial itself lasted for 3 and 1/2 months. Monroe County District Attorney said that he would seek a new trial, possibly outside of Monroe County. **(76)**

## Ten Men Go On Trial For Murder and Conspiracy

The ten men who went on trial **September 17, 1984,** for racketeering and conspiracy charges in U.S. District Court included the power structure of organized crime in Rochester, prosecutors said. They each faced the possibility of up to 20 years in federal prison and a $25,000 fine. The indicted defendants and their lawyers were:

**Anthony M. Colombo 41**, of 34 Brentwood St.. Rochester. He was named as a member of the organization in the indictment and was accused of pulling the trigger in the machine-gun staying of Thomas C. Didio, which was one of the crimes detailed in the 1982 indictment. He was represented by Buffalo lawyer Robert M. Murphy.

**Richard J. Marino, 44**. of 68 Venice Circle, Irondequoit. He was identified in the indictment as "Underboss." He was tried in late 1978 separately from six other defendants in connection with Massaro's slaying. His lawyer, Paul J. Cambria Jr, of Buffalo, Friday requested an adjournment of the trial because of his client's condition.

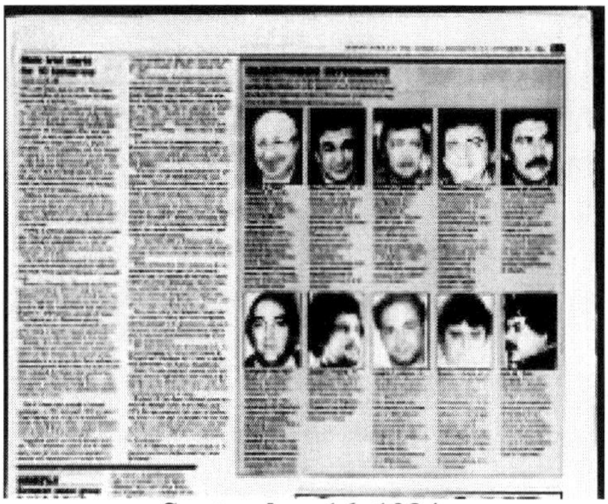

**September 16, 1984**
**Democrat and Chronicle**
**Rochester, N.Y.**

**Thomas E, Marotta. 42**, no address available. The indictment listed him as a "Captain." He was wounded twice in shootings during 1983, once as he walked from his home. He was one of several men convicted in the Massaro homicide. He suffered a heart attack in November 1977 in prison before the conviction was overturned. He was represented by Rochester lawver Richard A. Miller.

**Samuel Russotti**, of 52 Creekside Drive, Irondequoit. Russotti was named in the 1982 indictment as the "Boss" of the organization. His indictment in 1977 for the Massaro murder marked the first time Russotti had been charged with a serious crime. Russotti, represented by Buffalo lawyer John F. Humartin, spent much of his time at a Florida home.

**Rene Piccarreto**, 128 Carmas Drive, Greece. The indictment named Piccarreto as "Counselor," or top adviser to the "Boss." At the time of the indictment, authorities said Piccarreto ran the organization with Russotti's approval. Piccarreto was represented by Harold J. Boreanaz, who was appointed lead defense counsel to coordinate the pre-trial activities.

**Joseph J. Trieste, 39**, of 112 Yorkshire Road Irondequoit. Trieste was named in the indictment as a "member" of the organized crime group. Trieste was represented by Rochester lawyer Charies T. Noce.

**John M. "Flap" Trivigno. 40**, of 147 Nichols St., Rochester. The indictment said that Trivigno was employed by and associated with the crime organization. At the time of the indictment he was a steward for Teamsters Local #398 and owned a Clifford Avenue bar. Trivigno was represented by Rochester lawyer John R. Parrinelio.

**Joseph J. LaDolce, 42**, of 128 Gray St., Rochester. The indictment named LaDolce as a member of the organization. His first brush with law enforcement authorities was in 1969 when he was convicted of second-degree assault and given five years probation for breaking a man's jaw in a restaurant fight. LaDolce was represented by Buffalo lawyer Robert P. Freedman.

**Donald J. Paone, 40**, of 258 Stonehenge Road, Rochester. The indictment named Paone as a member of the organization. At the time of the indictment, authorities said he was an "up and comer" in the group. Paone pleaded guilty in 1983 to third-degree criminal possession of a weapon, but had appealed. He was represented by Rochester lawyer John F. Speranza.

**Joseph "the Hop" Rossi, 47**, of Monroe Avenue, Rochester. Rossi was named as a "Captain" in the indictment. He was convicted with Salvatore "Sammy G" Gingello in 1970 of possessing gambling records after a raid at Gingello's home. He pleaded guilty in 1983 to third-degree criminal possession of a weapon, but had appealed. He was represented by Herbert L. Green.

The complexity and expected duration of the trial caused U.S. District Judge Michael A. Telesca to ask that another judge take the case so Rochester's other federal cases would not be backlogged. The trial was expected to last at least two months, but U.S. District Judge Thomas C. Piatt of Brooklyn, who was presiding, told the lawyers he wanted it completed in four to six weeks.

Piatt had set a demanding schedule, telling the lawyers that court would begin at 8:30 a.m. daily and not finish before 6:30 p.m. He also warned them to keep their weekends free because Saturdays and Sundays may be used for testimony. Defense lawyers and prosecutors had whittled the number of prospective jurors from almost 600 to about 140 who were expected to appear at 9 a.m. the following day before Piatt. Twelve jurors and six alternates were to be picked.

During a pretrial conference soon after, Piatt told the lawyers he would have jury selection completed by 11 a.m. that day so they could begin opening statements and "we'll get this rolling."

The federal indictments were not the first time law enforcement authorities believed they had struck against

Rochester's reputed mob. Russotti, Piccarreto, Marotta and Marino were convicted in 1976 in state court of Massaro's murder. Also convicted were Salvatore "Sammy G" Gingello, at the time reputed to be the "Underboss" of the mob, and Eugene A. DiFrancesco, accused of being the triggerman in Massaro's slaying.

The convictions were overturned on Jan. 31, 1978, when a sheriffs deputy admitted fabricating key evidence used at the trial. During 1977, the year the men were in prison before the verdicts were overturned, police say the mobsters left control of the organization to a group that later refused to relinquish power when their one-time bosses were released. So began what authorities have dubbed "The Alphabet War." The insurgents, nicknamed the "B Team", were trying to take power from the established leaders, called the "A Team." The "B Team" was accused of several bombings in 1977 and early 1978 to warn "A Team" leaders not to try to re-establish power.

On April 23, 1978, a bomb exploded under a black Buick sedan parked in downtown Rochester, killing Sammy Gingello. Gingello's death spurred a bloody mob war. The indictment against the 10 defendants said that all but LaDolce had conspired to murder and attempted to murder two "B Team" members in May and June 1978. Plus all 10 were accused of Didio's slaying on July 6, 1978.

The bombings, shootings and homicides spurred a coordinated police effort that culminated in the 1982 indictments which also name Salvatore Gingello and John N. Fiorino, who had both been killed earlier, as participants in the crime ring. Fiorino was shot to death Dec. 17, 1981, outside an Irondequoit restaurant. Two men accused of planning Fiorino's death Thomas E. Taylor and Thomas M. Torpey were awaiting trial in state court.

A task force of investigators from the Rochester Police Department, Sheriffs Department, State Police and several town police forces banded together in 1978 to stem the violence. "The unit conducted investigations of persons who were believed to be members of the mob factions. Periodic surveillances of the gambling establishments and those frequenting them were done. Also staked out were the residences of persons who were believed to have been a threat to others, or whose lives might be in danger. They were conducted on a regular basis." (77)

## 2nd government informant takes the stand tomorrow

Racketeering trial of 10 entering its third week;

By Andy Pollack
Democrat and Chronicle

A crucial government witness, Anthony F. Oliveri, is scheduled to take the witness stand tomorrow as the federal racketeering trial of 10 men accused of being part of Rochester's organized-crime family opens its third week.

And in something of a surprise, prosecutors might call Thomas A. Pelusio, 37, to the witness stand later in the trial. Pelusio, linked by police to a splinter group of organized-crime figures, was not originally listed as a witness.

He only recently agreed to testify in exchange for entrance into the witness protection program. It is unknown what his testimony will cover.

Pelusio's brother, Gerald, was gunned down Aug. 27, 1982, in Irondequoit in a slaying police say might have been meant for Thomas Pelusio.

Thomas Pelusio and another brother, Michael, were sentenced in May 1983 to five years in federal prison after being convicted of federal weapons charges.

They also were convicted with Thomas E. Taylor in state court of beating a man at a gambling club. They were sentenced in August 1983 to two to six years in state prison for the assault conviction.

Oliveri, a self-proclaimed member of the crime family who turned informant, will be the second prosecution witness to testify who is part of the federal witness protection program.

Since the trial began, defense lawyers have attacked the credibility of Oliveri and the other paid government witnesses, saying they have lied to save their own skins. Both sides have said the outcome of the trial may turn on whether the jury accepts the testimony of the informants.

The government's first informant in the racketeering trial, Angelo Monachino, testified about the structure of the criminal organization and the 1973 slaying of Vincent "Jimmy the Hammer" Massaro. Oliveri is expected to testify about the 1978 machine-gun slaying of Thomas C. Didio and several attempted murders.

Prosecutors say the crimes Oliveri will testify about came in the midst of a struggle between rival factions for control of the criminal organization.

Oliveri, 45, has testified numerous times before federal grand juries during the three-year investigation that led to the indictment

TURN TO PAGE 2B

**September 30, 1984 Democrat and Chronicle**

# Anthony Oliveri Scheduled To Testify

With Anthony Oliveri's appearance scheduled for October 1, 1984, the tight security at the Federal Courthouse in Rochester was even stricter. The 10 defendants were accused of racketeering and conspiracy that encompassed more than a decade of crimes, including the Massaro and Didio homicides.

Unlike Angelo Monachino, a veteran courtroom witness, Anthony Oliveri had never testified at a trial before. Oliveri first came to the attention of federal authorities in the spring of 1980, while he was in a Utah state prison serving zero to five years after an August 1979 conviction for forgery and possession of stolen property. There he told them about a "bloody, bomb-filled war between organized crime groups in Rochester."

In July 1980, Oliveri joined the Federal Witness Protection Program. Like Monachino, he was given a new identity, relocated and granted immunity from prosecution. Oliveri had a long list of prior arrests, pleas and convictions that dated to 1955 when as a youth he was charged with stealing a car in Illinois, a criminal record prosecutors acknowledged to the jury during their opening statement.

Oliveri was said to be a close friend of Anthony M. Colombo, one of the 10 defendants. Colombo was accused of shooting Didio July 6, 1978, at a Victor motel and wounding Rosario "Ross" Chirico with a rifle shot about a month earlier. The indictment stated that Oliveri was with Colombo during both incidents. Oliveri and Colombo were together March 13, 1979, when they were arrested after a high-speed chase in Gates. Police found a .357 Magnum, a sawed-off shotgun and ski masks along Firestone Drive. Prosecutors said the pair were waiting to kill Angelo "Oskie" DiMarco, a gambling club owner, to stop him from testifying before a federal grand jury.

Defense lawyers said they would put Oliveri through lengthy, sharp cross-examination because his testimony was expected to be damaging to all 10 defendants. During his opening statement to the jury, Colombo's lawyer, Robert M. Murphy, set the stage for the defense attacks against Oliveri. Murphy, belittling Oliveri's story, said, "It's amazing when you're facing 15 or 16 years in a Utah prison how you can find the truth and tell it." Then, referring to Oliveri and Monachino, Murphy said: "Isn't it interesting that anybody who gets immunity is at a murder, but never pulls the trigger." (78)

## Oliveri Testifies About the Didio Murder

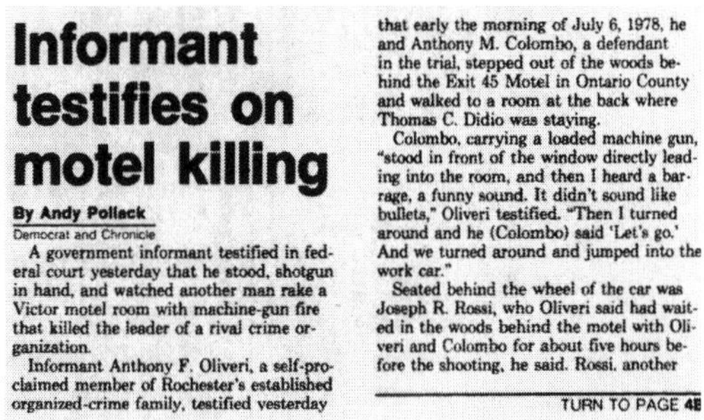

**Informant testifies on motel killing**

By Andy Pollack
Democrat and Chronicle

A government informant testified in federal court yesterday that he stood, shotgun in hand, and watched another man rake a Victor motel room with machine-gun fire that killed the leader of a rival crime organization.

Informant Anthony F. Oliveri, a self-proclaimed member of Rochester's established organized-crime family, testified yesterday that early the morning of July 6, 1978, he and Anthony M. Colombo, a defendant in the trial, stepped out of the woods behind the Exit 45 Motel in Ontario County and walked to a room at the back where Thomas C. Didio was staying.

Colombo, carrying a loaded machine gun, "stood in front of the window directly leading into the room, and then I heard a barrage, a funny sound. It didn't sound like bullets," Oliveri testified. "Then I turned around and he (Colombo) said 'Let's go.' And we turned around and jumped into the work car."

Seated behind the wheel of the car was Joseph R. Rossi, who Oliveri said had waited in the woods behind the motel with Oliveri and Colombo for about five hours before the shooting, he said. Rossi, another

TURN TO PAGE 4B

**October 2, 1984 Democrat and Chronicle**

Anthony Oliveri testified for a total of seven hours. During his testimony, he painted a vivid picture of how the murder of Thomas Didio went down.

Oliveri said that Joseph Rossi, Anthony Columbo and himself followed Thomas Didio's girlfriend to the Exit 45 Motel several times, including the day of the murder. Didio, the leader of the "B Team," was in hiding due to the mob war.

On the day of the murder, Oliveri said, the three waited in the woods behind the motel for about five hours before the shooting. Then he and Anthony Columbo stepped out of the woods behind the Exit 45 Motel and walked to a room in the back where Thomas Didio was staying. Joe Rossi was driving and stayed in the car. Oliveri said he was standing guard with a shotgun and Anthony Columbo, carrying a loaded machine gun, "stood in front of the window directly leading into the room, and then I heard a barrage, a funny sound. It didn't sound like bullets. Then I turned around and he (Columbo) said, "lets go," and we turned around and jumped into the work car."

Rossi sped out of the motel's back parking lot, cutting across the front lawn and down a hill to Route 96 while Columbo and Oliveri tossed their weapons, ski masks and gloves out the car windows, Oliveri testified. (79)

# Rackets trial going to jury this week

## Government's case drawn with help of 5 granted immunity

By Andy Pollack
Democrat and Chronicle

For the past five weeks in a federal courtroom in Rochester, the government has painted scenes of organized-crime violence that has rocked the city for the past decade.

The 10 men on trial in U.S. District Court for racketeering and conspiracy are the most active members of Rochester's organized-crime family and most responsible for the violence, Special U.S. Attorneys Douglas E. Rowe and Charles B. Wydysh have told the jury.

During final arguments today, Rowe is expected to put the finishing touches on the government's case. The jury is expected to begin its deliberations Wednesday after arguments from defense lawyers.

Some of the most damaging evidence government witnesses have provided since the trial began Sept. 17 has attempted to show:

- Samuel J. "Red" Russotti and Rene

TURN TO PAGE 5B

## Defense lawyers try to destroy credibility of federal witnesses

By Andy Pollack
Democrat and Chronicle

Doggedly, often with theatrical flair, defense lawyers have tried to counter the impact of dramatic statements from prosecution witnesses that could prove damaging to the 10 defendants on trial in federal court for racketeering and conspiracy.

During the past five weeks, defense lawyers relentlessly attacked the credibility of those witnesses, trying to tear apart the prosecution's tale of more than a decade of organized-crime activity in Rochester.

The defense lawyers, who called only one witness themselves, attacked the prosecution's version of events in a variety of ways, always relying upon their cross-examination to challenge the witnesses' stories.

"These cases don't hit you over the head. You have to be a detective to get to the truth," said defense lawyer Paul J. Cambria. "Nobody stands up like in Perry Mason and says, 'Yeah, you got me (in a lie).' "

TURN TO PAGE 5B

**October 22, 1984 Democrat and Chronicle**

# Rackets Trial Going To Jury This Week

On **October 22, 1984** the Democrat and Chronicle ran the article above. It outlined the entire trial, naming each defendant and his corresponding crime. The trial encompassed several charges such as conspiracy and murder including the "Jimmy The Hammer" and Thomas Didio murders. Five government informers testified; all of them were former Rochester Mafia members or associates who had turned states evidence. Each of them were then placed into the Federal Witness Protection Program. **(80)**

# 7 Rochester Mafia Leaders Are Convicted In Rico Indictment

# Seven mobsters convicted of racketeering, conspiracy

Richard Marino, left, and Rene Piccarreto after their conviction.

Donald Paone, left, Anthony Colombo, center, and Joseph Rossi being led from Federal Building after their convictions on racketeering and conspiracy charges.

## Federal jury acquits three others after week's deliberations

By Andy Pollack, Jody McPhillips and Laura Meade
Democrat and Chronicle

Seven men — including three of the most powerful leaders of Rochester's organized crime syndicate — were convicted yesterday of racketeering and conspiracy charges.

Three co-defendants were acquitted by a federal jury that deliberated seven days.

The 10 were accused of conspiring to form a criminal organization that planned and executed two murders, three attempted murders and extortion. Prosecutors said they gained control of Rochester's illicit gambling, loan sharking and arson-for-hire schemes in the early 1970s, fought to solidify their position, then waged a bloody, bomb-filled battle to remain in power.

Those found guilty were: mob boss Samuel J. "Red" Russotti, 72, second-in-command Rene Piccarreto, 60; third-in-command Richard J. Marino, 43; captains Thomas E. Marotta, 42, and Joseph R. Rossi, 47; Anthony M. Colombo, 41, a member who prosecutors said was the crime family's hit man; and Donald J. Paone, 40.

Acquitted of charges were Joseph J. Trieste, 39, Joseph J. LaDolce, 42, and John M. Trivigno, 40.

"We were extremely careful. That's what took so long," said juror John Mack of Penfield. "I wouldn't have come back with the verdict I did if I hadn't been convinced. It was a tough thing to do . . . making decisions about someone's life is tough."

The seven convicted defendants, handcuffed and in leg shackles, were taken from the federal courthouse to the Monroe County Jail to await their sentencing on Dec. 17. Each faces up to 20 years in prison and a $25,000 fine.

None of the acquitted defendants would comment, saying lawyers would speak for them.

"I thought that John shouldn't have been in the indictment in the first place," said Trivigno's lawyer, John R. Parrinello, calling some of the testimony "just incredible."

The trial began Sept. 17 before U.S. District Judge Thomas C. Platt of Brooklyn. More than 70 people took the witness stand during 25 days of testimony and lawyer arguments.

Among the most damaging evidence was a tape of Marino as he talked to government informant Vincent J. Rallo three times at his home in 1981. Rallo had been fitted

TURN TO PAGE 2A

## 27 years of organized crime leave legacy of murder, jail

By Jody McPhillips
Democrat and Chronicle

In 1960, an organized-crime prosecutor summed up a quarter-century of underworld violence in Rochester in his testimony before a U.S. Senate subcommittee.

"Rochester, the home of Kodak, Xerox and other thriving corporations . . . , is a wealthy city, a ripe plum ready to be plucked by the strongest and most ruthless mob," said Gregory Baldwin, then a lawyer with the Rochester strike force.

Gannett News Service reporter John Hanchette covered the subcommittee hearings. "While other gangsters relied upon more traditional and quieter rub-out techniques — bullets, piano wire, meathooks, baseball bats — the Rochester boys threw bombs," he wrote.

They also set fires at businesses, shot each other, and made *The Gang Who Couldn't Shoot Straight*-style gaffes en route to controlling the city's rackets.

With seven organized-crime leaders convicted of racketeering and conspiracy yesterday in U.S. District Court, authorities say Rochester once again is an open market for a new syndicate takeover.

**THE HISTORY** of organized crime in Rochester stretches back at least as far as November 1957, when brothers Frank and Stanley Valenti attended the famous gathering of mobsters at Apalachin in the Southern Tier.

Frank Valenti later explained the trip as an errand of mercy. "I was visiting a sick friend," he told a reporter.

Over the next 27 years, the cast of characters, motives and loyalties shifted with bewildering speed as the Rochester underworld tried to stay one step ahead of the police — and each other.

According to federal investigations:

Stanley Valenti controlled the city's rackets in 1957, when he attended the Apalachin conference with his brother Frank

TURN TO PAGE 3A

Samuel Russotti, right, reputed head of local crime family, and Thomas Marotta.

**October 31, 1984 Democrat and Chronicle**

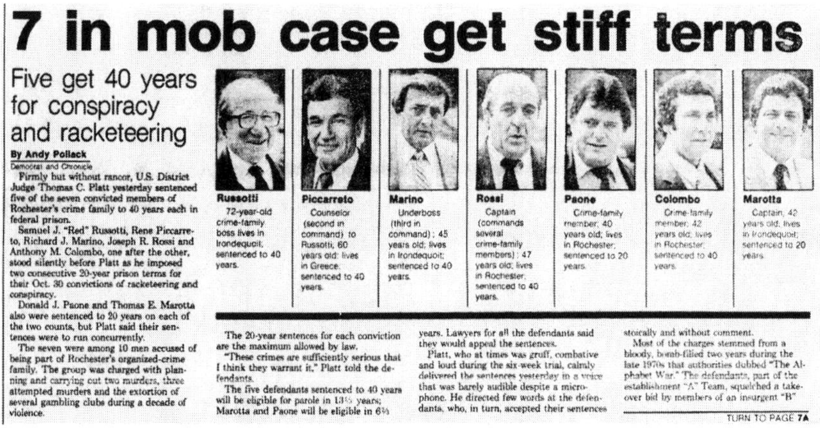

# 7 in mob case get stiff terms

## Five get 40 years for conspiracy and racketeering

**By Andy Pollack**
Democrat and Chronicle

Firmly but without rancor, U.S. District Judge Thomas C. Platt yesterday sentenced five of the seven convicted members of Rochester's crime family to 40 years each in federal prison.

Samuel J. "Red" Russotti, Rene Piccarreto, Richard J. Marino, Joseph R. Rossi and Anthony M. Colombo, one after the other, stood silently before Platt as he imposed two consecutive 20-year prison terms for their Oct. 30 convictions of racketeering and conspiracy.

Donald J. Paone and Thomas E. Marotta also were sentenced to 20 years on each of the two counts, but Platt said their sentences were to run concurrently.

The seven were among 10 men accused of being part of Rochester's organized-crime family. The group was charged with planning and carrying out two murders, three attempted murders and the extortion of several gambling clubs during a decade of violence.

**Russotti** 72-year-old crime-family boss lives in Irondequoit; sentenced to 40 years.

**Piccarreto** Counselor (second in command) to Russotti; 60 years old: lives in Greece. sentenced to 40 years.

**Marino** Underboss (third in command) ; 45 years old; lives in Irondequoit; sentenced to 40 years.

**Rossi** Captain (commands several crime-family members) ; 47 years old; lives in Rochester. sentenced to 40 years.

**Paone** Crime-family member; 40 years old; lives in Rochester; sentenced to 20 years.

**Colombo** Crime-family member; 42 years old; lives in Rochester; sentenced to 40 years.

**Marotta** Captain, 42 years old; lives in Irondequoit; sentenced to 20 years.

The 20-year sentences for each conviction are the maximum allowed by law.

"These crimes are sufficiently serious that I think they warrant it," Platt told the defendants.

The five defendants sentenced to 40 years will be eligible for parole in 13⅓ years; Marotta and Paone will be eligible in 6⅔ years. Lawyers for all the defendants said they would appeal the sentences.

Platt, who at times was gruff, combative and loud during the six-week trial, calmly delivered the sentences yesterday in a voice that was barely audible despite a microphone. He directed few words at the defendants, who, in turn, accepted their sentences stoically and without comment.

Most of the charges stemmed from a bloody, bomb-filled two years during the late 1970s that authorities dubbed "The Alphabet War." The defendants, part of the establishment "A" Team, squelched a take-over bid by members of an insurgent "B"

TURN TO PAGE 7A

**December 18, 1984 Democrat and Chronicle**

# 7 Mob Leaders Get Stiff Prison Terms

All seven of the Rochester Mafia leaders were found guilty of murder, racketeering and conspiracy. Each were given two 20 year sentences. Five of the defendants received consecutive terms (back to back). Samuel "Red" Russotti, Rene Piccarreto, Richard Marino Joseph Rossi and Anthony Columbo were sentenced to 40 years each in prison. Thomas Marotta and Donald Paone were sentenced to concurrent terms, which meant that they got to serve their sentences at the same time, giving them 20 years each in prison.

The five defendants sentenced to 40 years would be eligible for parole after 13 and 1/3 years: Marotta and Paone would be eligible for parole after 6 and 2/3 years. **(82)**

## Teamsters Local #398 Officer and Mob Leader, Dick Marino Is Sentenced to 20 Years In Prison for Murder and Conspiracy

**Dick Marino**

Dick Marino, Business Agent of Teamsters Local #398 was one of the seven men convicted of murder and conspiracy for running a criminal enterprise known as the Rochester La Cosa Nostra. He was sentenced to 20 years in prison.

Teamsters Local #398 President Phil Koch recalled that on the night before Richard Marino was to be incarcerated, Marino and Koch went for a drink. Marino told Koch that he must take care of Local #398 members LaDolce, John Travigno and George Trieste. LaDolce and John Travigno were the mobsters acquitted in the Rico indictment. George Trieste is the brother of Joseph Trieste, the other mobster acquitted in that indictment. Koch understood that this meant that he was to keep them on the payroll. **(81)**

## Torpey and Taylor Sentenced To 25 to Life For Murder of John Fiorino

**Thomas Torpey**

**Thomas Taylor**

On **April 9, 1985**, Thomas Torpey and Thomas Taylor, Rochester Mafia "C Team" leaders, were both sentenced to 25 years to life for ordering the murder of Rochester La Cosa Nostra "Captain," John Fiorino of the "A Team," on December 17, 1981.

John was Vice-President of Teamsters Local #398 at the time of his death. Thomas Torpey and Thomas Taylor were both former bodyguards for the late Sammy Gingello, Rochester Mafia "Underboss."

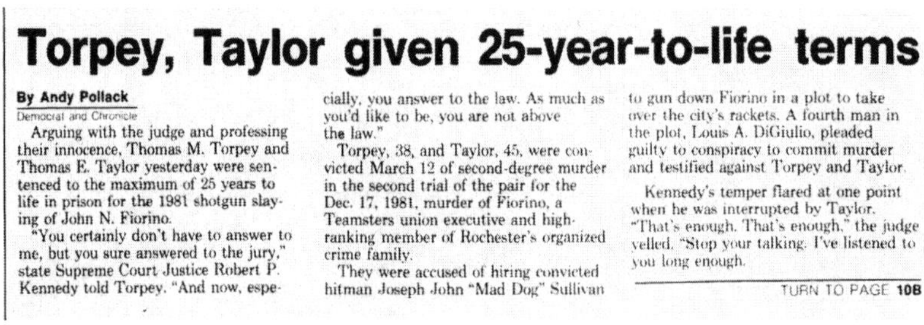

**Torpey, Taylor given 25-year-to-life terms**

By Andy Pollack
Democrat and Chronicle

Arguing with the judge and professing their innocence, Thomas M. Torpey and Thomas E. Taylor yesterday were sentenced to the maximum of 25 years to life in prison for the 1981 shotgun slaying of John N. Fiorino.

"You certainly don't have to answer to me, but you sure answered to the jury," state Supreme Court Justice Robert P. Kennedy told Torpey. "And now, especially, you answer to the law. As much as you'd like to be, you are not above the law."

Torpey, 38, and Taylor, 45, were convicted March 12 of second-degree murder in the second trial of the pair for the Dec. 17, 1981, murder of Fiorino, a Teamsters union executive and high-ranking member of Rochester's organized crime family.

They were accused of hiring convicted hitman Joseph John "Mad Dog" Sullivan to gun down Fiorino in a plot to take over the city's rackets. A fourth man in the plot, Louis A. DiGiulio, pleaded guilty to conspiracy to commit murder and testified against Torpey and Taylor.

Kennedy's temper flared at one point when he was interrupted by Taylor. "That's enough. That's enough," the judge yelled. "Stop your talking. I've listened to you long enough.

TURN TO PAGE 10B

**April 10, 1985**

## Torpey and Taylor Sentenced To 3 Years For Cocaine Trafficking

On **November 21, 1985**, Thomas Torpey and Thomas Taylor, Rochester Mafia "C Team" leaders, were both sentenced to another three years in prison for trafficking in cocaine. **(83)**

United States v. Thomas Taylor, No. 84-126, W.D.N.Y., 5/15/84. This was a prosecution of one of the leaders of "Team C" (see No 82-156, page 21) for trafficking in cocaine. On November 21, 1985, Taylor was sentenced to serve three years in prison following a plea. Taylor had been sentenced along with his faction co-leader, Thomas Torpey, to 25 years to life in state court in April 1985. That conviction was for the murder-for-hire of LCN captain John N. Fiorino on December 17, 1981, during the mob war detailed in No. 82-156.

# 2 Gambling Clubs Raided

In **November of 1985**, Rochester police raided two known Mafia gambling establishments, one on **November 14, 1985** and the other on **November 17, 1985,** resulting in the arrest of 9 people.

Five people were arrested at the Young Man's Social Club at 431 Jay Street on November 14th for gambling and selling alcohol without a license.

## 2 clubs raided, 9 people arrested

**By John O'Brien**
Democrat and Chronicle

City police arrested nine people on gambling and illegal sale of alcohol charges in pre-dawn raids at two alleged after-hours clubs yesterday and Saturday, ending a two-month investigation.

About 3 a.m. Saturday, eight police officers raided the Young Men's Social Club at 431 Jay St. and charged five people with second-degree promoting gambling and selling alcohol without a license, Sgt. Albert Joseph of the city vice squad said yesterday.

The club was taking in about $1,500 a night in gambling on blackjack card games, Joseph said.

Two city police officers, Gregory Raggi and Raymond Fischette, posed as customers in the club four different times until enough information was gathered to obtain an arrest warrant, Joseph said.

The undercover probe by the vice squad began two months ago, he said.

Arrested in that raid were:

Phillip DiNapoli, 45, of 79 McArdle St., charged with a count of second-degree promoting gambling; Albert Ryan Jr., 23, 137 Warner St., four counts of second-degree promoting gambling, one count of selling alcohol without a license; Joseph John Amico, 71, 55 Creighton Lane, four counts of second-degree promoting gambling; Leonard Stebbins, 44, of 2116 Maiden Lane, Greece, one count of second-degree promoting gambling; Paula Bojnoff, 23, of 4 Bonesteel Circle, Greece, four counts of selling alcohol without a license; and Carlos Rivera, 19, of North Clinton Avenue, a count of criminal possession of controlled substance.

Police confiscated 25 bottles of liquor and six cases of beer in the raid.

About 3 a.m. yesterday, 11 police officers raided the Venitian Social Club at 547 State St. and charged three people with selling alcohol without a license.

Arrested in that raid, each charged with one count of selling alcohol without a license, were Robert C. Cocilova, 28, of 10 Florida St., Greece; Jack Rivoli, 38, of 29 Joellen Drive; and Isabell Bryant, 29, of 51 Pearl St.

Police confiscated 12 bottles of liquor and 15 cases of beer in the raid, Joseph said. All of the suspects were released after posting bail.

Joseph said police hope a proposed city law will make it easier to shut down gambling houses in the future and keep them closed. The legislation, which City Council has not yet approved, allows police to padlock any building where criminal activity has been occurring over the course of a year.

**November 18, 1985**

Four more people were arrested on November 17th at the Venetian Social Club which was located at 547 State Street.

The arrests were a result of a two month long undercover operation conducted by the police. Undercover officers posing as customers frequented the establishments for several weeks gathering information before making arrests. **(84)**

# *Chapter 9*
# Cleaning House
# The Second RICO Indictment

## Wiretap Intercepts Mobster Angelo Amico Giving Instructions to Teamsters Local #398 Business Agent Angelo Misuraca

**Angelo Amico "Acting Boss"**

The September 1984 convictions of the seven upper echelon members of the Rochester Mafia had left the "organization" virtually leaderless. Despite his own reservations, Angelo Amico stepped up to the plate and became "Acting Boss" of the Family.

On the night of **March 4, 1986**, the Rochester Police Department was conducting routine wiretap surveillance of the gambling establishment run by Amico. That particular day the police picked up a conversation between Angelo Amico and Angelo Misuraca, who was the Vice-President of Teamsters Local #398 in Rochester, New York. Angelo Misuraca was also Rochester Mafia "Underboss" Richard Marino's brother-in-law.

At one point during the conversation Amico told Misuraca, "I don't care who it is, before you get going, ya gotta check with me, regardless of who the job is for." and "You know it gotta, it's gotta to the point where ya just can't assume that somebody is alright when he's going ta work. They have to check with us first, no matter who it is." Finally Amico told Misuraca, "I don't want anybody moved."

Clearly, that conversation detailed how the Mafia interfered with union business. The Vice-President of Local #398 was being instructed (by the "Acting Boss" of the Rochester Mafia) on how to assign, appoint and clear people for employment within Teamsters Local #398. **(87)**

# 2 Rochester Mafia Crime Family Members Denied Bail

On **February 2, 1987**, two accused counterfeiters were portrayed by a Federal Agent as being Rochester Crime Family members who participated in mob related attempts to kill two people.

Because of those allegations, U.S. Magistrate David Larimar refused to set bail for Charles T. "Charlie The Ox" Indovino and Christopher Pelitera.

Four out of 5 of the government informants, who were Crime Family members themselves, identified the pair as being members of Rochester's Cosa Nostra. They (the informants) also expressed concern for their safety if Indovino and Pelitera were to be released, since they had a history of attempting to kill witnesses. **(85)**

**A dark tale of 'hit men' in the mob**

U.S. agent testifies in counterfeiting case

By John O'Brien
Democrat and Chronicle

Two accused counterfeiters were portrayed by a federal agent yesterday as organized crime figures who participated in mob-related attempts to kill two men in 1985.

Because of those allegations, U.S. Magistrate David G. Larimer refused to set bail on Charles T. "Charlie the Ox" Indovino and Christopher Pelitera, saying there was "substantial evidence" that the men might threaten witnesses or flee the jurisdiction.

Eric Harnischfeger a special agent with the U.S. Secret Service, testified that Indovino and Pelitera were members of Rochester's "organized crime family" and Indovino has run loan-sharking operations in Rochester for the past 10 to 15 years.

The agent also linked both men to an attempt to kill Joseph J. DiBattisto in 1985.

DiBattisto was a target because he was a witness in the death of Eugene Ragland, who was killed in 1981 by an associate of Indovino, Assistant U.S. Attorney Rosemary G. Roberts told Larimer.

DiBattisto was linked to Ragland's slaying in a federal grand jury indictment handed down last week.

Harnischfeger said his sources against Indovino and Pelitera were four of five confidential informants, all of whom had expressed concern for their safety if Indovino or Pelitera were released.

He said he also based his information on police files, physical evidence and wire taps.

"I think the testimony has been rather startling," Larimer said. "There has been (testimony of) an inclination by the defendants to intimidate witnesses in the past, and two murders for hire. I can't think of anything more serious."

TURN TO PAGE 5A

**February 3, 1987**
**Democrat and Chronicle**

# Greece Man Pleads Guilty To Bombing

**'Charlie the Ox' enters guilty plea in 1985 bombing**

By Michelle Fountaine Williams
Democrat and Chronicle

Reputed mobster Charles T. Indovino pleaded guilty yesterday to taking part in a botched contract killing and faces up to 15 years in prison when he is sentenced in September.

But U.S. District Judge Michael G. Telesca, in "conditionally" accepting Indovino's plea, said the plea agreement could be called off if Indovino's pre-sentencing report is unsatisfactory to the court.

"If I think your background is such that I do not think this is a sufficient sentence," Telesca told Indovino, then the guilty plea would be rejected and the case would go to trial.

Sentencing is set for Sept. 16, when Telesca also will impose a fine that has yet to be determined.

Indovino has run loan-sharking operations in Rochester for the past 10 to 15 years, a special agent with the U.S. Secret

TURN TO PAGE 7A

**Greece man pleads guilty in bombing**

Reputed mobster may get 15 years

By Michelle Fountaine Williams
Democrat and Chronicle

Reputed mobster Charles T. Indovino pleaded guilty yesterday to taking part in a botched contract killing and faces up to 15 years in prison when he is sentenced in September.

But U.S. District Judge Michael G. Telesca, in "conditionally" accepting Indovino's plea, said the plea agreement could be called off if Indovino's pre-sentencing report is unsatisfactory to the court.

"If I think your background is such that I do not think this is a sufficient sentence," Telesca told Indovino, then the guilty plea would be rejected and the case would go to trial.

Sentencing is set for Sept. 16, when Telesca also will impose a fine that is yet to be determined.

Indovino has run loan-sharking operations in Rochester for the past 10 to 15 years, a special agent with the U.S. Secret Service testified before a federal magis-

TURN TO PAGE 7A

On **July 29, 1987**, "Charlie The Ox" plead guilty to taking part in a "botched" contract killing. He faced up to 15 years in prison when he was due to be sentenced on September 16, 1987. **(86)**

**July 30, 1987**
**Democrat and Chronicle**

## 2nd Guilty Plea Closes case

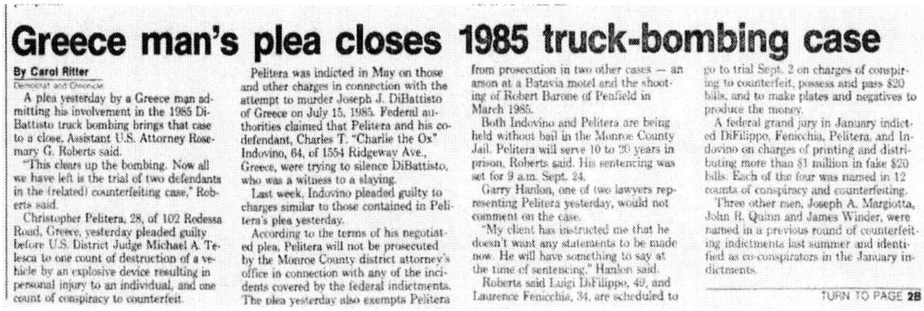

**Greece man's plea closes 1985 truck-bombing case**

By Carol Ritter
Democrat and Chronicle

A plea yesterday by a Greece man admitting his involvement in the 1985 DiBattisto truck bombing brings that case to a close, Assistant U.S. Attorney Rosemary G. Roberts said.

"This clears up the bombing. Now all we have left is the trial of two defendants in the (related) counterfeiting case," Roberts said.

Christopher Pelitera, 28, of 102 Rodessa Road, Greece, yesterday pleaded guilty before U.S. District Judge Michael A. Telesca to one count of destruction of a vehicle by an explosive device resulting in personal injury to an individual, and one count of conspiracy to counterfeit.

Pelitera was indicted in May on those and other charges in connection with the attempt to murder Joseph J. DiBattisto of Greece on July 15, 1985. Federal authorities claimed that Pelitera and his co-defendant, Charles T. "Charlie the Ox" Indovino, 64, of 1554 Ridgeway Ave., Greece, were trying to silence DiBattisto, who was a witness to a slaying.

Last week, Indovino pleaded guilty to charges similar to those contained in Pelitera's plea yesterday.

According to the terms of his negotiated plea, Pelitera will not be prosecuted by the Monroe County district attorney's office in connection with any of the incidents covered by the federal indictments. The plea yesterday also exempts Pelitera from prosecution in two other cases — an arson at a Batavia motel and the shooting of Robert Barone of Penfield in March 1985.

Both Indovino and Pelitera are being held without bail in the Monroe County Jail. Pelitera will serve 10 to 20 years in prison, Roberts said. His sentencing was set for 9 a.m. Sept. 24.

Garry Hanlon, one of two lawyers representing Pelitera yesterday, would not comment on the case.

"My client has instructed me that he doesn't want any statements to be made now. He will have something to say at the time of sentencing," Hanlon said.

Roberts said Luigi DiFilippo, 49, and Laurence Fenicchia, 34, are scheduled to go to trial Sept. 2 on charges of conspiring to counterfeit, possess and pass $20 bills, and to make plates and negatives to produce the money.

A federal grand jury in January indicted DiFilippo, Fenicchia, Pelitera, and Indovino on charges of printing and distributing more than $1 million in fake $20 bills. Each of the four was named in 12 counts of conspiracy and counterfeiting.

Three other men, Joseph A. Margiotta, John R. Quinn and James Winder, were named in a previous round of counterfeiting indictments last summer and identified as co-conspirators in the January indictments.

TURN TO PAGE 2B

**August 7, 1987 Democrat and Chronicle**

A guilty plea by the second man involved in the 1985 attempted murder of Joseph J. DiBattisto on **August 6, 1987**, has closed that case. The other defendant, Charles T. "Charlie The Ox" Indovino, also pleaded guilty the previous week on July 29th.

Christopher Pelitera pleaded guilty to one count of destruction of a motor vehicle with an explosive device resulting in personal injury to an individual and one count of conspiracy to counterfeit. He was expected to get 10 to 20 years in prison when he was due to be sentenced on **September 24, 1987**. **(87)**

## 15 Years in Prison for "Charlie The Ox"

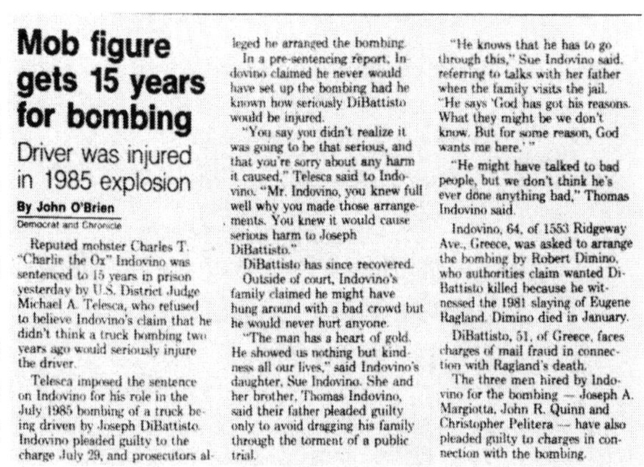

**Mob figure gets 15 years for bombing**

Driver was injured in 1985 explosion

By John O'Brien
Democrat and Chronicle

Reputed mobster Charles T. "Charlie the Ox" Indovino was sentenced to 15 years in prison yesterday by U.S. District Judge Michael A. Telesca, who refused to believe Indovino's claim that he didn't think a truck bombing two years ago would seriously injure the driver.

Telesca imposed the sentence on Indovino for his role in the July 1985 bombing of a truck being driven by Joseph DiBattisto. Indovino pleaded guilty to the charge July 29, and prosecutors alleged he arranged the bombing.

In a pre-sentencing report, Indovino claimed he never would have set up the bombing had he known how seriously DiBattisto would be injured.

"You say you didn't realize it was going to be that serious, and that you're sorry about any harm it caused," Telesca said to Indovino. "Mr. Indovino, you knew full well why you made those arrangements. You knew it would cause serious harm to Joseph DiBattisto."

DiBattisto has since recovered.

Outside of court, Indovino's family claimed he might have hung around with a bad crowd but he would never hurt anyone.

"The man has a heart of gold. He showed us nothing but kindness all our lives," said Indovino's daughter, Sue Indovino. She and her brother, Thomas Indovino, said their father pleaded guilty only to avoid dragging his family through the torment of a public trial.

"He knows that he has to go through this," Sue Indovino said, referring to talks with her father when the family visits the jail. "He says 'God has got his reasons. What they might be we don't know. But for some reason, God wants me here.'"

"He might have talked to bad people, but we don't think he's ever done anything bad," Thomas Indovino said.

Indovino, 64, of 1553 Ridgeway Ave., Greece, was asked to arrange the bombing by Robert Dimino, who authorities claim wanted DiBattisto killed because he witnessed the 1981 slaying of Eugene Ragland. Dimino died in January.

DiBattisto, 51, of Greece, faces charges of mail fraud in connection with Ragland's death.

The three men hired by Indovino for the bombing — Joseph A. Margiotta, John R. Quinn and Christopher Pelitera — have also pleaded guilty to charges in connection with the bombing.

**September 19, 1987 Democrat and Chronicle**

Reputed mobster Charles T. "Charlie The Ox" Indovino was sentenced to 15 years in prison for his role in the bombing.

Indovino was asked to arrange the bombing by Robert Dimino, who authorities claimed wanted DiBattisto killed because he witnessed the 1981 slaying of Eugene Ragland. Dimino died in January of 1987. **(88)**

# 2 Men Indicted for Refusal to Testify

Two indictments were handed up Thursday **October 1, 1987**, for two men who refused to testify. Charles Russo, 63, of 980 Titus Ave., Irondequoit, and Sebastian Gangemi Jr., 53, whose address was listed as 1588 Norton St, Rochester, were charged with contempt of court for refusal to provide testimony to the Grand Jury after having been granted immunity and being ordered to testify. Russo and Gangemi had been in custody since the previous May when they refused to testify. The contempt statute does not provide for a specific sentence, but recent federal court decisions have permitted sentences of up to 10 years. **(89)**

# 5 Indicted In Mafia Probe

**Angelo Amico**

**Loren Piccar-reto**

**Joseph LaDolce**

**Joseph Geniola**

**Donald Paone**

The second RICO indictment involving the leaders of the Rochester Mafia was released on **October 2, 1987**. Indicted this time were Angelo Amico, Loren Piccarreto, Joseph Geniola, and Donald Paone. All of them were charged with violating federal anti-racketeering laws.

Paone, at the time of the indictment was serving a twenty-year sentence from his conviction on the previous RICO indictment. In addition to these four men, Joseph La Dolce, who was also charged in the last indictment but found not guilty, was charged with conspiracy.

The indictment stated that Angelo Amico was the "Acting Boss" of the Rochester Family, and that Loren Piccarreto was the "Acting Underboss." Loren Piccarreto and Joseph Geniola were Union Stewards and Joseph LaDolce was a Teamsters Local #398 member.

In June 1984, Amico and others collected a $500 gambling debt from Angelo Bianchi, a court reporter from Seneca County. Bianchi could not be reached for comment.

The defendants were charged with running a criminal enterprise. That 'enterprise' was worth about $1 million a year. The indictment accused 5 defendants of 33 acts. Donald Paone, Joseph LaDolce and three other reputed Rochester Mafia members were accused in a 51-page federal grand jury indictment of violating the federal Racketeer Influenced and Corrupt Organizations Act. The racketeering acts include allegations of extorting "protection payments" or "juice payments" from illegal sports bookmakers and operators of illegal gambling clubs in the city. In exchange for the payments, the bookies and club owners were given permission by the enterprise to run their operations.

The indictment specifically accused five men of extorting protection payments between 1981 and 1986 from the owners of five illegal gambling clubs located at 234 Portland Ave., 44 Lake Ave., 241 Andrews St, 164 Avenue D, and 431 Jay St. The men were also accused of extorting payments between Sept 1, 1981, and March 31, 1986, from eight sports bookmakers in the city.

The charges accused the defendants of extorting illegal debts from 17 individuals, including a Rochester lawyer and two court stenographers. The loan sharking charges accuse the defendants of loaning money to people and then making them pay back the money plus exorbitant interest.

Those allegations included: Between December 1985 and April 1986, Amico "and others" twice extorted a total of $2,500 in gambling debts from Kenneth Vorassi, a defense lawyer. Vorassi denied any knowledge of those alleged transactions. In the fall of 1985, Amico and others collected a $4,000 gambling debt from Bianchi's brother, Richard Bianchi, a court reporter in Monroe County. Richard Bianchi declined to comment .

In October 1985 and March 1986, Amico, Piccarreto and others collected two gambling debts from a Webster man totaling $8,500. In 1984 and 1985, Amico and others collected four gambling debts totaling $4,500 from a Rochester man. The indictment also alleged that the enterprise was engaged in interstate commerce in furthering the conspiracy. It alleged that In November 1985, Amico met with Richard Marino in Leavenworth, Kansas. Marino was serving a 40-year sentence at a federal penitentiary in Leavenworth for his 1984 conviction on racketeering, extortion and conspiracy charges. Six other Rochester Mafia leaders also were convicted in that trial.

# 5 'crime leaders' indicted

## U.S. charges city mob figures with extortion

**By Katie Kilfoyle and John O'Brien**
Democrat and Chronicle

The Rochester organized crime family was stripped of its leadership for the second time in three years yesterday when five key members were indicted on federal charges, authorities said.

Angelo Amico, Loren Piccarreto, Joseph Geniola and Donald Paone each are charged with violating federal anti-racketeering and conspiracy statutes, and Joseph LoDolce is charged with conspiracy, according to the 51-page indictment.

The arrests crippled the already-weakened top echelon of organized crime in Rochester, said Roger P. Williams, acting U.S. attorney for western New York.

"These individuals are the last remnants of what we know to be organized crime in Rochester," Williams said.

"Usually, someone comes along to fill the void. Who and when that will be, we just don't know."

The five indicted yesterday assumed power after seven reputed Mafia leaders — including Paone — were convicted of racketeering and conspiracy in Rochester in 1984, according to the indictment.

On the heels of the sentencing of the seven, officials said, a 2½-year investigation was undertaken to determine who would take control next.

Those sentenced in 1984 were Samuel J. "Red" Russotti, the boss; Rene Piccarreto, second-in-command; Richard Marino, underboss; Joseph R. Rossi, captain; Paone, crime family member; Anthony M. Columbo, crime family

TURN TO PAGE 4A

A federal marshal unshackling Joseph Geniola so he can step into a van after arraignment. With him are city officers Thomas Parks, left, and James Tuite.

## Hi-tech setup had secret eye on 4 suspects

**By John O'Brien and Katie Kilfoyle**
Democrat and Chronicle

A *Candid Camera*-like surveillance gave police an insider's view to four reputed mobsters conspiring to extort about $1 million a year, authorities said.

The sophisticated equipment also captured conversations on how to detect police surveillance as well as which defense lawyers are the best and worst in town, according to sources who spoke on the condition their names not be used.

In an elaborate surveillance setup, Rochester police and state and federal authorities hid video cameras and sound-detection equipment in the offices of two illegal gambling clubs, taping dozens of conversations for at least five months ending in May, authorities said.

"We actually watched organized crime in the making," said Rochester police Capt. James O'Brien, commander of the Special Criminal Investigation Section.

O'Brien said yesterday that investigators entered two gambling establishments, which he would not name, and installed voice monitors and videotape machines in the offices.

"They were court-ordered surreptitious

TURN TO PAGE 4A

**ON 4A**

- **The suspects:** Profiles of the accused.
- **The charges:** What the accusations mean.

**October 3, 1987 Democrat and Chronicle**

The defendants were Angelo Amico, Loren Piccarreto, Joseph Geniola and Joseph LoDolce, 45. LoDolce, a construction worker, was named in the indictment as an "enforcer." He was acquitted in 1984 on federal charges of conspiracy and racketeering. He was charged with violating the federal conspiracy statute.

Amico was named in the indictment as the "Boss." He was charged with violating the anti-racketeering conspiracy statutes, filing false tax returns, and conspiring to defraud the government. No employment was listed. Loren Piccarreto was the son of Rene Piccarreto, top adviser to former "Boss" Samuel J. "Red" Russotti, who was convicted with the senior Piccarreto in 1984.

Loren Piccarreto, a steward and an employee of Nory Construction Co. Inc. in Gates, was named in the indictment as the "Acting Underboss." He was charged with violating the federal anti-racketeering and conspiracy statutes. Sources who spoke on the condition they not be identified said two of the remaining four defendants also are "made" members. Sources did not name which two defendants. **(90)**

"Because of previous attempts by law enforcement to eradicate the Mafia presence in Rochester, organized crime was having a very difficult time operating there. 'Organized' is a misnomer, said Capt James O'Brien, commander of the Rochester Police Special Criminal investigation Section. Loren, the son of Rene Piccarreto apparently took command with the family's blessing, authorities said. (91)

In November 1985, or shortly there after, Amico met with Marino in a Leavenworth, Kansas prison, and then he met with Paone in El Reno, Oklahoma. Then after Amico returned, he met with the younger Piccarreto later that month, according to the indictment. "This was not an insurgent group. It was an extension of the original conspiracy," said Rochester Police Chief Gordon Urlacher.

At Amico's arraignment, Assistant U.S. Attorney Douglas E. Rowe revealed that Amico was sworn in as a Mafia member several years prior, apparently one of the last few original members. Authorities said at the time that the videotapes would likely be key evidence in the prosecution of Angelo Amico, Loren Piccarreto, Joseph Geniola, Donald Paone and Joseph La Dolce, who were charged with extortion, racketeering and conspiracy.

Richard Endler, the lawyer in charge of the U.S. Organized Crime Strike Force in Buffalo, said the electronic surveillance was court-authorized and the video tapings show the defendants "while the alleged criminal activities were occurring."

District Attorney Howard Relin, whose office worked with police in setting up the surveillance, said he believed it was the first time videotapes were used in organized-crime surveillance. "The investigation took extraordinary measures for a long period of time," Relin said.

The "candid" conversations that were recorded included discussions among the defendants about where the extortion money was coming from and where it was going, sources said. Donald Paone, 43, was serving a 20-year sentence at the El Reno, Oklahoma Federal Correctional Institution for his 1984 conviction on federal racketeering and conspiracy charges at the time.

Joseph Geniola, a steward with Teamsters Local #398 and an employee of Schiavone Construction Co., based in Secaucus, N.J., was named in the indictment as an "enforcer." He was charged with violating the federal anti-racketeering and conspiracy statutes. Business dropped dramatically because knowledge of the grand jury probe caused members to maintain low profiles, O'Brien said. This meant the mob had to curtail its "enforcement" tactics, prompting some operators of gambling establishments to slack off paying their dues, O'Brien said. Testimony from other mob-related detention hearings revealed incidents of assaults and threats of physical intimidation in recent years, but the violence had lessened considerably. Since 1970, there had been at least 10 homicides and five attempted slayings related to the mob, O'Brien said. Most were directed at insurgents.

"It takes care of the problem and also sends out a tremendous message," he said. Authorities said at the time they were prepared for a resurgence of the mob following the resolution of those cases. The seven mobsters indicted in 1984 exerted influence on Amico and the others from behind bars.

"We didn't need people inside," said city Police Chief Gordon Urlacher, referring to the high-tech equipment In addition to the high-tech methods, old-fashioned surveillance techniques of following suspects in cars and on foot also were used by officers participating in the investigation, police said. As many as 50 local, state and federal officers at a time worked on the investigation over the past 22 years, authorities said. (92)

## Hitman named in 3 killings

### Former mob chief ordered slayings, cop says in affidavit

By John O'Brien
Democrat and Chronicle

Reputed mobster Dominic Taddeo committed three gangland slayings in the early 1980s under the orders of former mob leader Rene Piccarreto, a police investigator claimed publicly yesterday for the first time.

Taddeo killed Nick Matrodonato, Jerry Pelusio and Dino Tortatice in revenge for the murder of a mob leader, and to eliminate an insurgent faction of the Mafia, Rochester police Investigator Paul R. Camping said in an 11-page affidavit. He said confidential informants gave him the information.

Camping's affidavit, along with those of an FBI agent and another Rochester police investigator, were submitted yesterday at hearings to determine whether bail should be set for Piccarreto's son, Loren Piccarreto, Angelo Amico and Joseph LoDolce. They were indicted along with two other men last week on extortion, racketeering and conspiracy charges.

U.S. Magistrate David G. Larimer presided at the hearings, which will continue next week.

Camping also said confidential informants told him that unindicted mob leaders are upset because — in reaction to publicity of the impending indictments — some bookmakers have failed to make extortion payments to the mob. A reputed Mafia member is quoted in the affidavit as saying, "we are going to have to make examples of some of" the bookmakers.

The mob, also referred to as La Cosa Nostra, "would have to take some violent forceful actions against" bookmakers who weren't paying up, according to Camping's confidential informants, who quoted a mob leader.

Although FBI special agent Richard F. Foley testified in February that confidential informants told him Taddeo was the triggerman in the so-called ".45-caliber slayings," allegations that Taddeo was acting as Piccarreto's hit man had never before been made in public.

Taddeo, 29, has never been charged with the slayings. He's been missing since March, after Larimer released him on $25,000 cash bail on a federal firearms violation. A nationwide alert is still in effect for Taddeo's arrest.

TURN TO PAGE 3B

**October 8, 1987 Democrat and Chronicle**

# Former Mob Chief Ordered 3 Killings

Reputed mobster Dominic Taddeo committed three gangland slayings in the early 1980's under the orders of former mob leader Rene Piccarreto. Taddeo killed Nicholas Mastrodonato, Gerald Pelusio and Dino Tortatice in revenge for the murder of mob leader John Fiorino, and to eliminate an insurgent faction of the Mafia, said Rochester Police Investigator Paul Camping.

Camping submitted an 11 page affidavit on **October 7, 1987,** at hearings that were being held to determine whether bail should be set for reputed mobsters Loren Piccarreto, Angelo Amico and Joseph LoDolce, who were indicted the previous week on extortion, racketeering and conspiracy charges.

Camping also claimed that local mob leaders were upset because due to all the publicity surrounding the indictments, some local bookmakers have failed to make extortion payments to the mob. A reputed Mafia member was also quoted in the affidavit as saying, "We are going to have to make "examples" of some of the bookmakers." **(93)**

# John Quinn, Informant Sentenced to 5 Years in Prison

## 'Important' federal witness sentenced to a five-year term

By John O'Brien
Democrat and Chronicle

A man who became a key government witness against three reputed mobsters in an attempted slaying was sentenced to five years in prison yesterday by a federal judge who said the defendant's information was "very important to this community."

U.S. District Judge Michael A. Telesca imposed the sentence on John R. Quinn, who became a government witness in the July 1985 bombing of a truck being driven by Joseph J. DiBattisto of Greece.

Quinn, 47, formerly of 234 ...

... guilty in December to a count of counterfeiting and a count of unlawful possession of a firearm. He admitted possessing a silencer when police raided a restaurant and confiscated bogus money last year.

A federal agent testified in February that Quinn received $15,000 from Charles T. "Charlie the Ox" Indovino in 1985 to plan and carry out DiBattisto's slaying. Quinn then brought Christopher Pelitera and Joseph A. Margiotta into the homicide plot, paying them $1,000 each, Secret Service Special Agent Eric Hartmschleger testified.

Telesca previously sentenced ...

Pelitera to 20 years and Indovino to 15 years.

"Your information and potential to testify in this case are very important to this community," Telesca told Quinn.

As part of his plea agreement, the government agreed to apply for Quinn's entry into the federal Witness Security Program, based on the danger he faces as a result of his cooperation with prosecutors, according to Quinn's plea agreement that was sealed until recently.

The Witness Security Program allows the government to give special protection to cooperating witnesses ... them and give them new identities after they're freed.

Quinn agreed to cooperate with authorities by testifying before a federal grand jury or in any trial or other court proceeding, the plea agreement said.

"At this point, he has completed his cooperation," said Rosemary G. Roberts, assistant U.S. attorney in charge of the Rochester office.

DiBattisto was the target of the bombing because he was a witness to the death of Eugene Ragland Sr., who was killed in 1981 by an associate of Indovino's, authorities have said.

DiBattisto, 51, of Greece, was indicted in January on mail fraud and conspiracy charges accusing him of working with a co-conspirator to kill Ragland and collect $1.7 million in Ragland's life-insurance claims.

Robert A. Dimino, 51, the apparent co-conspirator in Ragland's death, died in January of lung cancer at Rochester General Hospital. He was never charged in connection with the slaying.

**October 9, 1987 Democrat and Chronicle**

John R. Quinn, who was the government's key witness against three mobsters in the attempted slaying of Joseph Battista, was sentenced to five years in prison for his role in that plot. Authorities said that Charles "Charlie The Ox" Indovino paid Quinn $15,000 to murder Joseph Battista. Quinn then brought two others into the plot. As part of the agreement reached in the case, the government agreed to allow Quinn to apply for entry into the Witness Protection Program, due to the danger he could still face as a result of his testimony. **(94)**

## Angelo Amico Denied Bail In Mob Case

Rochester Police Investigator Robert E. Gill gave a rare insider's view of alleged underworld figures through the use of electronic surveillance when he submitted a 42 page affidavit to the court, at Angelo Amico's bail hearing. The affidavit described some of the things recorded during the surveillance of Rochester mobsters.

Angelo Amico was caught both on audio and video tape plotting violence against competing gambling rings and casually discussing things like murder and different ways to terrorize people. Due to the information contained in this affidavit, Amico was denied bail and remained in jail pending his trial on racketeering and conspiracy charges. **(95)**

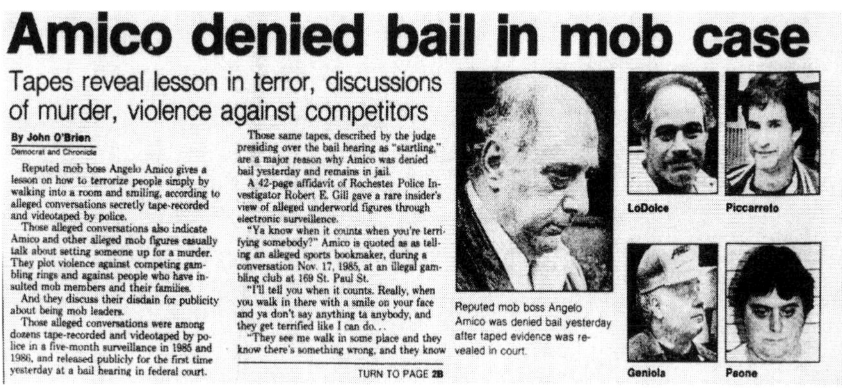

**Amico denied bail in mob case**

Tapes reveal lesson in terror, discussions of murder, violence against competitors

By John O'Brien
Democrat and Chronicle

Reputed mob boss Angelo Amico gives a lesson on how to terrorize people simply by walking into a room and smiling, according to alleged conversations secretly tape-recorded and videotaped by police.

Those alleged conversations also indicate Amico and other alleged mob figures casually talk about setting someone up for a murder. They plot violence against competing gambling rings and against people who have insulted mob members and their families.

And they discuss their disdain for publicity about being mob leaders.

Those alleged conversations were among dozens tape-recorded and videotaped by police in a five-month surveillance in 1985 and 1986, and released publicly for the first time yesterday at a bail hearing in federal court.

Those same tapes, described by the judge presiding over the bail hearing as "startling," are a major reason why Amico was denied bail yesterday and remains in jail.

A 42-page affidavit of Rochester Police Investigator Robert E. Gill gave a rare insider's view of alleged underworld figures through electronic surveillence.

"Ya know when it counts when you're terrifying somebody?" Amico is quoted as as telling an alleged sports bookmaker, during a conversation Nov. 17, 1985, at an illegal gambling club at 169 St. Paul St.

"I'll tell you when it counts. Really, when you walk in there with a smile on your face and ya don't say anything ta anybody, and they get terrified like I can do...

"They see me walk in some place and they know there's something wrong, and they know

TURN TO PAGE 2B

Reputed mob boss Angelo Amico was denied bail yesterday after taped evidence was revealed in court.

LoDolce

Piccarreto

Geniola

Peone

**October 15, 1987 Democrat and Chronicle**

# Police Raid and Close 3 Local Gambling Parlors

Early morning on **April 30, 1988** three illegal gambling clubs were raided by police and shut down. Two of those clubs were on Lyell Avenue and the other was at 234 Portland Avenue. The Club at 266 Lyell Avenue had been operating for at least 20 years before this raid and had been raided several times before. The other two clubs were relatively new at the time.

## 3 illegal gambling clubs shut by police in raids

### Officers seize $3,000 cash, paraphernalia

By Laura Buterbaugh
Democrat and Chronicle

Three illegal Rochester gambling clubs with alleged ties to organized crime were raided and closed down early yesterday, with police seizing $3,000 in cash and gaming tables and gambling paraphernalia.

No arrests were made during the 3 a.m. raids of the clubs at 266 Lyell Ave., 413 Lyell Ave. and 234 Portland Ave. But federal grand jury indictments are expected that could implicate anyone from the club managers to the cleanup crews, said Sgt. Mark Blair of the city police Special Criminal Investigation Section's intelligence unit.

The raids came after a four-month investigation of illegal gambling by the Rochester Police Department. Federal search warrants were obtained for the raids and the seizing of the commercial buildings, which have a total real estate value of $500,000, Blair said.

About 125 patrons filled each gambling parlor when a total of 50 city police officers arrived, but none of the patrons were arrested, he said. The buildings were boarded up after the raids.

Blair said yesterday's raids were an attempt to disrupt Rochester's organized crime network, reputed to run parlors around the city.

"The mob here is already disorganized," he said. "This is just another way for us to keep it that way."

The Rochester investigation is an offshoot of a federal probe that led to similar raids of four gambling parlors last May. Those raids were a joint effort of the Rochester police, the FBI and the U.S. Marshals Service, resulting in 19 federal indictments to date.

Under federal law, anyone convicted of operating an ongoing gambling establishment can be fined up to $20,000 and sentenced to up to five years in prison.

Two of the parlors seized yesterday operated seven days a week, with the third open six days, Blair said. They brought in as much as $10,000 a week, he said.

The club at 266 Lyell Ave. operated for at least 20 years, and has been raided several times before. The other clubs were relatively new, Blair said.

**Democrat and Chronicle May 1, 1988**

No arrests were made, but buildings were seized and boarded up in an ongoing effort to disrupt Rochester's organized crime network. The raids were the result of a four month investigation and indictments were still expected. (96)

# Judge Scolds "Born-Again" Mobster Loren Piccarreto

## Judge scolds mobster who is 'born-again'

By Carol Ritter
Democrat and Chronicle

Suspected mobster Loren Piccarreto says he is heeding God's call by joining the prison ministry and traveling to Attica. But Judge David Larimer wants more down-to-earth proof of his involvement.

Piccarreto, who is awaiting trial on racketeering and gambling charges, admitted yesterday in U.S. District Court that he has been violating his court-ordered curfew and travel restrictions by making weekly trips to the state prison to counsel inmates.

Holding a Bible as he stood in court, the born-again Christian told Larimer he wasn't trying to hide anything.

"I did not try to do this thing out of the way of the court, and I don't do other things the court doesn't know about."

But Larimer said he was skeptical.

'I did not try to do this thing out of the way of the court, and I don't do other things the court doesn't know about.'

— Loren Piccarreto

"Knowing that in general people tend to do more than they ever get caught doing, I share the government's concern that maybe this wasn't the first time you have violated your terms."

Piccarreto, 37, of 385 Churchill Drive South, Greece, must prove that he has been actively involved in the Full Gospel Businessmen's Fellowship International prison ministry before he will get permission to continue, Larimer said.

"It is an admirable request, and I'm inclined to grant it if I get a letter from someone involved in this ministry that he is in fact participating and the work is beneficial," Larimer told Piccarreto's lawyer, Patrick Baker.

Larimer said he was concerned about Piccarreto's disregard of the strict conditions he set last October when he released Piccarreto on $100,000 bail.

Federal investigators claimed that Piccarreto was controlling local mob operations in the absence of his father, Rene Piccarreto, who was sentenced in 1984 to a lengthy prison term.

Larimer allowed the younger Piccarreto to go free on bail on the condition that he meet a 6 p.m. to 6 a.m. curfew, stay in Monroe County and avoid involvement with anyone

TURN TO PAGE 28

Loren Piccarreto, daughter, Amanda, in March photo.

**August 31, 1988 Democrat and Chronicle**

Reputed mobster Loren Piccarreto who had recently become a "born again Christian" was in court before Judge Larimer for violating his court ordered curfew and travel restrictions while he was out of jail on bail, on racketeering and conspiracy charges. As a condition of being released on bail,

Piccarreto was given a 6 P.M. to 6 A.M. curfew and was not permitted to travel outside of Monroe County in New York State.

Holding a Bible as he stood in court, Piccarreto claimed he was not trying to hide anything. He said that he had been actively involved in the Full Gospel Business Men's Fellowship International Prison Ministry, making weekly trips to the state prison to counsel prisoners.

Judge Larimer said that he was skeptical. While admirable, said the judge, he wanted some kind of proof, like a letter, from someone else involved in the ministry that could attest to the fact that Loren Piccarreto was indeed involved in the ministry, and that it was beneficial, before he would allow the prison visits to continue. (97)

## Amico Pleads Guilty to Racketeering and Conspiracy

**Amico may testify at mob trial**

He pleads guilty to racketeering, income tax evasion

By Carol Ritter
Democrat and Chronicle

Angelo Amico is no longer a defendant, but he remains a potential witness in the federal court trial of three alleged mobsters accused of racketeering and conspiracy.

Amico, 56, of 177 Colebourne Road, Rochester, pleaded guilty in secret last week to both counts of the current indictment and an additional count of income tax evasion from a previous indictment.

His name is on a list of about 60 people who may be called by federal prosecutors to testify against his former co-defendants, who are charged with operating illegal gambling clubs at several locations.

The defendants also are accused of using strong-arm tactics to extort payments from several people involved in the gambling operations and using the money to pay legal bills and support the families of other alleged mob figures who are in prison.

The defendants are: Joseph Geniola, 59, of 128 Hempel St., Rochester, a Teamsters union official and construction employee, free on $50,000 bail; Joseph

Angelo Amico

LoDolce, 46, of 128 Gray St., Rochester a construction worker, free on $100,000 bail; and Loren Piccarreto, 37, of 395 Churchill Drive South, Greece, a construction worker, free on $100,000 bail.

Jury selection began Monday, continued through yesterday and is to resume at 9:30 a.m. today.

Records unsealed yesterday by U.S. District Judge David G. Larimer revealed that Amico entered a guilty plea last Tuesday to one income tax count includ-

SELECTING JURORS A TEDIOUS TASK 2B

ed in a three-count indictment. On the following day, he pleaded guilty to the racketeering and conspiracy charges.

Larimer said he took the pleas in his chambers because he feared publicity could hinder the chances of a fair and impartial jury for the others.

He noted that the activities of alleged mobsters in Rochester had received extensive news coverage for several years.

"Should Mr. Amico's decision to plead guilty today be known to the press, there would be a very noticeable detailed article in the press about (it) and the terms

TURN TO PAGE 2B

**November 2, 1988 Democrat and Chronicle**

By **November of 1988**, Angelo Amico was no longer a defendant. He pleaded guilty to racketeering and conspiracy in late **October of 1988**. He remained a potential witness against his co-defendants along with about 60 others who were expected to testify against Joseph Geniola, Joseph LoDolce and Loren Piccarreto. The remaining defendants were all accused of operating illegal gambling establishments in the city of Rochester and extorting money from others, then using that money to pay the legal bills and support the families of other imprisoned mobsters. (98)

# Tapes Make Good Witnesses

Federal prosecutors were banking on dozens of video and audio tape recordings to prove their case of racketeering and conspiracy against three alleged mobsters.

The tapes were compiled through court-ordered hidden microphones and video cameras intending to prove that three reputed Rochester mobsters operated illegal gambling establishments in the city of Rochester and extorted money from other gambling establishments, then used that money to pay the legal bills and support the families of other imprisoned mobsters. (99)

## Tapes in mob case called 'most important witnesses'

**By Carol Ritter**
Democrat and Chronicle

Federal prosecutors are banking on dozens of video and audio tapes to prove their case against three men on trial for conspiracy and racketeering.

"Here, the most important witnesses are not the people that take the stand, but the tapes," Assistant U.S. Attorney Anthony Bruce said yesterday in his opening statement.

He said the tapes, compiled through court-ordered surveillance using hidden cameras and microphones, will show that three alleged mobsters conspired to control illegal gambling in the city and distribute the proceeds to support the families of imprisoned mob members and pay legal fees.

As Bruce talked, members of the six-man, six-woman jury and the six alternates sat attentively, some with note pads on their laps.

In an unusual move, U.S. District Judge David G. Larimer told the jurors he would permit them to take notes during the trial, which is expected to last six weeks or more. He said the evidence would be complicated and difficult to follow.

But he warned the jury to pay close attention to the testimony. He said notes must be left each night in individual jurors' folders in the jury room and would be destroyed by the court at the end of the trial.

Fellow U.S. District Judge Michael A. Telesca said he had never allowed a jury to take notes.

"It's at the discretion of the judge, but

TURN TO PAGE **3B**

**November 3, 1988 Democrat and Chronicle**

# 3 linked to mobster initiation

## But lawyers attack witness's credibility in racketeering trial

By Carol Ritter
Democrat and Chronicle

Anthony Oliveri told a federal court jury yesterday that Joseph LoDolce, Loren Piccarreto and Joseph Geniola all were present when he was initiated into the Rochester mob one December night 10 years ago.

But in cross-examination, prosecution witness Oliveri admitted that he never mentioned any of those names when he testified about the same incident at the 1984 trial of several former mob leaders.

"You have lied under oath before, haven't you?" defense lawyer Anthony Leonardo asked Oliveri.

"Yes, once," Oliveri answered.

Defense lawyers objected singly or in chorus to nearly every question in his direct examination. And it was obvious from the start of testimony that no detail is likely to be overlooked by any of the five lawyers involved in the racketeering and conspiracy trial of LoDolce, Piccarreto and Geniola.

The three men are charged in connection with illegal gambling operations at several social clubs in Rochester. They are alleged to have taken over leadership of the local mob after several of their associates were convicted of racketeering and sent to prison in 1984.

The indictment alleges that LoDolce, Piccarreto and Geniola extorted payments from operators of gambling clubs and used the money to pay for lawyers and support the families of the men in prison.

Joseph LoDolce    Loren Piccarreto    Joseph Geniola

Oliveri, a former Rochester resident, is in the federal witness protection program and was given a new identity when he became an informer while serving a prison term in Utah in 1980.

Yesterday he testified that he had committed "thousands of burglaries" and participated in several robberies, including a $200,000 heist of actress Sophia Loren's jewelry in New York City several years ago. He wasn't arrested or prosecuted for that crime, he said.

Between prison terms for various offenses, he said, he settled in Rochester and was invited to join the mob 10 years ago.

Describing his initiation in the basement of an Irondequoit home, he said his finger was pricked to drip blood onto a

TURN TO PAGE 2B

**November 4, 1988 Democrat and Chronicle**

Government informant and self proclaimed former "made" member of the Rochester Mafia, Anthony Oliveri, testified against his three former Mafia brothers at their racketeering and conspiracy trial that had started in early **November of 1988**. Oliveri testified that all three men, Joseph LoDolce, Loren Piccarreto, and Joseph Geniola, were present when he was officially inducted into the Rochester Mafia in a secret ceremony in the basement of an Irondequoit home. (100)

# Club Owner Testifies at Mob Trial

# Mob trial witness recalls gambling payments

## He says he paid $500 a week from illegal blackjack games as 'a right-to-operate fee'

By Carol Ritter
Democrat and Chronicle

Operating an illegal gambling club in Rochester was like running a fast-food restaurant, a witness said yesterday at the racketeering and conspiracy trial of three alleged mobsters.

Robert Barone testified that he had to pay $500 a week to alleged mob member Donald Paone from the proceeds of his blackjack games at 232 Portland Ave.

"He said, 'Think of it like a franchise fee that McDonald's pays — a right-to-operate fee,'" Barone testified.

Barone was the second prosecution witness to testify against defendants Joseph Geniola, 59, of 128 Hempel St.; Joseph LoDolce, 46, of 128 Gray St.; and Loren Piccarreto, 37, of 395 Churchill Drive S., Greece.

Paone also had been named in the indictment, but he and Angelo Amico pleaded guilty before the trial began.

The trial before U.S. District Judge David G. Larimer resumes at 1 p.m. today.

Barone, 34, of County Line Road, Ontario, Wayne County, said he knew what he had to do when he decided in 1981 to take over a social club and run illegal card games there.

"In order to open up a gambling joint in Rochester, you had to get an OK from the guys representing the Rochester mob," he testified.

He said he raked off 5 percent of the kitty in his blackjack games, which were netting as much as $1,500 a day five or six days a week. The rakeoff went for protection payments to the mob and other expenses, Barone said.

"If you couldn't make the payments, they'd tell you to shut down, or there could be physical violence," he said. "The more money you make, the more you can

TURN TO PAGE 4B

**November 8, 1988 Democrat and Chronicle**

Robert Barone, the operator of an illegal gambling club located at 232 Portland Avenue, testified that he had to pay Rochester Mafia member Donald Paone $500 every week for the privilege of running a gambling parlor in Rochester.

Barone described the "juice payments" as being similar to paying a "franchise fee," like MacDonald's pays, sort of a right-to-operate fee. Barone testified that he raked off 5 percent of the kitty in his blackjack games, which were netting $1,500 daily, to cover the protection payments to the mob and other expenses. (101)

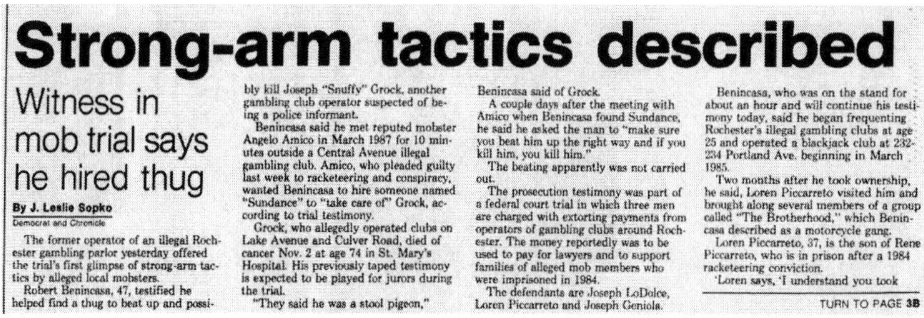

# Strong-arm tactics described

## Witness in mob trial says he hired thug

By J. Leslie Sopko
Democrat and Chronicle

The former operator of an illegal Rochester gambling parlor yesterday offered the trial's first glimpse of strong-arm tactics by alleged local mobsters.

Robert Benincasa, 47, testified he helped find a thug to beat up and possibly kill Joseph "Snuffy" Grock, another gambling club operator suspected of being a police informant.

Benincasa said he met reputed mobster Angelo Amico in March 1987 for 10 minutes outside a Central Avenue illegal gambling club. Amico, who pleaded guilty last week to racketeering and conspiracy, wanted Benincasa to hire someone named "Sundance" to "take care of" Grock, according to trial testimony.

Grock, who allegedly operated clubs on Lake Avenue and Culver Road, died of cancer Nov. 2 at age 74 in St. Mary's Hospital. His previously taped testimony is expected to be played for jurors during the trial.

"They said he was a stool pigeon," Benincasa said of Grock.

A couple days after the meeting with Amico when Benincasa found Sundance, he said he asked the man to "make sure you beat him up the right way and if you kill him, you kill him."

The beating apparently was not carried out.

The prosecution testimony was part of a federal court trial in which three men are charged with extorting payments from operators of gambling clubs around Rochester. The money reportedly was to be used to pay for lawyers and to support families of alleged mob members who were imprisoned in 1984.

The defendants are Joseph LoDolce, Loren Piccarreto and Joseph Geniola.

Benincasa, who was on the stand for about an hour and will continue his testimony today, said he began frequenting Rochester's illegal gambling clubs at age 25 and operated a blackjack club at 232-234 Portland Ave. beginning in March 1985.

Two months after he took ownership, he said, Loren Piccarreto visited him and brought along several members of a group called "The Brotherhood," which Benincasa described as a motorcycle gang.

Loren Piccarreto, 37, is the son of Rene Piccarreto, who is in prison after a 1984 racketeering conviction.

'Loren says, 'I understand you took

TURN TO PAGE 3B

**November 9, 1988 Democrat and Chronicle**

Robert Benincasa, former operator of another gambling parlor in Rochester, also testified to the strong-arm tactics employed by the Mafia in order to collect "protection" money from illegal gambling clubs.

He testified that he was hired by mobster Angelo Amico to find and beat up and possibly kill another club operator who was suspected of being a police informant. (102)

# Jurors Shown Surveillance Video of Mobsters

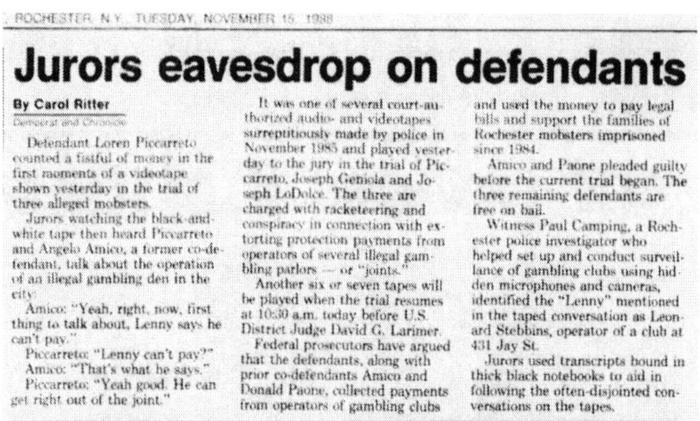

ROCHESTER, N.Y., TUESDAY, NOVEMBER 15, 1988

# Jurors eavesdrop on defendants

By Carol Ritter
Democrat and Chronicle

Defendant Loren Piccarreto counted a fistful of money in the first moments of a videotape shown yesterday in the trial of three alleged mobsters.

Jurors watching the black-and-white tape then heard Piccarreto and Angelo Amico, a former co-defendant, talk about the operation of an illegal gambling den in the city:

Amico: "Yeah, right, now, first thing to talk about, Lenny says he can't pay."

Piccarreto: "Lenny can't pay?"

Amico: "That's what he says."

Piccarreto: "Yeah good. He can get right out of the joint."

It was one of several court-authorized audio- and videotapes surreptitiously made by police in November 1985 and played yesterday to the jury in the trial of Piccarreto, Joseph Geniola and Joseph LoDolce. The three are charged with racketeering and conspiracy in connection with extorting protection payments from operators of several illegal gambling parlors — or "joints."

Another six or seven tapes will be played when the trial resumes at 10:30 a.m. today before U.S. District Judge David G. Larimer.

Federal prosecutors have argued that the defendants, along with prior co-defendants Amico and Donald Paone, collected payments from operators of gambling clubs and used the money to pay legal bills and support the families of Rochester mobsters imprisoned since 1984.

Amico and Paone pleaded guilty before the current trial began. The three remaining defendants are free on bail.

Witness Paul Camping, a Rochester police investigator who helped set up and conduct surveillance of gambling clubs using hidden microphones and cameras, identified the "Lenny" mentioned in the taped conversation as Leonard Stebbins, operator of a club at 431 Jay St.

Jurors used transcripts bound in thick black notebooks to aid in following the often-disjointed conversations on the tapes.

**November 15, 1988 Democrat and Chronicle**

Jurors in the racketeering trial against three Rochester Mafia members were shown the first of several police surveillance videos, getting a rare first-hand glimpse of life in the underworld. The video showed Loren Piccarreto counting a large sum of money.

Then there was a conversation about a gambling club operator "Lenny," Leonard Stebbins, who wasn't paying his "protection" payments. The videotapes surreptitiously made by police in November of 1985 were audio and video tapes of surveillance conducted on illegal gambling parlors in the city. Another six or seven tapes were expected to be played for the jurors when the trial resumed.

# Piccarreto wrote he was a mafioso

## Letter to pastor, church says Jesus redeemed him

**By Carol Ritter**
Democrat and Chronicle

**Loren Piccarreto**
racket-trial defendant

Loren Piccarreto was in jail when he wrote to his pastor and fellow church members in 1987 and described himself as a former Mafia member who had changed his life.

A copy of his handwritten letter was read yesterday to the federal court jury hearing evidence in a racketeering and conspiracy case against Piccarreto, Joseph Geniola and Joseph LoDolce. U.S. District Judge David G. Larimer overruled defense objections to having the letter entered in evidence.

In the letter dated Oct. 9, 1987, Piccarreto wrote:

"The newspaper portrays me as a mafia leader and you know me as a servant in the army of the Lord Jesus Christ. As a fellowship let us proclaim to the public that because of Jesus our Lord and Savior the old man is dead and we claim victory that we are New Creatures in Christ. Use my situation to proclaim the Glory, the Mercy, the compassion that Jesus has. Yes he took a member in the mafia who was dead in the world and because I believed on Him he made a new creature out of me."

Piccarreto, a professed born-again Christian, is a member of the Greece Assembly of God Church.

He was arrested on a federal indictment warrant and jailed a week before he wrote the letter. Now he and the other two defendants are free on bail.

They are alleged to have coordinated illegal gambling operations in Rochester, extorting protection payments from gambling club owners and using the money to pay legal bills and support the families of imprisoned mobsters.

The government contends that Piccarreto and another man, Angelo Amico, took over leadership of the local mob after Rene Piccarreto, Loren's father, was sent to federal prison in 1984, along with several associates.

Amico was indicted along with the three present defendants, but he plead-

TURN TO PAGE 4B

**November 17, 1988 Democrat and Chronicle**

# Letter to Pastor and Church Congregation Read in Court

A letter written by Loren Piccarreto on October 9, 1987 to his pastor and fellow church members while in jail, was read in open court despite objections made by the defense.

In the letter, Piccarreto claimed that the media portrayed him as a Mafia leader but Piccarreto said that he had become a new creature in Christ, becoming born-again after accepting Jesus Christ as his Lord and Savior. (103)

# Trial Throws Light on Rochester's Gambler Underworld

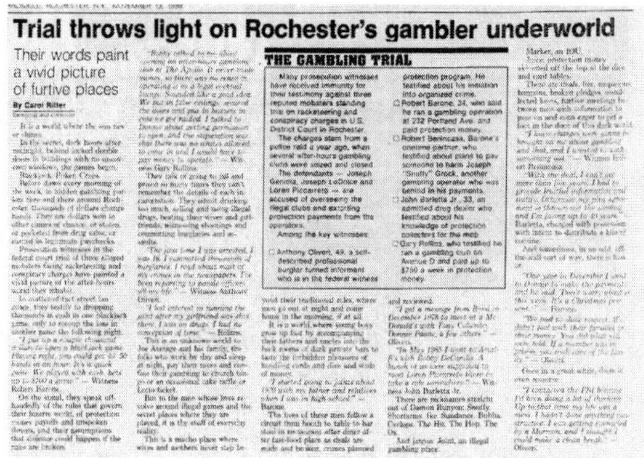

Trial throws light on Rochester's gambler underworld

Their words paint a vivid picture of furtive places

By Carol Ritter

THE GAMBLING TRIAL

Many prosecution witnesses have received immunity for their testimony against three reputed mobsters standing trial on racketeering and conspiracy charges in U.S. District Court in Rochester.

The charges stem from a police raid a year ago, when several after-hours gambling clubs were seized and closed.

The defendants — Joseph Geniola, Joseph LoDolce and Loren Piccarreto — are accused of overseeing the illegal clubs and extorting protection payments from the operators.

Among the key witnesses:

- Anthony Oliveri, 49, a self-described professional burglar turned informant who is in the federal witness protection program. He testified about his initiation into organized crime.
- Robert Barone, 34, who said he ran a gambling operation at 232 Portland Ave. and paid protection money.
- Robert Benincasa, Barone's onetime partner, who testified about plans to pay someone to harm Joseph "Snuffy" Grock, another gambling operator who was behind in his payments.
- John Barletta Jr., 33, an admitted drug dealer who testified about his knowledge of protection collectors for the mob.
- Gary Rollins, who testified he ran a gambling club on Avenue D and paid up to $750 a week in protection money.

**November 13. 1988**
**Democrat and Chronicle**

In the secret, dark hours after midnight, behind locked double doors in buildings with no uncovered windows, the games began. Blackjack, Poker and Craps.

Before dawn every morning of the week, in hidden gambling parlors here and there around Rochester, thousands of dollars changed hands. They were dollars won in other games of chance, or stolen, or pocketed from drug sales, or earned in legitimate paychecks.

Prosecution witnesses in the Federal Court trial of three alleged mobsters facing racketeering and conspiracy charges have painted a vivid picture of the after-hours world they inhabited, in matter-of-fact street language, they testified to dropping thousands in cash in one blackjack game, only to recoup the loss in another game the following night.

"You put up a couple thousand dollars to open a blackjack game. Playing right, you could get 40 to 50 hands in an hour. It's a quick game. We played with cash, bets up to $100 a game." said witness Robert Barone. On the stand, they spoke offhandedly of the rules that governed their bizarre world, of protection money payoffs and unspoken threats, and their assumptions that violence could happen if the rules were broken. **(104)**

Witness John Barletta Jr. testified, "There are nicknames straight out of Damon Runyon: Snuffy, Shortarms, Ike, Sundance, Bubba, Cyclops, The Hit, The Hop, and The Ox. And jargon: joint, an illegal gambling place. A "marker" was an IOU, "juice" was protection money skimmed off the top at the dice and card tables.

There were deals, lies, suspicions, bargains, broken pledges, uncollected loans, furtive meetings between men with information to pass on and cops eager to get a foot in the door of this dark world.

It was a world where the sun never shined, where men went out at night and came home in the morning, if at all. It was a world where young boys grew up fast, by accompanying their fathers and uncles into the back rooms of dark private bars to taste the forbidden pleasures of handling cards and dice and wads of money.

That was an unknown world to Joe Average and his family, the folks who work by day and sleep at night, pay their taxes and confine their gambling to church bingo or an occasional cake raffle or Lotto ticket. But to the men whose lives revolved around illegal games and the secret places where they were played, it was the stuff of everyday reality. It was a macho place where wives and mothers never stepped," explained Gary Rollins.

They talked of going to jail and prison so many times they couldn't remember the details of each incarceration. They admitted to drinking too much, selling and using illegal drugs, beating their wives and girlfriends, witnessing shootings and committing burglaries and assaults. "The first time I was arrested, I was 16. I committed thousands of burglaries. I read about most of my crimes in the newspapers. I've been reporting to parole officers all my life," exclaimed witness John Barletta Jr. (105)

## Summary of Witness Testimony in Mob Trial

Many prosecution witnesses had received immunity for their testimony against three reputed mobsters standing trial on racketeering and conspiracy charges in U.S. District Court in Rochester. The charges stemmed from a police raid the previous year, when several after-hours gambling clubs were seized and closed. The defendants Joseph Geniola, Joseph LoDolce and Loren Piccarreto were accused of overseeing the illegal clubs and extorting protection payments from the operators.

Among the key witnesses was Anthony Oliveri, 49, a self-described professional-burglar-turned-informant who was already in the Federal Witness Protection Program.

"I contacted the FBI because I'd been doing a lot of thinking. Up to that time my life was a mess. I hadn't done anything constructive. I was getting counseled by a Mormon, and I thought I could make a clean break," said witness Anthony Oliveri, while testifying about his role in the gambling operation.

He also had this to say. "Hobby talked to me about opening an after-hours gambling club at The Apollo. It never made money, so there was no sense in operating it as a legal cocktail lounge. Sounded like a good idea. We put in false ceilings, secured the doors and put in buzzers in case we got raided. I talked to Donnie Paone about getting permission to open, and the stipulation was that there was no whites allowed to come in and I would have to pay money to operate." "I lost interest in running the joint after my girlfriend was shot there. I was on drugs. I had no conception of time." He also testified about his initiation into organized crime.

Gary Rollins testified that he ran a gambling club on Avenue D and paid up to $750 a week in protection money.

Witness Robert Barone, 34, said he ran a gambling operation at 232 Portland Ave. and paid protection money. Sometimes, in an odd, off-the-wall sort of way, there is honor.

"One year in December, I went to Donnie to make the payment, and he said, Don't worry about it this week, it's a Christmas present," said Barone. "We had to show respect. We didn't fool with their families or their money. You did what you were told. If a member was in prison, you took care of the family. "

John Barletta Jr., 33, an admitted drug dealer, also testified about his knowledge of protection collectors for the mob. Barletta was charged with possession with intent to distribute a kilo of cocaine.

Robert Benincasa, Barone's onetime partner, testified about plans to pay someone to harm Joseph "Snuffy" Grock, another gambling operator who was behind in his payments.

"I knew charges were gonna be brought on me about gambling and that, and I wanted to work something out," said witness Robert Benincasa.

"With the deal, I can't get more than five years. I had to provide fruitful information and testify. Otherwise my agreement was thrown out the window and I would have been facing up to 40 years." **(106)**

# Amico Associate Testifies at Mob Trial

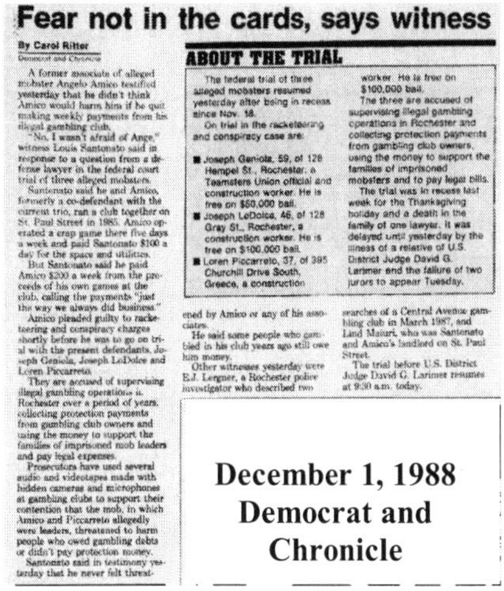

## Fear not in the cards, says witness

By Carol Ritter
Democrat and Chronicle

A former associate of alleged mobster Angelo Amico testified yesterday that he didn't think Amico would harm him if he quit making weekly payments from his illegal gambling club.

"No, I wasn't afraid of Ange," witness Louis Santonato said in response to a question from a defense lawyer in the federal court trial of three alleged mobsters.

Santonato said he and Amico, formerly a co-defendant with the current trio, ran a club together on St. Paul Street in 1985. Amico operated a crap game there five days a week and paid Santonato $100 a day for the space and utilities.

But Santonato said he paid Amico $200 a week from the proceeds of his own games at the club, calling the payments "just the way we always did business."

Amico pleaded guilty to racketeering and conspiracy charges shortly before he was to go on trial with the present defendants, Joseph Geniola, Joseph LoDolce and Loren Piccarreto.

They are accused of supervising illegal gambling operations in Rochester over a period of years, collecting protection payments from gambling club owners and using the money to support the families of imprisoned mob leaders and pay legal expenses.

Prosecutors have used several audio and videotapes made with hidden cameras and microphones at gambling clubs to support their contention that the mob, in which Amico and Piccarreto allegedly were leaders, threatened to harm people who owed gambling debts or didn't pay protection money.

Santonato said in testimony yesterday that he never felt threatened by Amico or any of his associates.

He said some people who gambled in his club years ago still owe him money.

Other witnesses yesterday were E.J. Lergner, a Rochester police investigator who described two searches of a Central Avenue gambling club in March 1987, and Land Maiuri, who was Santonato and Amico's landlord on St. Paul Street.

The trial before U.S. District Judge David G. Larimer resumes at 9:30 a.m. today.

**ABOUT THE TRIAL**

The federal trial of three alleged mobsters resumed yesterday after being in recess since Nov. 18.

On trial in the racketeering and conspiracy case are:

- Joseph Geniola, 59, of 128 Hempel St., Rochester, a Teamsters Union official and construction worker. He is free on $50,000 bail.
- Joseph LoDolce, 46, of 128 Gray St., Rochester, a construction worker. He is free on $100,000 bail.
- Loren Piccarreto, 37, of 395 Churchill Drive South, Greece, a construction worker. He is free on $100,000 bail.

The three are accused of supervising illegal gambling operations in Rochester and collecting protection payments from gambling club owners, using the money to support the families of imprisoned mobsters and to pay legal bills.

The trial was in recess last week for the Thanksgiving holiday and a death in the family of one lawyer. It was delayed until yesterday by the illness of a relative of U.S. District Judge David G. Larimer and the failure of two jurors to appear Tuesday.

**December 1, 1988**
**Democrat and Chronicle**

Louis Santonato, a former associate of mobster Angelo Amico testified that he did not think Amico would harm him if he stopped making his weekly "juice" payments.

Santonato said that he and Amico ran a club together on St. Paul St. Amico operated a crap game there five days a week and paid Santonato $100 a day for the space and utilities.

But Santonato said he gave back $200 a week of that money to Amico for "protection" for running his own games there. Santonato said that was "just the way we always did business." (107)

# Witness Collapses On Witness Stand

## Medics take witness from court

Mob-case trial disrupted when Colangelo appears ill

By Carol Ritter

**HIGHLIGHTS OF MOB TRIAL**

In the federal court trial of three alleged mobsters that began Nov. 1, prosecutors have called 35 witnesses and introduced videotaped testimony from another who died of cancer last month.

Five or six government witnesses remain to be heard, according to prosecutors Anthony Bruce and Gregory West. Defense lawyers have not said whether they plan to call any witnesses.

U.S. District Judge David G. Larimer is hearing the case against three men accused of conspiring to control illegal gambling in Rochester, extorting protection money and using it to support the families of imprisoned mob leaders and pay legal bills.

The defendants are:

- Joseph Geniola, 59, of 128 Hempel St., Rochester, a Teamsters Union official and construction employee. He is free on $50,000 bail.
- Joseph LoDolce, 46, of 128 Gray St., Rochester, a construction worker. He is free on $100,000 bail.
- Loren Piccarreto, 37, of 395 Churchill Drive South, Greece, a construction worker. He is free on $100,000 bail.

**December 7, 1988**
**Democrat and Chronicle**

Witness Nicholas Colangelo was wheeled out of a Federal Courtroom on an ambulance stretcher after he began breathing heavily and complaining of chest pain.

Colangelo turned pale on the witness stand while he was on redirect examination from the prosecutor. LoDolce's lawyer was the first to inform the judge that Colangelo had a heart condition.

"He has a very bad heart," Geniola added. "He gets emotional, very emotional. I seen him gambling one time and he almost passed out."

The conspiracy and racketeering trial for three of Rochester's leading Mafia members was temporarily postponed until the following day. (108)

# Mob 'turned upside down'

Guilty

**Loren Piccarreto**
- **Age:** 37
- **Address:** 395 Churchill Drive South, Greece
- **Occupation:** Construction worker and Teamsters union steward
- **Verdict:** Convicted of conspiracy and racketeering.
- **Maximum sentence:** 40 years in prison and a $500,000 fine

Guilty

**Joseph Geniola**
- **Age:** 60
- **Address:** 128 Hempel St., Rochester
- **Occupation:** Construction worker and Teamsters union official
- **Verdict:** Convicted of conspiracy and racketeering
- **Maximum sentence:** 40 years in prison and a $500,000 fine.

Guilty

**Joseph LoDolce**
- **Age:** 46
- **Address:** 128 Gray St., Rochester
- **Occupation:** Construction worker
- **Verdict:** Convicted of conspiracy, acquitted of racketeering
- **Maximum sentence:** 20 years in prison and a $250,000 fine.

Democrat and Chronicle

## Rackets trial ends in three convictions

By J. Leslie Sopko
Democrat and Chronicle

The conviction of three reputed Rochester mobsters on conspiracy charges yesterday "turned the gambling world upside down," a police investigator said after a federal court jury delivered its verdict.

"It takes four more members off the streets and does put a crimp in gambling efforts in the city," said Paul Camping, a Rochester police special investigator who tracks organized crime.

Federal prosecutors originally indicted four men. But Angelo Amico pleaded guilty shortly before the trial began.

The two-month trial was the result of police raids a year ago when several after-hours gambling clubs were seized. Authorities said the investigation and trial

ZEIGLER INTERVIEWS PICCARRETO 1B

dramatically curbed the illegal collection of gambling debts and left only one club operating in the city.

"Whew. I'm just relieved and very happy," said Assistant U.S. Attorney Anthony Bruce, chief prosecutor in the trial that began Nov. 1.

The three defendants showed little emotion when the jury foreman read the verdict at 1:45 p.m. But moments later, outside the courtroom, their eyes welled with tears as they kissed and hugged family members and friends, who wept softly.

"There's nothing to say, really," said Joseph LoDolce, the only one of the three acquitted of racketeering. He faces up to 20 years in prison and a $250,000 fine for his conviction of conspiring to control illegal gambling activity.

The other men, Joseph Geniola and Loren Piccarreto, were convicted of both racketeering and conspiracy charges from a two-count, 53-page indictment. They each face up to 40 years in prison and $500,000 in fines.

U.S. District Court Judge David G. Larimer allowed the men to remain free on bail until sentencing Feb. 21. Piccarreto and Geniola posted $100,000 bail, and LoDolce is free on $50,000 bail.

Defense lawyers argued throughout the trial that prosecutors blew the case out of proportion. They said it had no place in federal court under the Racketeer Influenced and Corrupt Organizations Act, known as RICO.

TURN TO PAGE 8A

## Fact couldn't compare with fiction

### Courtroom-drama fan, juror said mob trial wasn't TV's 'Matlock'

By Jonathan Saltzman
Democrat and Chronicle

For Marjorie Hartford, a fan of Mickey Spillane crime novels and television courtroom dramas, serving as a juror in the racketeering trial of reputed Rochester mobsters was something of a disappointment.

"This wasn't run like *Matlock*," the Avon grandmother said, referring to the TV courtroom show starring Andy Griffith. "It wasn't as entertaining. It's real life. Nobody wrote the script."

Hartford and 11 other jurors yesterday convicted Loren Piccarreto, Joseph Geniola and Joseph LoDolce of conspiracy charges related to organized crime activities. The federal jury deliberated 40 hours over seven days before the foreman, Kevin McWilliams, delivered the verdicts.

Hartford, 54, who assembles eyeglass cases at Bausch & Lomb Inc., was relieved that her first experience as a juror was over.

"It's been a long trial. There was a lot of tension. You're deliberating on somebody else's life, which is hard to do for anybody."

The jury of six men and six women struggled to understand racketeering and conspiracy laws, Hartford said. Jurors sent U.S. District Judge David G. Larimer more than 35 notes asking him to clarify legal points.

"It was quite complicated for us. After we went out and asked the judge the definitions, it would start clearing up more and more."

Several times, the jury asked the judge to replay videotapes Rochester police secretly obtained in the offices of two illegal gambling clubs in 1985 and 1986.

"Some of the tapes were muffled. You had to hear them two or three times to get what they were saying."

The jury, which also convicted Piccarreto and Geniola of racketeering in the two-count indictment, repeatedly was split while deliberating verdicts. But the votes usually were 6-6 or 7-5, never 11-1, Hartford said.

Jurors sat around a big table with a pot of coffee provided by the judge. Salvatore's Pizza-Subs Inc. delivered sandwiches and chicken fingers.

Hartford said the trial was her introduction to gambling.

"I'm used to playing euchre around the tables. That's my card game."

**December 1, 1988 Democrat and Chronicle**

# Mobsters Found Guilty

Loren Piccarreto, Joseph LoDolce and Joseph Geniola were found guilty of conspiracy charges relating to control of organized gambling in Rochester. Piccarreto and Geniola were also found guilty of racketeering, a charge LoDolce was acquitted of.

Piccarreto and Geniola each faced a maximum sentence of up to 40 years in prison. Joseph LoDolce faced a maximum of 20 years.

The convictions removed the leadership of the Rochester Mafia from the streets, leaving the established Mafia organization a mere shell of what it once was.

In it's hey-day the established Mafia in Rochester boasted more than 40 members plus associates. By 1988, the majority of the mob's members were in prison, were murdered or they had turned informant, and they were relocated into the Federal Witness Protection Program.

# *Chapter 10*
# The Fall of Teamsters Local #398
# and
# (Dominic Taddeo's Mob Hits)

## Dominic Taddeo is Indicted for Slaying 3 Mobsters

Dominic Taddeo of Rochester, N.Y., described by authorities as an organized crime figure, was indicted on **August 1, 1990**, on two racketeering counts that linked him to three homicides and two attempted homicides in the Rochester area, U.S. Attorney Dennis C. Vacco said.

Back again

Wayne Scarberry Democrat and Chronicle

Dominic Taddeo, escorted yesterday from courthouse, is to be arraigned today on conspiracy charges.

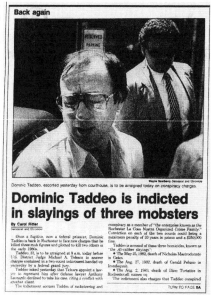

**Dominic Taddeo is indicted in slayings of three mobsters**

By Carol Ritter
Democrat and Chronicle

Once a fugitive, now a federal prisoner, Dominic Taddeo is back in Rochester to face new charges that he killed three mob figures and plotted to kill two others in the early 1980s.

Taddeo, 33, is to be arraigned at 9 a.m. today before U.S. District Judge Michael A. Telesca to answer charges contained in a two-count indictment handed up yesterday by a federal grand jury.

Taddeo asked yesterday that Telesca appoint a lawyer to represent him after defense lawyer Anthony Leonardo declined to take his case, citing a conflict with another client.

The indictment accuses Taddeo of racketeering and conspiracy as a member of "the enterprise known as the Rochester La Cosa Nostra Organized Crime Family." Conviction on each of the two counts could bring a maximum penalty of 20 years in prison and a $250,000 fine.

Taddeo is accused of these three homicides, known as "the .45-caliber slayings":

- The May 25, 1982, death of Nicholas Mastrodonato in Gates.
- The Aug. 27, 1982, death of Gerald Pelusio in Irondequoit.
- The Aug. 2, 1983, death of Dino Tortatice in Rochester.all names cq

The indictment also charges that Taddeo conspired

TURN TO PAGE 8A

**August 2, 1990**
**Democrat and Chronicle**

At the time, Taddeo, 33, was already in prison. He had been implicated in **July of 1990** in a plot to use guns and camouflage gear stored in rented lockers in the Lehigh Valley to bust Colombian cocaine lord Carlos Lehder out of federal prison and sell him back to the Medellin Drug Cartel. Taddeo randomly chose the Lehigh Valley, officials said. That plan was interrupted with Taddeo's March 1989 arrest in Cleveland and the subsequent seizure of the weapons and cash stored in lockers in Bethlehem and Wescosville, police said. Taddeo was serving a 17-year federal sentence for possession of illegal weapons and bail jumping.

The federal grand jury indicted Taddeo under the Racketeer Influenced Corrupt Organizations Act. Evidence presented to the grand jury by Assistant U.S. Attorneys Christopher Buscaglia and Anthony Bruce was developed over a 3-1/2-year investigation.

Count one of the indictment alleged that Taddeo was part of the Rochester La Cosa Nostra Crime Family, participated in the May 25, 1982, murder of Nicholas Mastrodonato, the Aug. 27, 1982, murder of Gerald Pelusio, the April 12 and Nov. 10, 1983, attempted murders of Thomas Marotta, the Aug. 2, 1983, murder of Dino Tortatice, and a conspiracy to murder Thomas Taylor, Vacco said.

It also alleged that Taddeo conducted an illegal gambling business in Rochester and used extortion to take over another gambling business, then ran a gambling operation from that business. Count two charged Taddeo with conspiring to conduct affairs named in the first count. Each count of the indictment carried a maximum penalty of 20 years in prison and a $250,000 fine. **(89)**

# Angelo Misuraca Resigns as Vice President and Business Agent of Teamsters Local #398 And IBT Joint Council #17 After He Is Charged With Associating With Mafia Member Angelo Amico

In 1990, Angelo Misuraca was the Vice President and Business Agent of Teamsters Local Union #398 in Rochester, New York. He resigned both of those positions in **October of 1990**, after the IRB, the Independent Review Board, filed a charge against him. The IRB was a governmental oversight agency designed to rid the Teamsters Union of Mafia influence. The charge against Misuraca read, "During the time you were an officer of Teamsters Local #398 in Rochester, New York, you knowingly associated with Angelo Amico, a member of organized crime."

A hearing on that charge was held on **November 20, 1990**, at which the Investigations Officer proved, by a fair preponderance of the evidence, the charge against Misuraca. While testifying at the hearing, Agent Ulmer, an FBI agent, had indicated that "Amico" was considered by the Federal Bureau of Investigation to be a highranking member of the Rochester Crime Family." Amico was also identified as a member of the faction of the Rochester Family of La Cosa Nostra, known as the "A Team."

That conclusion was corroborated by many sources. In 1987, Amico was listed by the Permanent Subcommittee on Investigations of the United States Senate as the "Acting Boss" of the Rochester Family of La Cosa Nostra. Amico was also named as a defendant and described as a leading member of a criminal racketeering "enterprise" in the Western District of New York in the case of United States v. Angelo Amico, et al.. CR-87-00177L. Agent Ulmer described the "enterprise" in that case as identical to the Rochester Family of La Cosa Nostra. Amico entered a guilty plea in that prosecution to two counts.

The entire case revolved around a conversation on March 4, 1986 between Angelo Amico and Angelo Misuraca. That conversation was recorded by the Rochester Police, and ultimately led to the charge of "knowingly associating with a member of organized crime" being filed, followed by Misuraca's resignation. (111)

# New York State Police Interview
# Teamsters Local #398 President Philip Koch

Phil Koch

On **December 20, 1990**, investigators of the United States Department of Labor and the New York State Police interviewed Local #398 President and Business Representative, Philip Koch, shortly before Koch died. Koch had been a Local #398 member since 1947. Koch advised the investigators that from at least 1967 organized crime had infiltrated Teamsters Local #398. Koch stated that during his administration there was a group of approximately 25 Local #398 members who had connections to organized crime. Koch related numerous examples during his presidency of organized crime members directing him to make certain Local appointments or to take particular action in Local #398 matters.

For example, in 1967 or 1968, Angelo Monachino, who later admitted his own organized crime membership, told Koch to "take it easy" on an employer trucking firm with which Koch was having difficult dealings. In December 1980, organized crime member John Fiorino told Koch that he was to appoint either Angelo Misuraca, Rochester LCN Family Underboss Richard Marino's brother-in-law, or Rochester LCN Member Joseph Rossi to assist Fiorino to monitor Teamster driven trucks. Koch appointed Misuraca.

In addition, according to Koch, in December 1983 Local #398's secretary was Richard Marino's daughter. When she left, Misuraca directed Koch to replace her with Donna Paone, the daughter of another Rochester mobster Donald Paone.

Phil Koch, the former President of Teamsters Local #398, since 1974 passed away on **August 9, 1991**. Phil was President of Local #398 for 17 years, he was also a Delegate to Joint Council #17.

## Local #398 Elects Mobster's Brother As New Secretary-Treasurer

In **January of 1991**, George Trieste was elected to Secretary-Treasurer of **Local #398**. The FBI considered George's brother Joseph to be a made member of the Rochester Mafia. (4) Organized crime member Anthony Oliveri testified in the Russotti trial, that Joseph Trieste worked in the crew of LCN captain Thomas Marotta.

Hit man Dominic Taddeo, another self-admitted Rochester LCN member, told the FBI in May 1990 that Trieste attended a January 1987 meeting Taddeo organized for certain made members of the Rochester LCN Family. Taddeo told the FBI that Rochester LCN Family, Boss Angelo Amico attended the meeting also. (113)

## Mobster's Sister-In-Law Becomes Local #398 Fund Manager

On the same day that her husband became the new Secretary-Treasurer of **Local #398**, in **January 1991**, Debbie Trieste became the Teamster Local's Fund Manager.

The fact that Debbie had no prior funds management experience whatsoever did not seem to be a factor in the appointment of this new job.(177) Debbie's brother-in-law was Rochester mobster Joseph Trieste.

## Local #398 Vice-President Is Permanently Barred From Teamsters

On **March 6, 1991**, Angelo Misuraca, Vice-President of Teamsters Local #398 in Rochester, New York, was found guilty by the Independent Administrator of the Independent Review Board (1), of knowingly associating with Rochester La Cosa Nostra Member, Angelo Amico. As a penalty, Misuraca was permanently barred from IBT membership. The Order was affirmed by Judge Edelstein and took effect on **July 16, 1991**. (178)

## President Of Local #398 John Trivigno Charged With "Knowingly Associating" With Members Of The Rochester La Cosa Nostra

On **March 12, 1991**, a Hearing of the Independent Administrator, from the Independent Review Board, was held and John Trivigno, President of **Local #398** was formally charged with "knowingly associating with known members of organized crime." John Fiorino, Dick Marino, Joseph Rossi, Joseph Trieste, Joseph LaDolce, Anthony Oliveri and Joseph Geniola were specifically listed as known Mafia members that Trivigno was accused of associating with.

During the hearing it was well established that John Trivigno had associated with at least seven known members of organized crime in Rochester for a period of over 20 years.

As a penalty, Travigno was permanently removed from office and barred from all membership in the IBT, effective immediately. Judge Edelstein affirmed that decision on **April 27, 1992**. **(179)**

## Angelo Misuraca, Vice-President of Teamsters Local #398 Found Guilty of Knowingly Associating With Rochester La Cosa Nostra Member Angelo Amico, Permanently Barred From Teamsters Union

At Misuraca's trial, The Hearing Examiner found Agent Grande qualified to offer opinion testimony regarding organized crime and its structure in the Rochester, New York area. He (Agent Grande) testified as to his interpretation of the conversation between Misuraca and Amico. Agent Grande established that the conversation took place in Amico's office behind a newly opened gambling establishment in Rochester. To enter that office you either had to be accompanied by Amico or directed to enter by him. Agent Grande further testified that there was a specific purpose to the meeting.

Agent Grande stated that the conversation eventually turned to Teamsters Local #398, and employment with that Local. He noted that Misuraca and Amico were discussing the state of affairs in the union and the "apparent disdain that other labor organizations within the Rochester community had for the Teamsters."

At one point during the intercepted conversation, Amico told Misuraca, "I don't care who it is, before ya get going, ya gotta check with me. Regardless who the job is for." At another point Amico told Misuraca, "You know, it gotta, it's gotta to the point where ya just can't assume that somebody's allright when he's going ta work. They have to check with us first, no matter who it is."

As for these segments, Agent Grande stated that Amico was instructing Misuraca how to assign, appoint and clear people for employment in Teamsters #Local 398. As Agent Grande put it, "In my opinion, it refered to Amico giving instructions to Misuraca that he's not to put anyone to work without Amico and Rochester's LCN in a larger picture."

At another point doing the conversation, where Amico told Misuraca, "I don't want anybody moved," Grande indicated that

Amico was again directing Misuraca how to handle internal IBT Local #398 matters. Agent Grande stated that Amico again was addressing Local #398 business when he told Misuraca, "No, they made a deal along with the company that's there; we let 'em stay."

At his deposition taken by the Investigations Officer, Misuraca testified that he read newspaper articles that Amico "ran the Rochester organized crime family." In the ordinary course, newspaper allegations would not impart knowledge of Amico's organized crime associations to a casual reader of the newspapers, but Misuraca had direct access to Amico, met with him in his gambling establishment, and took directions from him regarding union activities.

In the absence of direct evidence of knowledge of the organized crime ties of an associate . . . such knowledge may be inferred from the duration and quality of the association. In this case, Misuraca's admitted knowledge of the media publicity surrounding Amico, combined with the nature and circumstances surrounding their March 4, 1986, meeting, leads to the conclusion that Misuraca knew of Amico's mob connections when he met with him in 1986.

The Investigations Officer met his burden of proving this charge. Misuraca met with Amico in March of 1986, knowing Amico to be a leader of the La Cosa Nostra Rochester Family. While a single meeting of relatively short duration may, under other circumstances, require some mitigation of the penalty to be imposed, in this case no mitigation was warranted. The nature of this meeting concerned Teamsters Local #398, Misuraca's Local. Amico was giving orders to Misuraca concerning Local #398 and Misuraca posed no objection to accepting the orders. This conversation is all the more troubling when considered against the factual background that numerous individuals, identified as members and associates of the Rochester Family of La Cosa Nostra, have been members, shop stewards, business agents, or elected officers of that Local over the years.

Angelo Misuraca was found guilty as charged and he was permanently barred from holding membership in the International Brotherhood Of Teamsters on **July 16, 1991**. Misuraca was not found to have been a member of organized crime, but rather was found to have associated with a member of organized crime. (112)

# Angelo Misuraca, Vice-President of Teamsters Local #398 is Kicked out of Union Because of Mafia Ties for "Knowingly Associating With Angelo Amico"

Despite the fact that Angelo Misuraca resigned as Vice-President of Teamsters Local #398 in October of 1990, the administrator bounced Misuraca out of the Teamsters local completely and barred him from holding any further office in the International Brotherhood of Teamsters. That latest action underscored not only a local and national link between the Teamsters and organized crime, but the unprecedented effort by the federal government to break those ties. The Teamsters had been one of the nation's most controversial unions since its founding in 1903. The 1.54 million member organization, historically representing truck drivers and construction workers, had battled with the federal government for decades over charges of Mafia influence.

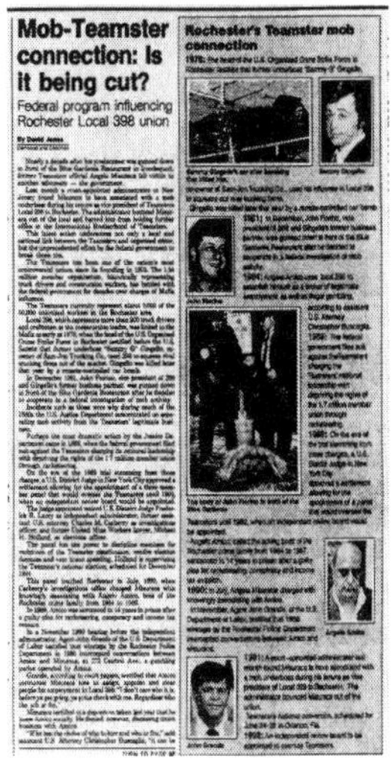

Mob-Teamster connection: Is it being cut?

Federal program influencing Rochester Local 398 union

Rochester's Teamster mob connection

**Rochester, New York Democrat and Chronicle Sunday April 21, 1991**

In the early nineties, the Rochester Teamsters represented about 5,000 of the 50,000 unionized workers in the Rochester area. Local #398, which represented more than 900 truck drivers and craftsmen in the construction trades, was linked to the Mafia in 1978, when the head of the U.S. Organized Crime Strike Force in Rochester testified before the U.S. Senate that former "Underboss" "Sammy G" Gingello, co-owner of Sam-Jon Trucking Co., used Local #398 to squeeze rival trucking firms out of the market. Gingello was killed later that year by a remote-controlled car bomb.

In December 1981, John Fiorino, Vice President of Teamsters Local #398 and Gingello's former business partner, was gunned down in front of the Blue Gardenia Restaurant after he decided to cooperate in a federal investigation of mob activity. Incidents such as those were why during much of the 1980s the

U.S. Justice Department concentrated on separating mob activity from the Teamsters' legitimate business. Perhaps the most dramatic action by the Justice Department came in 1988, when the Federal Government filed suit against the Teamsters charging its national leadership with depriving the rights of the 1.7 million-member union through racketeering.

On the eve of the 1989 trial stemming from those charges, a U.S. District Judge in New York City approved a settlement allowing for the appointment of a three-member panel that would oversee the Teamsters Union until 1992, when an independent review board would be appointed. The judge appointed retired U.S. District Judge Frederick B. Lacey as independent administrator; former assistant U.S. attorney Charles M. Carberry as investigations officer, and former United Mine Workers lawyer, Michael H. Holland, as elections officer. The panel had the power to discipline members for violations of the Teamster constitution, resolve election disputes and veto union spending. Holland was supervising the Teamster's national election, scheduled for December 1991.

That panel touched Rochester in July, 1990, when Carberry's investigations office charged Angelo Misuraca with knowingly associating with Angelo Amico, "Boss" of the Rochester Mafia Crime Family from 1984 to 1989. In 1989, Amico was sentenced to 14 years in prison after pleading guilty to racketeering, conspiracy and income tax evasion.

## Taddeo Admits He Sold Drugs

Reputed mobster Dominic Taddeo pleaded guilty on **December 6, 1991**, to both counts of a federal indictment charging him with selling illicit drugs. Taddeo, who was 33 at the time, was a former Greece resident. He was serving a 17-year sentence for illegal weapons possession and bail-jumping convictions. He was supposed to have faced trial the following week on the two drug-related charges. No sentencing date had been set by U.S. District Judge David G. Larimer.

The indictment accused Taddeo and six others of conspiring to distribute about 50 grams of cocaine. In addition, Taddeo alone was charged with selling the drug to five other people. Four of the co-defendants who were to go to trial with Taddeo pleaded guilty that week to federal drug distribution charges: Wayne Schwasman, 43, of 1393 Lehigh Station Road, Henrietta; Richard LeStrange, 41, formerly of 134 Goodburlet Road, Henrietta; Robert Cocilova, 34, of Rochester; and Richard R. Cocilova, 36, formerly of Hilton. The remaining two co-defendants, Samuel Joseph "Joe" Primerano and John Cocilova, signed plea agreements, said federal prosecutor Charles Pilato.

Tadeo still faced trial in Rochester, on a second, unrelated indictment for which he was scheduled to go to trial in March of 1992. That indictment accused Taddeo of planning five mob slayings in the early 1980s and carrying out three of them. Taddeo also was also accused of conspiring to operate illegal gambling establishments at several Rochester locations. Victims of the so-called ".45-caliber slayings" described in that indictment were: Nicholas Mastrodonato, shot to death May 25, 1982. Gerald Pelusio, shot Aug. 27, 1982. Dino Tortatice, killed Aug. 2, 1983. **(115)**

# Taddeo Pleads Guilty In Mob Hits
## Saturday, January 25, 1992

**Dominic Taddeo**

Nearly a decade after the last of the so-called .45-caliber slayings rocked the Rochester underworld, suspected hit man Dominic Taddeo finally appeared before a federal judge and said five significant words: Guilty. Guilty. Guilty. Guilty. Guilty. It was a surprise unannounced development in the long-standing case that was scheduled to go to trial in March of 1992. The 34 -year-old former Greece man admitted that he had plotted five mob killings and succeeded in carrying out three of them.

Taddeo pleaded guilty to both counts of a two-count indictment charging him with racketeering for the 1981 and 1982 slayings and for operating illegal gambling establishments in Rochester. He also pleaded guilty on three weapons counts.

Appearing before U.S. District Judge Michael A. Telesca, Taddeo said, "Yes" when asked if facts outlined by the prosecutor were true: 1) That, a crime organization known as La Cosa Nostra existed in Rochester in 1982. 2) That he was paid by the organization to kill certain people. 3) That he conducted surveillance of intended targets and executed several crimes.

Victims of the so-called "45-caliber slayings" described in that indictment were: Nicholas Mastrodonato, shot to death May 25, 1982. Gerald Pelusio, shot Aug. 27, 1982. Dino Tortatice, killed Aug. 2, 1981. Taddeo also was accused of shooting mob leader Thomas Marotta twice in 1981 in failed attempts to kill him and plotting to kill Thomas Taylor, another mob figure.

The shootings had taken place during a period that produced considerable violence among rival factions of the local mob. Rochester Police Department Investigator Paul Camping, part of a strike force set up to monitor organized crime activity in Monroe County, said, "I've been tracking this guy (Taddeo) since 1976." (116)

## Samuel J. (Red) Russotti, "Boss" of Rochester's La Cosa Nostra Dies

**ROCHESTER, June 29, 1992** Samuel J. (Red) Russotti, the reputed head of Rochester's Mafia Crime Family, who once listed his occupation as "huckster," died in Federal prison. He was 81 years old. Mr. Russotti was in the Federal Correctional Institution in Milan, Mich., where a prison spokesman said the cause of death was an apparent heart attack.

. Russotti had been in prison since 1984, when he and six others were convicted of murdering two rivals, three attempted murders and extortion of money from several gambling clubs. Their convictions marked the downfall of an organized-crime family that made hundreds of thousands of dollars annually from gambling, loan sharking and arson-for-hire schemes. He would have been eligible for parole in October 1994.

. In the Rochester Suburban Directory, Mr. Russotti listed his employment as "huckster." He once testified that he supported himself by gambling and borrowing from his mother. Federal and local officials said Mr. Russotti and Rene Piccarreto seized control of the Rochester mob in 1972. .

. Mr. Russotti was survived by his wife, a daughter, a son, six grandchildren, five great-grandchildren, a brother and two sisters.

**(117)**

# Teamsters Local # 398 Placed Into Trusteeship For Lifetime Affiliation With the Mafia

Local 398's Union Hall was located at 190 Dodge Street, Rochester, NY 14606. Today it is a church.

Based upon information provided in a **January 28, 1997** IRB Report recommending trusteeship, which detailed continued contacts between officers of the Local and organized crime members and associates, Teamsters Local #398, located in Rochester, New York, was finally placed under trusteeship, on **February 18, 1997**,

The IRB Report stated that then Local #398 President Corinne Lippa and Secretary-Treasurer Charles Ross had purposeful contacts with former Local #398 President and Business Agent John Trivigno after he was permanently barred from the IBT for knowingly associating with Rochester La Cosa Nostra members. **(119)**

President of **Local #398**, Corrine Lippa, feigning innocence, was quoted as saying, "I find all this difficult to comprehend." Although the article went on to say that Lippa testified in September of 1996 that Anthony Gingello was her boyfriend.

Local truckers union seized 2-21-97

Teamsters act after mob allegations arise

By KATHLEEN DRISCOLL
STAFF WRITER

TEAMSTERS, PAGE 5A

In charge Trustees Tony Valenti, left, and Howard Bennett leave Teamsters headquarters on Dodge Street yesterday.

**Democrat & Chronicle**
**February 21, 1997**

Anthony Gingello was the brother of Sam "Sammy G" Gingello, Rochester Mafia "Underboss," who was killed by a car bomb in 1978. Anthony was at one time an alleged member of Rochester's LCN himself, although he was never convicted of a major crime. **(194)**

Leader defends local's actions

Teamster officials suspend her, others

By SUSAN J. SMITH
STAFF WRITER

**Democrat & Chronicle**
**February 22, 1997**

## Joseph LoDolce Is Found Guilty of Being a Member Of Rochester's La Cosa Nostra He Is Permanently Barred From the Teamsters Union

The Independent Review Board, the government oversight committee of the Teamsters Union, held a hearing on **June 4, 1997**, and thereafter made a determination, on the charge filed against Joseph LoDolce. LoDolce was charged with being a member of organized crime while he was a member of Teamsters Local Union #398. After having reviewed the evidence and post-hearing submission, by the Chief Investigator, the IRB found that the charge against LoDolce was proved. As a penalty, LoDolce had been permanently barred from membership in the IBT and may not hereafter obtain employment, consulting or other work with the IBT or any IBT-affiliated entity.

Prior to the IRB hearing, in a sworn examination on October 28, 1996, LoDolce had testified that he became a member of the IBT in late 1979. Thereafter, LoDolce worked on construction projects in the Rochester, New York, area and occasionally, between the late 1970's and late 1980's, he was a Teamster shop steward on union construction projects.

On June 30, 1987, LoDolce was convicted of a federal racketeering conspiracy in United States v. Amico, CR. 87-177L-05, and was sentenced to seven years' imprisonment and a $15,000 fine. While LoDolce was in prison, Teamsters Local #398 placed him on withdrawal status. Upon his early release in January 1991, LoDolce returned to Rochester and Teamsters Local #398. Local #398 Business Agents and officers Corinne Lippa and Charles Ross then found work for LoDolce.

The FBI considered LoDolce to be a member of the Rochester LCN Family. Anthony Oliveri testified about LoDolce's organized crime membership and activities. In the Russotti and Amico trials Oliveri testified that he and LoDolce were involved in organized crime activities together and that they were inducted into the Rochester LCN Family on the same day in December 1978. LoDolce was a member of Rochester LCN "Captain" Thomas Marotta's "crew."

Oliveri attended at least two meetings of members of organized crime that LoDolce also attended. In September 1977,

**Joseph LoDolce**

Oliveri heard LoDolce and other members of the Rochester LCN Family explain that they had assaulted three men, with LoDolce putting a gun in the mouth of a man named Vaccaro. At another meeting in late 1977 or early 1978, Oliveri saw LoDolce at a meeting at the Centurion Restaurant on Goodman Street in Rochester. That meeting was called by Rochester LCN member Gingello so that he could determine which organized crime members were on his side in an internal power struggle between Rochester LCN members.

Oliveri also testified that in June 1978 he, LoDolce and others, in separate cars, had trailed a woman named Karen Cleveland to the Exit 45 Motel in Victor, New York. She was Rochester LCN member Thomas Didio's girlfriend. One week later Didio was murdered at that motel. LoDolce's organized crime membership was also suggested by other facts. LoDolce's conviction in the Amico trial was for his part in a criminal enterprise. LoDolce's conduct in "Amico" involved his running gambling operations and extorting gambling operations for the Rochester LCN Family. In the absence of evidence to the contrary, it was assumed that LaDolce continued to be an LCN member.

The undisputed evidence established the charge that Joseph LoDolce brought reproach upon the IBT and violated the IBT Constitution through his organized crime membership. Accordingly, LoDolce was permanently barred from holding membership in or any position with the IBT, or any IBT-affiliated entity, in the future. LoDolce also could not thereafter obtain employment, consulting or other work with the IBT or any IBT-affiliated entity. (118)

On **September 30, 1997**, Judge David Edelstein issued an order granting the Teamsters' Independent Review Board's request to impose sanctions on Teamsters Local #398 member, and member of the Rochester Mafia, Joseph LoDolce. After several hearings, LoDolce was found to have brought reproach upon the Teamsters Union due to his membership in the Rochester's La Cosa Nostra. The FBI considered LoDolce to be a "made" member of organized crime in Rochester and testified accordingly at his hearing.

# Teamsters Joint Council #17 Investigated and Placed in Trusteeship

## Teamster council here investigated

▪ International union takes control while allegations of fund misuse are checked.

BY STAFF WRITER
**MARK REILLY**

A local Teamsters coordinating body has been taken over by International Teamsters officials, over allegations that the group used thousands of dollars from a union fund for unauthorized payments and personal items.

Joint Council 17, a group that combines members of Teamsters Locals 398, 118 and 791, was placed into trusteeship by an order of General President Ron Carey, who leads the International Teamsters organization.

In February, Local 398 was seized by international leadership after a federal panel reported links between the local group and organized crime.

The order puts the council under new control while the allegations are investigated. Three officers and two trustees of the Joint Council were suspended.

The order springs from a recommendation by a court-appointed independent review board, which was named earlier this month to investigate the Joint Council.

The council is intended to serve as a political force for Teamsters locals and to organize functions for members, according to Nancy Stella, a Teamsters representative. According to the review board's report, that was never done.

The independent review board said the council used 60 cents out of every dollar it received from union dues to pay for unauthorized severance payments to departing union officials and staff. Other funds were used for social events for union officials, the IRB said.

From 1989 to 1995, the council disbursed $198,765, the IRB report alleged that nearly 87 percent of that went to the sole benefit of union officers and representatives of the council.

According to the IRB, one retiree — now deceased — received $55,000 from the severance fund in 1994. Another union member, expelled because of ties to organized crime, received $5,000 from the severance fund in 1990, the review board said.

In the report, the IRB

TEAMSTERS, PAGE 4B

**Teamster coverage**

**Local 118:** Represents about 2,000 members including workers at Wegmans Food Markets, United Parcel Service and other freight carriers.

**Local 398:** Represents 500 workers, including members at the American Red Cross and ADT Security Systems.

**Local 791:** Represents about 1,200 members, including workers at Genesee Brewing Co. and Upstate Dairy in Rochester and Kraft Foods in Avon, Livingston County.

**Democrat and Chronicle**
**June 20, 1997**

Teamsters Joint Council #17, which represents all Teamsters in the greater Rochester area was placed under trusteeship by the Teamsters International Union while an investigation into alleged abuses was conducted.

The Joint Council was eventually dissolved and Rochester was absorbed into Joint Council #46 located in Buffalo, New York.

# Charles Ross, Secretary Treasurer of Local #398 and David Valerio, Local #398 Union Steward are Barred from IBT for Knowingly Associating With Barred Former President John Travigno

On **February 3, 1997**, a hearing was held on the charges against Charles Ross, Secretary Treasurer of Local #398 and David Valerio, Local #398 Union Steward. They were both found guilty on **July 7, 1997** of bringing reproach upon the IBT for knowingly associating with banned former President of **Local #398**, John Travigno.

The Hearing Panel recommended that they both be barred for life from holding a Union Officer's position and a three-year suspension from membership for Ross and a five-year suspension from membership for Valerio. The General President of The IBT, Ron Carey, modified the Hearing Panels recommendation by changing the Membership bans to lifetime ban for Valerio and a seven-year ban for Ross.

David Valerio, John Travigno and Joseph Trieste had been lifelong friends since elementary school. Valerio had testified that he and Travigno had hunted together several times even after Travigno's ban from the IBT. Valerio was also invited to attend a Baptism celebration for Travigno's child. Valerio also knowingly associated with known LCN member John Trieste. Valerio stated that he did not know that he was not allowed to "hang out" with Trieste just because he was a Mafia member. Furthermore Valerio expressed no remorse for his actions and indicated that he planned to continue to associate with Travigno and Trieste, hence the modification of his penalty to a lifetime ban on membership as well as his lifetime ban on Union Office.

Charles Ross knew that John Travigno had been removed from the office of President of Local #398 and freely admitted to the IRB that he maintained a regular and continuous social relationship with Travigno, but he claimed that he did not know that he (Travigno) was banned from membership as well. Ross testified that he felt that he was still required to represent Travigno whether he was a member of the Union or not. Ross expressed remorse for his actions and indicated that he would not have associated with Travigno had he known he was not supposed to, and that he would not associate with Travigno in the future. Also Ross had two witnesses testify to his good moral character and submitted letters of reference from employers for whom he had worked. Therefore his penalty was somewhat less severe than that of Valerio's.

# *Chapter 11*
# Lifetime Affiliation with the Mafia

In 1997, Teamsters Local #398 was one of just three Teamster Locals left in the city of Rochester, New York. At one time, there had been ten. Lifetime affiliation with the Mafia was the stated reason for dissolving the local. For some people, that penalty seemed unduly harsh. "Lifetime affiliation with the Mafia;" was that really a fair assessment of an entire Teamsters Local that had been in business for six decades?

Sure, at the time, Corrine Lippa, President of Local #398, was by her own admission dating Tony Gingello, an "alleged" member of the Rochester Mafia. Tony Gingello's brother was Sammy Gingello, the Rochester Mafia "Underboss" who was blown up in his car in April of 1978. **(120)**

Sure, Lippa and Charles Ross, Local #398 Secretary-Treasurer, had found work for Joseph LoDolce, Rochester Mafia Soldier, after his release from prison. LoDolce was kicked out of the Teamsters Union himself on September 30, 1997 because he was a known member of the Rochester Mafia. Even the FBI considered LoDolce to be a known member of the Rochester LCN Family. **(123)**

OK, the former President of Local #398 was John Travigno. Travigno was removed from office five years prior, on April 27, 1992 for knowingly associating with seven Mafia members for a period of more than 20 years. Travigno was a known Rochester Mafia member himself, but it was not necessary to prove that in order to kick him out of the union. **(121)** He was removed from office by the IRB, The Independent Review Board, a governmental oversight agency of the Teamsters Union, which was designed specifically, to keep the Mafia out of the Teamsters Union. John Travigno was not even the first officer to be removed from Local #398 by the IRB.

Prior to Travigno's removal, Angelo Misuraca , the Vice-President of Local #398 was also removed from office on July 16, 1991 for associating with known mob member Angelo Amico. Misuraca was also the brother–in-law of Richard Marino, Rochester Mafia "Underboss." Angelo Amico was listed in the United States Subcommittee on Investigations as the "Acting Boss" of the Rochester Mafia in 1991 since all the former leaders were already imprisoned. (122)

Between 1989 and 1997, the IRB removed at least six members of Teamsters Local #398 from the union for Mafia related offences, not counting Corrine Lippa and her Executive Board. Three other members of the Local, David Valerio, Robert Triano and Secretary-Treasurer, Charles Ross, were also barred from union membership for associating with known mafia members or other "barred" persons.

Prior to the inception of the Independent Review Board, there was no effective way to rid the Teamsters Union of Mafia influence. Teamsters Local #398 Secretary-Treasurer, Charles Ross admitted in 1994, that in or about 1985 he flew twice to Leavenworth Kansas to visit Anthony Michael Columbo in federal prison there. Columbo was serving a 40 year sentence for racketeering and conspiracy for his part in the murders and other crimes committed by the Rochester Crime Family. (124) John Fiorino, while Business Agent and Vice-President of Local #398, had once visited Dick Marino in prison.

Richard Marino, Rochester Mafia "Underboss" controlled Teamsters Local #398 as Business Agent and Trustee, from 1972 to December of 1984 when he was incarcerated for the Massaro murder. He was assisted in that role by Rochester Mafia "Capo" John Fiorino, until Fiorino's untimely shotgun death on December 19, 1981. Marino and Fiorino had replaced Mafia Soldiers Sam Campanella and James Canarozza as the unions' mob controllers.

Sam Campanella and James Canarozza both quit their Teamsters Local #398 union positions and were forced out of town in 1978 by the "A Team" leaders of the Rochester Mafia at the height of the Rochester Mob Wars. They had both mistakenly pledged allegiance to Thomas Didio, the insurgent "B Team" mafia leader who was murdered.

Sam Campanella had long been the major connection between Rochester's Organized Crime Family and Teamsters Local #398 for almost two decades, ever since 1959 when he was involved in a conspiracy to remove the existing Vice-President of Local #398. Campanella then, coincidentally, acceded to that very position himself and kept that position until he too was removed, that time by his own Mafia bosses.

## Organized Crime Takes Control of Teamsters Local #398

Democrat Chronicle

D&C BARES LABOR RACKETS; CRIME PROBERS HERE TODAY

Castro Forces Smash Invasion, Reports Claim

Mob Delegates, Teamsters Tied To Shakedowns

Rebel Teamsters Keep Fighting In Spite of Threats, 'Accidents'

**Rochester, N.Y.**
**Democrat and Chronicle**
**August 10, 1959**

The New York State Crime Commission came to Rochester, New York on **August 10, 1959**, holding private hearings, listening to allegations of extortion, labor racketeering and violence in Rochester's construction industry.

Information leading to the hearings was gathered during an intensive five-month investigation by The Democrat and Chronicle, the Crime Commission, State Police, the Federal Bureau of Investigation, city police and other agencies. Affidavits and testimony that were introduced at the closed hearings linked the rackets with Local #398 of the International Brotherhood of Teamsters.

Also disclosed in the testimony were the names of several delegates to the notorious Apalachin Mafia "convention" of November 14, 1957. Investigators for the Crime Commission had been in Rochester several times since the widespread inquiry had gotten under way, most recently to serve subpoenas commanding the appearance of witnesses at the private hearings.

The Crime Commission (formally designated as the State Commission of Investigation) decided to investigate conditions in Rochester after receiving a detailed report of alleged extortion and racketeering in the city. Based on affidavits and summaries of interviews supplied by the Democrat and Chronicle newspaper, the report listed alleged instances of shake down attempts on construction contractors and sub-contractors. It also claimed a connection between officials of Teamsters Local #398 and “a firm” which purportedly offered "labor peace" to construction companies in return for payment of $1 per truck per day. The

Commission also looked into charges that failure to accede to "the firm's" demand was the cause of damage inflicted on a local firm's trucks at a cost of $25,000. Among those due to be questioned were officials of "the firm."

Teamsters Local #398 officers were accused of financial misconduct and running the union for their own benefit, at the Teamster Local's December 1958 general membership meeting, by Gasper Alongi, former Vice-President of that local. **(125)**

**Rebel Teamsters Keep Fighting In Spite of Threats, 'Accidents'**

By JACK WILLIAMS

**How It All Started**

A SIX-PART series on the inside operations of Rochester's Teamsters Local 398 starts in tomorrow's Democrat and Chronicle. Written by reporter Jack Williams, it will give a blow-by-blow account of the "power vacuum" which led to the local's present difficulties, the battle for justice which raged to the desk of James R. Hoffa, and the absence of union constitutional safeguards which led to a behind-the-scenes union despotism. Watch for it in tomorrow's . . .

Democrat and Chronicle

**Democrat and Chronicle**
**Rochester, N.Y.**
**August 10, 1959**

When the State Crime Commission opened its hearings, it heard a variety of charges involving Teamsters Local #398 and its dealings with the Rochester construction industry. But in the periphery of the hearing was another story, the story of a two-year battle by a small group of Teamsters to rid their local of what they felt were corruption and fiscal irresponsibility. That story had involved threatening telephone calls in the night, undercover purchases of guns and ammunition for self-protection, alleged threats at pistol-point, and "accidents" suffered by men who opposed the union's leadership.

For several of the group, the battle had meant a cut in pay. The union leadership had given jobs to its friends and kept them from its foes, they charged, regardless of seniority protections or willingness to work.

In the article "Rebel Teamsters Keep Fighting In Spite of Threats, "Accidents," Gasper Alongi described to the Crime Commission how he was retaliated against for speaking out at the December 1958 union meeting. Alongi was kicked out of Teamsters Local #398 that year after a "sham trial" conducted by the union's current officers.

Formal charges were preferred against him by Samuel C. Campanella, who was allegedly a Teamster Local #398 member in good standing. Ironically, or perhaps not, Campanella would eventually accede to the position of Vice-President of Local #398 himself.

Actually Campanella was not even present at a secret meeting on Clifford Avenue were the charges were drawn up. Campanella merely just signed the charges. Attending that meeting were Teamsters Local #398 Business Agents John Savea and Joseph Catalano, President of Local #398 Nardo Buscemi and John "Johnny Treetop" Imburgia.

Samuel C. Campanella was a Rochester Cosa Nostra "Soldier" who was muscling his way in to the union hierarchy. He had only been a Local #398 member for about a month. The previous month, December of 1958, Campanella was still a cab driver, one of several questioned in a slaying at the Ivanhoe Hotel in Brighton. He became a Teamsters Local #398 member sometime after that December 23 incident. Campanella was also out on bail on unrelated charges that he and another man beat and robbed Richard J. Polizzi of Canandaigua.

# Threats, 'Accidents' Fail To Halt Teamster Rebels

(Copyright, 1959, by Rochester Democrat and Chronicle, Gannett Co., Inc.)

By JACK WILLIAMS

When the State Crime Commission opens its hearings here today, it will hear a variety of charges involving Teamsters Local 398 and its dealings with the Rochester construction industry.

But in the periphery of the hearing will be another story — the story of a two-year battle by a small group of Teamsters to rid their local of what they feel are corruption and fiscal irresponsibility.

That story has involved threatening telephone calls in the night, undercover purchases of guns and ammunition for self-protection, alleged threats at pistol-point, and "accidents" suffered by men who opposed the union's leadership.

For several of the group, the battle has meant a cut in pay. The union leadership has given jobs to its friends and kept them from its foes, they charge, regardless of seniority protections and willingness to work.

**Lost Membership**

For one, continued criticism of union leadership meant loss of membership in the local — and the start of a fight to regain it which raged from the Rochester Teamsters Joint Council to James Riddle Hoffa and finally to the court-appointed Teamsters Board of Monitors.

Gaspar J. Alongi, 46, of 14 Varian Lane, Gates, a former vice president of Local 298, was notified last January that he would be tried by the local's executive committee on a rag tag series of charges, one of which was "activities which tend to bring the local or the international into disrepute."

The notification followed hard on the heels of the Teamster local's December general membership meeting. During that meeting, Alongi accused the local's leaders of fiscal irresponsibility and conduct of union affairs for their own benefit.

The charges against Alongi were preferred by Samuel C. ("Sam Camp") Campanella, 26, of 36 Lorimer St., who was, as he said, a member in good standing of Local 398.

But Campanella hadn't been a Local 398 member for long. As recently as December, he had been one of the taxicab drivers involved in an ill-fated trip to the Ivanhoe Motel, Brighton, with Jeanne Wilson.

Miss Wilson, a self-admitted prostitute, was sentenced in June to 7½ to 15 years in connection with the bludgeon murder of George Fisher, a North Syracuse salesman.

Campanella testified during the trial of Joseph Sobb Jr. for first degree murder that he had not actually accompanied the other cabbies and Miss Wilson to the murder scene.

But he said that at that time, he was a driver for the Hamilton Cab Co. After Dec. 23, the date of the assault on Mr.

Continued on Page 9

**How It All Started**

**A SIX-PART series on the inside operations of Rochester's Teamsters Local 398 starts in tomorrow's Democrat and Chronicle. Written by reporter Jack Williams, it will give a blow-by-blow account of the "power vacuum" which led to the local's present difficulties, the battle for justice which raged to the desk of James R. Hoffa, and the absence of union constitutional safeguards which led to a behind-the-scenes union despotism. Watch for it in tomorrow's . . .**

Democrat and Chronicle

SAMUEL CAMPANELLA

**Rochester Mafia "Soldier" Sam Campanella "muscled" his way into the Teamsters union leadership beginning in 1959.**

The New York State Crime Commission Hearings held in Rochester, New York were rather extensive. Nine witnesses were called to testify. The outcome of the proceedings were undetermined. But an aide to Robert F. Kennedy, brother of President JFK, counsel to the Rackets Committee, said in New York City that his office would watch "with great interest" the proceedings of the commission in regard to Rochester. (126)

# FBI Investigates Teamsters In Rochester, New York

The New York State Crime Commission was not the only investigative body that had an interest in the ties between organized crime and organized labor, there was also the FBI. The results of an investigation of Teamsters Local #398 by the Federal

Bureau of Investigation were turned over to U.S. Attorney John O. Henderson of Buffalo. He declined to elaborate. Henderson stated at the time that he had received information on the Rochester study, but that he had not finished evaluating it.

The FBI investigation was carried on separately from the one which was pursued by the State Crime Commission Hearings. The Commission, acting on information supplied by The Democrat and Chronicle as long ago as April 1959, conducted its own private hearings in Rochester.

Among the allegations considered by the commission were those of labor racketeering and abuses in Teamsters Local #398. When reports of shakedown attempts on trucking firms allied with construction industry were first obtained by this newspaper, they were transmitted to Crime Commission investigators. Nine witnesses eventually testified that day. (127)

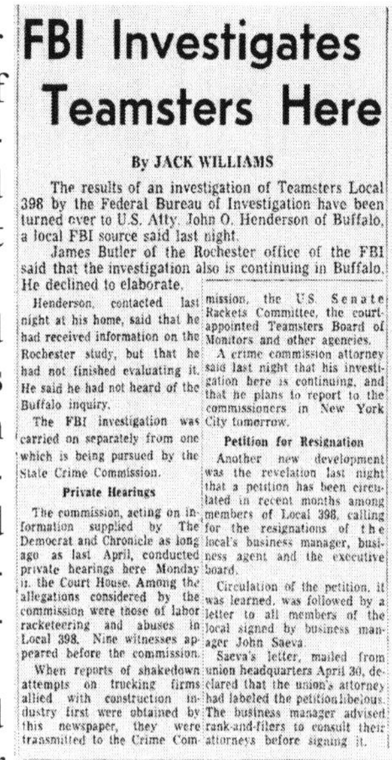

FBI Investigates Teamsters Here

By JACK WILLIAMS

The results of an investigation of Teamsters Local 398 by the Federal Bureau of Investigation have been turned over to U.S. Atty. John O. Henderson of Buffalo, a local FBI source said last night.

James Butler of the Rochester office of the FBI said that the investigation also is continuing in Buffalo. He declined to elaborate.

Henderson, contacted last night at his home, said that he had received information on the Rochester study, but that he had not finished evaluating it. He said he had not heard of the Buffalo inquiry.

The FBI investigation was carried on separately from one which is being pursued by the State Crime Commission.

Private Hearings

The commission, acting on information supplied by The Democrat and Chronicle as long ago as last April, conducted private hearings here Monday in the Court House. Among the allegations considered by the commission were those of labor racketeering and abuses in Local 398. Nine witnesses appeared before the commission.

When reports of shakedown attempts on trucking firms allied with construction industry first were obtained by this newspaper, they were transmitted to the Crime Commission, the U.S. Senate Rackets Committee, the court-appointed Teamsters Board of Monitors and other agencies.

A crime commission attorney said last night that his investigation here is continuing, and that he plans to report to the commissioners in New York City tomorrow.

Petition for Resignation

Another new development was the revelation last night that a petition has been circulated in recent months among members of Local 398, calling for the resignations of the local's business manager, business agent and the executive board.

Circulation of the petition, it was learned, was followed by a letter to all members of the local signed by business manager John Saeva.

Saeva's letter, mailed from union headquarters April 30, declared that the union's attorney had labeled the petition libelous. The business manager advised rank-and-filers to consult their attorneys before signing it.

**Rochester, NY Democrat and Chronicle August 13, 1959**

## Nardo Buscemi

**Nardo Buscemi 3-25-48**

In 1948, Nardo Buscemi was a taxi cab driver. Cab drivers in Rochester, N.Y. were Teamsters and at one time they had their own local, Teamsters Local #933. Buscemi's picture (on the left) was featured in the Democrat and Chronicle that year at Easter time because of his taxi drivers hat, in an article titled "Some Hats Change for Easter-Some Don't." (128)

Unfortunately for Nardo, that was not the only time that he made the newspaper that year. On May 17, 1948, Buscemi was arrested along with four other men in a gambling raid. One of those other men was Rene J. Piccarreto, who was 23 years old at the time. Piccarreto would later become the Rochester Mafia's "Consigliore" or "Counselor" and remain a leader of the Rochester Mafia for nearly two decades until his incarceration for murder and conspiracy in December of 1984. Also arrested with Buscemi that day were Louis J. "Treetop" Imburgia and his brother John J. Imburgia. (129)

Louis J. "Treetop" Imburgia would be together again with Nardo Buscemi, 10 years later, at a secret meeting with other Teamster Local #398 officials. At that meeting they conspired to remove the Vice-President of the Local, Gaspar Alongi, by having Rochester Mafia Soldier, Sam Campanella file internal union charges against Alongi.

Alongi's removal from office then opened the "door of opportunity" to Campanella, who eventually acceded to the position of Teamsters Local #398 Vice-President himself, and thereby solidified the ties between organized crime and organized labor. It would not be in the next election, but soon after.

PAGE THIRTEEN

## 5 ARRESTED IN NUMBERS GAME RAID

**1,000 Play Slips, $250 Seized By Police**

Top police officials took a hand in cracking down on local "numbers" lottery operations yesterday afternoon when they raided a room at 484 Ormond St. and arrested five men.

The raiders were Chief Henry T. Copenhagen and Inspector Charles Roth, who reported seizure of upwards of $250 in cash and about 1,000 play slips on a lottery involving the totals of New York Stock, Bond and Curb Market transactions.

Booked as a common gambler for allegedly maintaining a room for the operation of a lottery was Louis J. (Treetop) Imburgia, 33, of 316 Culver Pkwy., Irondequoit, who was released after posting $1,000 cash bail at the Franklin Street Station.

The other men, charged as inmates of a gambling room, were released in $25 bail each. They were identified as Imburgia's brother, John J. Imburgia, 31, of 2033 Clifford Ave.; Anthony T. Polvino, 62, of 37 Niagara St.; Rene J. Piccarreto, 23, of 134 Masseth St., and Nardo Buscemi, 27, of 260 Garson Ave.

Chief Copenhagen described the alleged lottery operation as a "family affair" and added that the raid was the routine followup of a complaint.

**5-18-48**
**Democrat and Chronicle**

## Teamsters Local #398 President Nardo Buscemi Indicted for Taking Employer Payoffs

MORNING, OCT. 5, 1963 — 10 CENTS

## Local Teamsters Chief Indicted on Accepting Payoffs from Employers

By ARTHUR DEUTSCH

The federal grand jury yesterday indicted Nardo Buscemi, president and business representative of Teamsters Local 398 of Rochester, on 17 counts of accepting illegal payments from employers.

Buscemi, 42, of 203 Alfonso Drive, Greece, was scheduled to be arraigned here Monday, Oct. 14, before Chief Judge Harold P. Burke of U.S. District Court, according to the U.S. district attorney's office here.

The indictment accuses the Teamsters president, who also is known as Leonardo Buscemi, of illegally receiving payments from two employers who held subcontracts on projects of the Monroe County Sewer Agency.

He is accused of taking the money for accepting into Local 398 membership the employes of the subcontractors.

If Buscemi is convicted, he faces a fine of up to $10,000, a year in prison or both.

One of the employers is expected to testify that he was warned by Buscemi that failure to make the payments would result in his job being shut down.

Seven of the counts accuse Buscemi of receiving a total of $1,000 in illegal payments between July 7 and Nov. 17, 1961, from Harold E. Tripp, Pontiac, Mich. Donald W. Russell, director of the Sewer Agency, identified Tripp as a subcontractor on sewer laterals for his brother, George Tripp, head of George Tripp, Inc., of Pontiac, the prime contractor.

The remaining counts allege Buscemi received payments totaling $180 between May 6 and Nov. 14, 1960, from Chester A. Dean, of 4 Talanne Road, Henrietta, a masonry contractor, and $350 between Oct. 13 and Dec. 4, 1961, from Dekel Contracting, Inc., a corporation headed by Dean.

The sewer agency awarded George Tripp, Inc., a $640,572 contract in October 1959 to construct 9½ miles of sewers and a $3 million-plus contract in November 1960 to construct more than 46 miles of sewers in the Gates-Chili-Ogden Sewer District.

The largest payments allegedly made to Buscemi were in the amount of $200, received Oct. 13 and Nov. 17, 1961, from Tripp.

The indictment specifies these instances of payments to Buscemi:

By Tripp — July 7, 1961, $80; July 14, $120; Aug. 11, $160; Sept. 1, $120; Sept. 22, $120; Oct. 13, $200; Nov. 17, $200, total, $1,000.

By Dean — May 6, 1960, $20; May 24, $40; June 18, $20; July 31, $20; Sept. 12, $40; Nov. 14, $40; total, $180.

By Dekel Contracting, Inc. — Oct. 13, 1961, $50; Oct. 17, $150; Nov. 7, $100; Dec. 4, $50; total, $350.

Continued on Page 17

**Democrat and Chronicle**
**October 5, 1963**

In **December of 1960** Nardo Buscemi was elected to President of Teamsters Local #398 in a bitterly contested election.(131)

Less than three years later, on **October 4, 1963** Buscemi was indicted for shaking down employers and accepting payoffs for labor peace.

One employer testified that he was warned by Buscemi that "failure to make the payments would result in his job being shut down." (130)

# Thousands in N.Y. Mobs, Valachi Tells Inquiry
# The Valenti Brothers are Named As "Soldiers"

**Joseph Valachi testifying before the Permanent Subcommittee on Investigations.**

Four days after Nardo Buscemi was indicted for accepting bribes, Joseph Valachi testified before the Permanent Subcommittee on Investigations. Valachi was a "Soldier in the New York City Genovese Crime Family from the early 1930's until his arrest for narcotics trafficking in 1959. Some time after his incarceration he became a government informant.

On **October 8, 1963**, Valachi testified that the Mafia not only existed, but it had thousands of members. Valachi was considered to be the first Mafia informant to reveal in detail the inner workings of the National Mafia.

In the hierarchy of the national Cosa Nostra, the Valenti brothers were named as 'Soldiers.' But they were also identified as being the representatives from Rochester, NY at the Appalachian Mafia Summit in 1957.

Thousands in N.Y. Mobs, Valachi Tells Inquiry

Talk of Guns, Violence

TIGHT GUARD—Mobster Joseph Valachi has John McShane, U.S. chief marshal, at his side during his hearing before the investigations group. (AP)

In Costa Nostra

Valentes Named as 'Soldiers'

Toy Soldiers Guard Their Flower Beds

JANITOR INJURED

**Democrat and Chronicle October 9, 1963**

Valachi told of 14 years as an underworld loan shark. He said he won a reputation as "the best Shylock around." And he testified labor racketeers kept unions out of a dress shop in which he held an interest. There were 356 names on the charts of Cosa Nostra's five "families" in New York, and almost every entry was marked with an asterisk meaning the man was identified by him.

"The ones there's a star on, are the ones I know," Valachi told the Senate Investigations Subcommittee.

Valachi testified, as he had previously, that he was "very close with Magad-deen (Stefano Magaddino) in Buffalo." He identified Magaddino as the leader of the Buffalo "Cosa Nostra" and said that "Buffalo and Canada were all one" in the apparently sprawling underworld organization. And yet, according to Valachi's testimony, it appeared that the Valentis of Rochester were related to the Bonanno family of Brooklyn, notwithstanding the proximity of Rochester to the Buffalo organization.

Valachi's testimony had given police their first in-depth view of the New York underworld, with the men at the bottom named as well as those at the top. It was an intelligence asset that police had never had previously. And he added it helps arouse the public in the fight against organized crime by pointing to the links between bookmaking and narcotics peddling, between burglary and gangland slayings. **(132)**

## Rochester Police Doubt Mafia Link

Joseph Valachi's testimony revealed that there were between 100 and 125 "Cosa Nostra" Members operating in the general Buffalo, New York area in 1963.

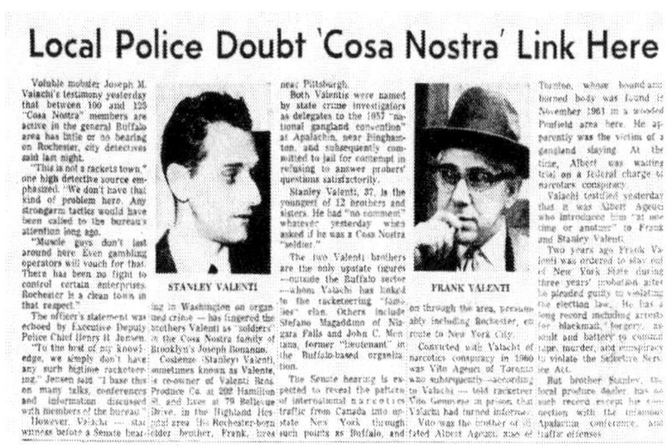

Local Police Doubt 'Cosa Nostra' Link Here

Voluble mobster Joseph M. Valachi's testimony yesterday that between 100 and 125 "Cosa Nostra" members are active in the general Buffalo area has little or no bearing on Rochester, city detectives said last night.

"This is not a rackets town," one high detective source emphasized. "We don't have that kind of problem here. Any strongarm tactics would have been called to the bureau's attention long ago.

"Muscle guys don't last around here. Even gambling operators will vouch for that. There has been no fight to control certain enterprises. Rochester is a clean town in that respect."

The officer's statement was echoed by Executive Deputy Police Chief Henry H. Jensen.

"To the best of my knowledge, we simply don't have any such bigtime racketeering," Jensen said. "I base this on many talks, conferences and information discussed with members of the bureau."

However, Valachi — star witness before a Senate hearing in Washington on organized crime — has fingered the brothers Valenti as "soldiers" in the Cosa Nostra family of Brooklyn's Joseph Bonanno.

Costenze (Stanley) Valenti, sometimes known as Valente, is co-owner of Valenti Bros. Produce Co. at 202 Hamilton St. and lives at 79 Bellevue Drive, in the Highland Hospital area. His Rochester-born elder brother, Frank, lives near Pittsburgh.

Both Valentis were named by state crime investigators as delegates to the 1957 "national gangland convention" at Apalachin, near Binghamton, and subsequently committed to jail for contempt in refusing to answer probers' questions satisfactorily.

Stanley Valenti, 37, is the youngest of 12 brothers and sisters. He had "no comment" whatever yesterday when asked if he was a Cosa Nostra "soldier."

The two Valenti brothers are the only upstate figures —outside the Buffalo sector —whom Valachi has linked to the racketeering "families" clan. Others include Stefano Magaddino of Niagara Falls and John C. Montana, former "lieutenant" in the Buffalo-based organization.

The Senate hearing is expected to reveal the pattern of international narcotics traffic from Canada into upstate New York through such points as Buffalo, and on through the area, presumably including Rochester, en route to New York City.

Convicted with Valachi of narcotics conspiracy in 1960 was Vito Agueci of Toronto who subsequently—according to Valachi — told racketeer Vito Genovese in prison that Valachi had turned informer.

Vito was the brother of ill-fated Albert Agueci, also of Toronto, whose bound and burned body was found in November 1961 in a wooded Penfield area here. He apparently was the victim of a gangland slaying. At the time, Albert was awaiting trial on a federal charge of narcotics conspiracy.

Valachi testified yesterday that it was Albert Agueci who introduced him "at one time or another" to Frank and Stanley Valenti.

Two years ago Frank Valenti was ordered to stay out of New York State during three years' probation after he pleaded guilty to violating the election law. He has a long record including arrests for blackmail, forgery, assault and battery to commit rape, murder, and conspiracy to violate the Selective Service Act.

But brother Stanley, the local produce dealer, has no such record except his connection with the infamous Apalachin conference, and traffic offenses.

STANLEY VALENTI

FRANK VALENTI

**October 10, 1963 Democrat and Chroni-**

Despite that newly discovered fact, Rochester Police were rather reluctant to believe it. "That fact has little or no bearing on Rochester" claimed Rochester detectives. "This is not a rackets town," one high detective source emphasized. We don't have that kind of problem here. "Any strongarm tactics would have been brought to the attention of the bureau long ago." The officer's statements were echoed by Executive Deputy Police Chief Henry H. Jensen. "To the best of my knowledge, we simply don't have any such big time racketeering. **(133)**

Statements like those would perhaps foreshadow how woefully unprepared Rochester Police were for the infiltration of organized crime into their city in the very near future.

# Jake Russo Missing, Assumed Murdered The Valenti's Regain Control of the Rochester Mafia

ROCHESTER, N. Y., MONDAY MORNING, DEC. 14, 1964 — 10 CENTS

## Where Is 'Jake' Russo? Valenti's Enforcer Missing

Where is "Jake" Russo?

A top lieutenant and enforcer in local gambling operations during the three-year "exile" of Frank Valenti, Russo has not been seen in Rochester in the past three months.

Several mysterious circumstances have surrounded his disappearance:

—He didn't appear at a "dinner date" with Valenti on a Sunday night last September. The two were to have had dinner at the Italian Village Restaurant in Main Street East.

—Within two weeks, a car bearing license plates issued to Russo was found in Galusha Street on the north side of the city.

—Russo's wife has returned to work as a nurse's aide in a local hospital.

Police refused to speculate on Russo's disappearance. Although he had faced minor (inmate) gambling counts in his early life, Russo has had no local police record in the last 15 years.

Near the top in Rochester gambling in the last decade, Russo, in his early 50s, was left in charge when Valenti was ordered out of the state in 1961 for violation of state election laws.

His designated duties also extended to the role of "peacemaker" among gamblers. He was supposed to care for difficulties arising over betting disagreements and violations of "territory" rights.

Russo wasn't a well man, had a heart condition.

Syndicate affairs were not prospering when Valenti returned to the city three months ago.

Interlopers were trying to crack the organization.

Al Mancuso, within a month after he had beaten a murder "rap" in the killing of Benjamin Oken in an Oak Street office hold-up, attempted to declare himself "in" for part of the racket collection.

When Mancuso and two partners were convicted of

*Continued on Page 13A*

**Rochester, New York Democrat and Chronicle**
**December 14, 1964**

In **September 1964**, mobsters Frank Valenti and Angelo Vaccaro returned to Rochester, N.Y., after a forced three year exile. They soon joined forces with Stanley Valenti. While he was gone, Frank Valenti, Rochester's Mafia "Boss," had left Jake Russo in charge of settling disputes between the gamblers, among other duties. When Valenti returned to Rochester, he discovered that "Syndicate" affairs were not prospering as well as they should.

Within three months of Frank Valenti's return to Rochester in December 1964, Jake Russo, who at the time was the current mob boss, had disappeared. The evening of Russo's disappearance, Frank Valenti was dining in "Eddie's Chop House," a well-known restaurant in Rochester, buying drinks and advising his guests that he was "the man to see" in Rochester.

It was apparent that Jake Russo disappeared during a power struggle initiated by Frank Valenti and Stanley Valenti, and Jake Russo, or his remains, have never been found. (134) Unfortunately, Jake Russo would only be the first in a long list of Rochester mobsters to be murdered during power vacuums that were created when established leaders were removed from their positions of power for any reason.

# Buscemi Convicted in Builder Payoffs

Buscemi Convicted
In Builder Payoffs

**Democrat & Chronicle**
**Rochester, N.Y.**
**October 17, 1964**

On **October 16, 1964**. Nardo Buscemi became Western New York's first labor boss to be convicted of accepting payoffs from employers. Buscemi, President and Business Representative of Rochester Teamsters Local #398, was found guilty in Federal Court of pocketing 17 kickbacks from builders of a suburban sewer project.

The Maximum penalty for each of the 17 federal misdemeanors was a $10,000 fine and one-year imprisonment. Sentencing was delayed, as Buscemi was granted a week to file for a new trial. The conviction was one of the Justice Department's toughest, despite its success on all counts of a 1963 indictment. It took three federal agencies almost three years and about $20,000 to marshal its case. Each charge had to be proved five ways, the most difficult being that Buscemi knowingly took funds illegally.

The Justice Department contended that Buscemi accepted funds, although performing no work or services and jurors huddled 42 hours before delivering the verdict. The jury included several unionists and former unionists from various Rochester locals.

Buscemi, 44, of 203 Alfonso Drive, Greece, led the 1,200 members of Teamster Local 398. He was convicted of violating a section of the Taft-Hartley Act that seeks to maintain clean relations between employers and employees. The prosecution said Buscemi collected $1,530 from sewer pipe and manhole installers by demanding that they pay $20 for every truck that he allowed them to run without a Teamster driver.

Other government sources said compulsory employers' reports, filed under the Landrum-Griffin Act, had indicated that payoffs to Buscemi reached at least $12,000. There were perhaps a dozen subcontractors on the 75-mile sewage works involved. The guilty verdict on all counts was an outstanding feat for the government.

The Justice Department normally runs into evidence troubles when prosecuting cases of this type. Employers as well as union chiefs were subject to kickback prosecution and earlier cases seeking to convict both parties produced few persons who were willing to incriminate themselves. The subcontractors testifying against Buscemi were not indicted. (135)

## Teamsters President Stripped of Offices

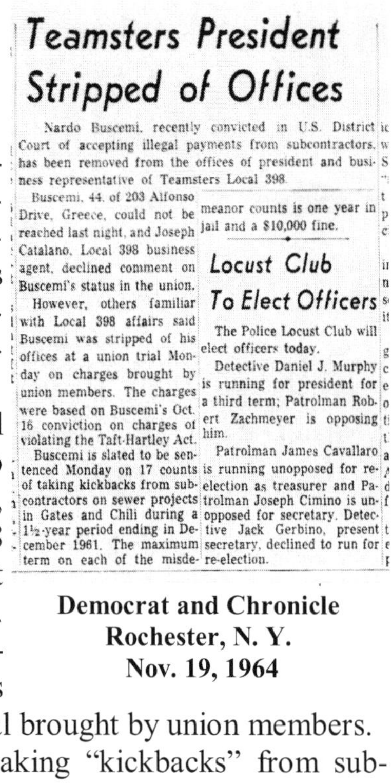

Teamsters President Stripped of Offices

Nardo Buscemi, recently convicted in U.S. District Court of accepting illegal payments from subcontractors, has been removed from the offices of president and business representative of Teamsters Local 398.

Buscemi, 44, of 203 Alfonso Drive, Greece, could not be reached last night, and Joseph Catalano, Local 398 business agent, declined comment on Buscemi's status in the union.

However, others familiar with Local 398 affairs said Buscemi was stripped of his offices at a union trial Monday on charges brought by union members. The charges were based on Buscemi's Oct. 16 conviction on charges of violating the Taft-Hartley Act.

Buscemi is slated to be sentenced Monday on 17 counts of taking kickbacks from subcontractors on sewer projects in Gates and Chili during a 1½-year period ending in December 1961. The maximum term on each of the misdemeanor counts is one year in jail and a $10,000 fine.

Locust Club To Elect Officers

The Police Locust Club will elect officers today.

Detective Daniel J. Murphy is running for president for a third term; Patrolman Robert Zachmeyer is opposing him.

Patrolman James Cavallaro is running unopposed for re-election as treasurer and Patrolman Joseph Cimino is unopposed for secretary. Detective Jack Gerbino, present secretary, declined to run for re-election.

**Democrat and Chronicle**
**Rochester, N. Y.**
**Nov. 19, 1964**

Nardo Buscemi, who had recently been convicted in U.S. District Court of accepting illegal payments from subcontractors, was removed from the offices of President and Business Agent of Teamsters Local #398.

President of Teamsters Local #398, Buscemi, 44, of 203 Alfonso Drive, Greece could not be reached, and Joseph Catalano, Local #398 Business Agent, declined comment on Buscemi's status in the union. However, others familiar with Local #398 affairs said he was stripped of his offices at a union trial brought by union members.

Buscemi was convicted of taking "kickbacks" from subcontractors on sewer projects in Gates and Chili, New York. (136)

# *Chapter 12*
# The Gamblers and Their Business

## Federal Gambling Tax Stamps

Despite the Rochester Police Department's denial of the existence of racketeering activities, illegal gambling was flourishing in the Rochester area that year. In 1964, twenty-nine (29) Federal Gambling Tax Stamps were issued in Rochester, New York. By comparison, only twenty-three (23) others were issued everywhere else in the entire state combined. A Federal gambling Tax Stamp was issued upon request for $50 to individuals in New York State who claimed that their main source of income was derived from gambling. On top of the $50 fee, holders of the "stamp" were supposed to send 10% of the income they "earned" from gambling directly to the IRS.

The funny thing was, holders of those "stamps" were not immune from prosecution on gambling related charges just because they held the stamp. They were only immune from prosecution by the Federal Government for tax evasion. Even more bizarre was the fact that stamp holders were required to list, by name, all persons working for them and the location that the gambling was taking place. It almost seemed as though the government was intentionally trying to get those gamblers to inform on themselves.

In spite of all that, 29 people in Rochester alone were willing to admit that gambling was their main source of income and purchased those stamps. Whether they were truthful on the applications and the reporting of their yearly income is unknown. Rochester's leading newspaper, the Democrat and Chronicle publicly stated that this outbreak of illegal gambling was an "indication of undue leniency by Rochester's police and judges." It was indeed a fact that convicted gamblers in Rochester just were not ever sent to jail.

The newspaper, Democrat and Chronicle, was not at all amused by that inconvenient truth. In fact they were running a full expose at the time, on the Gambling Tax Stamps, which included detailed histories about the individuals who held the stamps, exposing their criminal histories. Unfortunately two of the individuals who held these stamps, Carl Seide who was 46 in 1964 and Sam J. Accorso who was 40, filed an injunction against the newspaper to prevent the paper from publishing their police and court records.

They contended that publication of those records would prejudice their upcoming trials on gambling charges. The Democrat and Chronicle agreed to temporarily withhold their records until after the trials but they were not deterred from their position. "Whatever the reason for this large scale illegal gambling, whether it is lax police action, lenient judges, skillful criminal lawyers, indifferent prosecution, public apathy or a combination of all of these, we think our readers are entitled to know the facts," stated a representative of the paper. **(137)**

## 'Stamped' Gambler Number Two

**Phil Infantino**

Police raiders broke up a back-room blackjack game one May evening in 1964, at 257 Clinton Ave. N. Phil (Cincy) Infantino, who was 62 years old that year, had bought a $50 federal gambling-tax stamp three years previous. He had insisted that he was a "clerk" when the "cigar" store was raided, and sure enough, there were a few cigars there, eight boxes of them.

But Infantino, according to the then Capt. Clarence DePrez was positioned in a caged counter in the room where the blackjack action was. DePrez also said there was a large blackboard which carried results of sporting events. Of about $700 in bet slips confiscated, more than $600 was on Infantino's person, the raiders said. Fifteen players were arrested. Infantino was charged with being keeper of a gambling place and possession of bookmaking records.

While his case was still pending, raiders returned to the same place, exactly a week later, and Infantino was in double trouble. That time, 10 patrons were seized and Infantino was booked on the same charges as the previous week. What happened in court? After several adjournments, Infantino finally pleaded guilty to possession of bookmaking records and was fined $100. **(193)**

In **March of 1964**, Infantino was in his home at 132 Ridgeway Ave. Rochester, N.Y. when state and local police staged large-scale raids at five apartments, a store and the Ridgeway Avenue address.

Three members of Uncle Sam's $50 tax-stamp club were arrested, including Infantino. Charged with bookmaking and possession of bookmaking records, he paid a $150 fine by the time the cases had dragged on to late August of 1964. The eventual plea was violation of the city's anti-gambling ordinance.

257 CLINTON AVE. N.
. . . eight boxes of cigars

**257 Clinton Ave. was the scene of a back room blackjack game that was raided by police.**

Investigators said that the March raids were aimed at a bookie business grossing some $25 million annually at that time, in 40 upstate communities. The spots hit were described as layoff places for heavy bets. (138)

## The CIU Raids East End Smoke Shop Gambling Records Seized

One afternoon in September 1964, three detectives from the Police Bureau's CIU (Criminal Intelligence Unit) entered a familiar spot in a bustling small-business area near Goodman Street North and the New York Central freight yards. They bought no cigarettes from the East End Smoke Shop, at 1065 Main St. E., but they did arrest the proprietor, Joseph J. LoVerde, 53, one of 29 holders of a $50 federal gambling-tax stamp.

The CIU said, LoVerde had numerous bet slips for Batavia Downs in his possession, they charged him with bookmaking and possession of bookmaking records. In court, the defendant pleaded guilty to one count possessing bookie records in violation of state law and was fined $150. But in July of '63, when a CIU officer got into the same establishment (he wore a cap and jacket, carried a large bag of groceries and said he wanted to buy cigarettes) and confiscated alleged gambling evidence, LoVerde beat the rap. The charge was violating the city's anti-gambling ordinance. It was dismissed in court because, the judge ruled, bet slips found in a back room didn't necessarily belong to LoVerde who was arrested in a front room.

On earlier occasions through the years, LoVerde had paid a $50 fine and forfeited $50 bail in connection with gambling arrests. He no longer had telephone service, police said. But the East End Smoke Shop's owner of record had big-scale trouble with Uncle Sam, contrasted to his brushes with the local law enforcers.

In January of 1952, the Internal Revenue Service filed tax liens totaling $26,888.23 against Joe LoVerde and his wife, contending they were delinquent in taxes over a three-year period, an action which illustrated why gamblers bothered to buy the $50 annual federal stamps, fill out monthly taxation forms and part with 10 per cent of their gross take.

Concerning the other article in the newspaper that day, “Judges Ignore Leniency Charge” one judge remarked, "The other judges are all over 21, I don't advise them what to do; I'm not their boss." The judges had been criticized by some law enforcement officers because in many cases fines alone were imposed on gamblers rather than jail or penitentiary sentences. Gambling cases handled by City Court judges were misdemeanors.

Depending on the charge, defendants could be given sentences of up to one year in the Monroe County Penitentiary. The city's anti-gambling ordinance, under which many of Rochester's gamblers were charged, called for a maximum sentence of $150

2B ROCHESTER DEMOCRAT AND CHRONICLE
Thursday, Dec. 3, 1964

**Rochester's Brazen GAMBLERS**

**1065 MAIN ST. E.**
*. . . listed on gambling stamp*

One afternoon last September three detectives from the Police Bureau's CIU (Criminal Intelligence Unit) entered a familiar spot—in a bustling small-business area near Goodman Street North and the New York Central freight yards.

They bought no cigarettes from the East End Smoke Shop, at 1065 Main St. E., but they did arrest the proprietor, Joseph J. LoVerde, 53, one of 29 holders of a $50 federal gambling-tax stamp.

| BOX SCORE ON . . . JOSEPH LO VERDE | |
| --- | --- |
| Arrests . . . . . | 5 |
| Convictions . . . | 3 |
| Fines . . . . . . . | $250 |
| Dismissals . . . . | 1 |
| Acquittals . . . . | 1 |

The CIU, who said LoVerde had numerous bet slips for Batavia Downs in his possession, charged him with bookmaking and possession of bookmaking records. In court, the defendant pleaded guilty to one count — possessing bookie records in violation of state law — and was fined $150.

But in July of '63, when a CIU officer got into the same establishment (he wore a cap and jacket, carried a large bag of groceries and said he wanted to buy cigarettes) and confiscated alleged gambling evidence, LoVerde beat the rap.

The charge was violating the city's anti-gambling ordinance. It was dismissed in court because, the judge ruled, bet slips found in a back room didn't necessarily belong to LoVerde—who was arrested in a front room.

On earlier occasions through the years, LoVerde has paid a $50 fine and forfeited $50 bail in connection with gambling arrests. He no longer has telephone service, police say.

But the East End Smoke Shop's owner of record has had big-scale trouble with Uncle Sam, contrasted to his brushes with the local law-enforcers.

In January of 1952 the Internal Revenu Service filed tax liens totaling $26,888.23 against Joe LoVerde and his wife, contending they were delinquent in taxes over a three-year period—an action which illustrates why gamblers bother to buy the $50 annual federal stamps, fill out monthly taxation forms and part with 10 per cent of their gross take.

## Judges Ignore Leniency Charge

*Continued from Page 1B*

"The other judges," he remarked, "are all over 21. I don't advise them what to do. I'm not their boss."

The judges have been criticized by some law enforcement officers because in many cases fines alone are imposed on gamblers rather than jail or penitentiary sentences.

Gambling cases handled by City Court judges are misdemeanors.

Depending on the charge, defendants could be given sentences of up to one year in the Monroe County Penitentiary.

The city's anti-gambling ordinance, under which many of Rochester's gamblers are charged, calls for a maximum sentence of $150 in fines, 150 days in jail, or both.

If the gambler is convicted of the State Penal Code misdemeanor charge, a judge could fine him a maximum of $500 and send him to the penitentiary for up to one year.

In some local gambling cases, defendants are charged with both misdemeanors and if found guilty of both could be sentenced to serve consecutive maximum terms for both charges.

**Rochester, N.Y. Democrat And Chronicle Thursday, Dec. 3, 1964**

in fines, 150 days in jail, or both. If the gambler was convicted of the State Penal Code misdemeanor charge, a judge could fine him a maximum of $500 and send him to the penitentiary for up to one year. In some local gambling cases, defendants were charged with both misdemeanors and if found guilty of both could be sentenced to serve consecutive maximum terms for both charges. (139

## Clerics Rap Gamblers, Stamps or No

Democrat and Chronicle B

Clerics Rap Gamblers, Stamps or No

**Friday December 4, 1964**
**Democrat and Chronicle**

In **December of 1964** recently released figures had put the spotlight on Rochester as the city with the greatest number of acknowledged gambling operators in the state. The figures: Albany (district) 3, Buffalo 0, New York City 1, Niagara Falls 6, ROCHESTER 29, Syracuse 0, Utica 0, Elsewhere in state 13.

The question of why Rochester's gamblers couldn't be stopped legally was raised by local clergymen. Others described gambling as a "form of theft or laziness."

"Why so many licensed gamblers can continue operating here without apprehension is bewildering to me," said Rev. Richard J. Davey, D.D. Dr. Davey, senior pastor of Asbury First Methodist Church, had said at the time, "The fact that Rochester has more licensed gamblers than any other city in the state creates an 'unfortunate image' for the community."

"The fact that a man pays for a gambling license would seem to be proof enough, he's a gambler," the clergyman continued. Rev. Eugene Tennis, assistant pastor of Third Presbyterian Church, said,

"I know the problem of gambling exists and I certainly am not in favor of it."

He indicated the problem perhaps involves the wording of gambling laws rather than the agencies who enforce the statutes.

"The problem seems to be how to stop it.

Sometimes it seems that the arrests of gamblers are only token arrests because of legal technicalities," he said.

Another minister who discussed the evils of gambling was Rev. J. Ralph Shotwell, pastor of the Greece Baptist Church. He condemned gambling for being a form of theft or laziness:

"It promotes the philosophy of something for nothing in an age when value given for value received is often forgotten."

"Gambling can make one neurotic, dreaming of a ship coming in when you've forgotten that you never sent that ship out to sea." Rt. Rev. George W. Barrett, bishop of the Episcopal Dioceses of Rochester, said.

"While games of chance may be a legitimate form of amusement, provided they are not done to excess or interfere with a person's financial responsibility or his gifts to religious or charitable purposes, gambling easily lends itself to abuse and is almost always undesirable when conducted on a commercial basis."

Goodman A. Sarachan of Rochester, member and former chairman of the New York State Investigation (Crime) Commission, said: "Practically every time I read of a guilty plea to a gambling charge, or of convictions in my city, the penalty invariably was a nominal fine of $100, more or less. That was peanuts to a bookie." **(140)**

## Temporary Injunction Is Granted to Gamblers

A show-cause order was signed by Justice William G. Easton in a court action that sought to temporarily restrain the Democrat and Chronicle from publishing scheduled case histories on two Rochester gamblers in the newspaper's current editions on gambling. In N.Y. State Supreme Court, the order was obtained by attorney Robert C. Napier. Napier was counsel for Carl Seide, 46, of 3 Crosman Ter., and Sam J. Accorso, 40, of 405 1st St., listed by the Internal Revenue Service as among 29 Rochester men whom the Chamber of Commerce had initiated prosecution proceedings against.

Norris W. Vagg, managing editor of The Democrat and Chronicle, issued this statement in connection with the court action concerning the stories about Rochester gambling:

"We believe it is significant that Rochester has more 'stamped' operators than the rest of New York State. We believe the public has a right to know about this. Whatever the reasons for this large-scale illegal gambling here whether it is lax police action, lenient judges, skillful criminal lawyers, indifferent prosecution, public apathy, or a combination of these we think our readers are entitled to know the facts.

If the people of Rochester want the reputation as New York State's gambling Mecca, that is their decision to make. If they want their public servants to change the situation, that, too, is their decision. We will not let the threat of court action or any other pressure prohibit us from informing the public of what is going on in their community."

Detectives raided an establishment at 319 Lyell Avenue on Oct. 21, 1964 and arrested seven men including Carl Seide, inside, "no telephone" Anthony (Sabu) Cringoli, 25, has one of those what-about-the-other guy problems. His smoke shop at 349 Lyell Avenue has no phone. But up the street, at 410 Lyell Avenue, the Agbe Novelties store does. The proprietors of record at these establishments have $50 federal gambling-tax stamps. Seide was accused of possessing bookmaking records and keeping a place for Gambling.

Cringoli who had 4 arrests, 3 convictions, 3 fines and 1 dismissals, and Joe (Fat) Mastrodonato at 410 Lyell Avenue both own stamps. Cringoli didn't have a phone because he had been arrested and convicted on gambling charges as a result of police raids. Cringoli's phone was yanked at police request He last was raided June 3, 1964 by CIU detectives as keeper of gambling equipment. Following an adjournment, he pleaded guilty July 8, 1964 to violating the city's anti-gambling ordinance and was fined $150. City Court Judge Emmett L Doyle suspended a 30-day penitentiary sentence. Cringoli's smoke shop, at the corner of Orchard Street, is in the heart of a busy industrial-mercantile Lyell Avenue neighborhood.

Vern Rusrift had obtained an adjournment. His case came up for City Court trial Dec. 11, 1964. Accorso operated the Bay Aluminum Co. at 257 Bay St., and his adjourned gambling-arrest case came up Dec. 29, 1964. He and 15 other men were picked up by police raiders on Nov. 7, 1964 when an alleged blackjack game was broken up. Accorso was booked as keeper of a gambling place, then released on $250 bail. Mastrodonato did have an arrest-conviction record, but it was not linked to 410 Lyell Avenue where his occupation was described as "clerk." **(141)**

# *Chapter 13*
# Organizing The Bookmakers

By **December of 1964**, the police in Rochester began investigating reports that Frank Valenti had been trying to line up these local gamblers into an organization that would guarantee them protection against non-affiliated competition and collect debts from players who were slow in their payments. The gamblers were to pay from 10 to 20 per cent of their profits for these services. Valenti had just been identified the previous year before the Senate Permanent Subcommittee on Investigations as a member of Rochester's La Cosa Nostra. **(142)**

The idea of charging individuals for the right to operate illegal gambling establishments was eventually perfected down to a science. That right would eventually cost each proprietor between $400 and $1800 per week, depending on the circumstances. No one was exempt from this charge. Those refusing to pay would be "persuaded" to pay, killed if necessary. The vast majority of people paid and gambling became a very lucrative source of income for the organization. In fact gambling was the primary source of income for the Rochester Mafia.

That is the way it was in Rochester for many years until the "Mob Wars" started. The Mob Wars in Rochester would eventually be fought over who was to be in charge of the "organization" that would control literally millions of dollars in gambling profits. Frank Valenti may very well have organized the illegal gamblers in Rochester but the ultimate control of that very organization that he headed, would change hands several times in the years to come. The struggle for control of those rackets was commonly known as, the Rochester Mob Wars.

## Rochester Fears Underworld War

But in **December of 1964**, The Mafia, the nationwide criminal organization, was reportedly just starting to take over control of bookmaking and numbers gambling in Rochester from unaffiliated local racketeers. As a result, the city of 311,000 persons, the third largest in the state at the time, faced the possibility of an underworld war.

The situation developed as a result of Frank Valenti returning here from exile in Pittsburgh. Valenti, a 54-year-old ex-convict, was named before the Senate permanent subcommittee on investigations as a member of Cosa Nostra, which is another name for the Mafia. At public hearings in 1963, Valenti was identified by Joseph M. Valachi, a narcotics dealer and murderer and as a "Soldier" in the Cosa Nostra "Family" of Joseph Bonanno. Bonanno, alias Joe Bananas, was kidnapped on a New York City street recently on the eve of his scheduled appearance before a grand jury. The police believed that he was murdered.

Valenti, who was ordered out of the state for three years following a conviction for violation of election laws in 1961, returned to Rochester in September 1964 and began offering "protection" and "services" to local gamblers for a slice of their receipts, according to the local newspaper.

A check of police files in New York City showed that Valenti was listed as a "close associate" of Andrew M. Alberti, who was found dead of a shotgun wound in his home in the Bronx a few hours before he was to appear before a grand jury investigating an $88,000 gem swindle. The police listed his death as apparent suicide. Alberti, a partner in a baking company, had been identified as a member of the Carlo Gambino Crime Family.

The Democrat and Chronicle reported that Valenti's agents had been calling on bookmakers and other gamblers and demanding to be cut in for from 10 to 30 per cent of the take. Among the services they were said to have promised, were collection of debts from slow-paying players, "handling" of disgruntled losers and a guarantee against local competition.

Observers in Rochester reported that more than half of those approached had agreed to go along, but that some were holding out. Valenti's reappearance on the local scene coincided with the disappearance of Jake Russo, who reportedly had been left in charge of the gambling business for the Mafia during Valenti's court ordered exile. There were reports that the crime syndicate was dissatisfied with Russo's inability to keep nonaffiliated gamblers from encroaching on its territory. Russo was reported as having gone to Florida. (143)

# It's Arrest No. 26 For Joe Lippa

## It's Arrest No. 26 For Joe Lippa

'Biggest' Raids Here, Page 1A

It was arrest No. 26 for Big Joe Lippa, the policy racketeer with a genius for staying out of jail, during yesterday's police raids.

And it came at a time when The Banker—as police call him—already is waiting trial on a 14-count indictment handed up June 19.

The indictment charges Lippa, 48, of 44 Madison St., with felonies of operating a policy or betting business, and misdemeanors of possessing lottery slips.

* * *

CHARGED YESTERDAY with another felony as operator of a policy slip business, the supermarket operator was his usual taciturn self when taken to Police Headquarters.

"He knows from nothing about gambling, to hear him tell it," a detective said. "This guy wouldn't give you the time of day—unless there was a bet involved."

Lippa was jailed with a recommendation from Police Chief William M. Lombard that $10,000 minimum cash bail be placed.

Lombard was emphatic in saying that "the IRS (Internal Revenue Service) will be made aware of Lippa's activities." This action could mean a real financial headache for Big Joe and possibly could result in his purchasing a $50 federal gambling-tax stamp—or else.

* * *

LIPPA NEVER has got around to joining Uncle Sam's $50 Club, an organization which includes more professional gamblers in Rochester than in any other community in New York State.

Although The Banker—who controls a lucrative policy slip operation in a large sector of the city's west side, principally in the 3rd Ward—has been indicted, tried, convicted and sentenced in varied cases, he's served time in Monroe County Penitentiary only twice.

Lippa's dossier involves State Liquor Authority infractions and police seizure of questionable literature on his supermarket premises at 82 Prospect St., but mainly policy slip operations. For years he has employed upwards of 50 persons as runners who pick up daily bets.

* * *

BIG JOE was minding a new store yesterday when detectives Donald Bunce, Eugene LaChima and Elwood Smith cruised by at 91 Prospect St., across from his old market. The new market isn't open yet, but the proprietor was on the premises.

He also had visitors, the detectives said, in the form of underlings observed entering the place with bet slips.

When the raiders barged in, Joe's expression became pained but his reaction was quick. He dumped a quantity of policy slips from his pockets onto the floor, Bunce said.

Lippa had only $182 on his person but evidence showing some 250 bets also was seized, the raiders said. His only comment was:

"Oh, no . . . what's happening here?"

* * *

ON PREVIOUS occasions, Lippa has been known to hide some $10,000 worth of assets in the meat freezer—frozen so solidly they couldn't be counted until thawed.

Detective Supervisor Lucien DiGiovanni often has described The Banker as being in charge of a roughly $1,000-a-day illegal operation. He also sells groceries.

BIG JOE LIPPA

**Democrat and Chronicle on January 31, 1965 page 8**

On **January 30, 1965**, It was arrest No. 26 for "Big Joe" Lippa, the policy racketeer with a genius for staying out of jail. It came at a time when "The Banker," as police called him, already was waiting trial on a 14-count indictment handed up on June 19, 1964. The indictment charged Lippa, 48, of 44 Madison St., with felonies of operating a policy or betting business, and misdemeanors of possessing lottery slips.

Big Joe was charged with another felony as operator of a policy slip business, the supermarket operator was his usual taciturn self when taken to Police Headquarters. "He knows nothing about gambling, to hear him tell it," a detective said. "This guy wouldn't give you the time of day unless there was a bet involved."

Lippa was jailed with a recommendation from Police Chief William M. Lombard that $10,000 minimum cash bail be placed. Lombard was emphatic in saying that "the IRS (Internal Revenue Service) will be made aware of Lippa's activities."

That action could mean a real financial headache for Big Joe and possibly could result in his purchasing a $50 federal gambling-tax stamp or else. Lippa never had gotten around to joining Uncle Sam's $50 Club, an organization which includes more professional gamblers in Rochester than in any other community in New York State. Although "The Banker" who controls a lucrative policy slip operation in a large sector of the city's west side, principally in the 3rd Ward has been indicted, tried, convicted and sentenced in varied cases, he served time in Monroe County Penitentiarys only twice.

Lippa's dossier involves State Liquor Authority infractions

and police seizure of questionable literature on his supermarket premises at 82 Prospect St., but mainly policy slip operations. For years he had employed upwards of 50 persons as runners who picked up daily bets.

Big Joe was minding a new store when detectives Donald Bunce, Eugene LaChima and Elwood Smith cruised by 91 Prospect St., across from his old market. The new market wasn't open yet, but the proprietor was on the premises. He also had visitors, the detectives said, in the form of underlings observed entering the place with bet slips. When the raiders barged in, Joe's expression became pained but his reaction was quick. He dumped a quantity of policy slips from his pockets onto the floor, Bunce said. Lippa had only $182 on his person but evidence showing some 250 bets also was seized, the raiders said.

His only comment was: "Oh, no . . . what's happening here?" On previous occasions, Lippa had been known to hide some $10,000 worth of assets in the meat freezer frozen so solidly they couldn't be counted until thawed. Detective Supervisor Lucien DiGiovanni often had described “The Banker” as being in charge of a roughly $1,000-a-day illegal operation. He also sold groceries. **(144)**

# Dominick "The Deacon" Alloco Is Murdered

## Alloco's Last Pal Sought by Police

Dominick (The Deacon) Alloco hurriedly ate a large steak dinner, probably in a restaurant, about an hour before being murdered on a lonely country road in Walworth, an analysis of his stomach contents revealed yesterday.

Also, State Police investigators said, the slain gambler and shakedown artist changed his clothes sometime before his death, possibly in the restaurant where he ate his last meal.

Investigator George A. Loomis of Newark, who is directing the investigation into the gangland-style murder last night issued an appeal to anyone who might have seen Alloco and a companion late Tuesday night or early Wednesday to contact authorities.

Alloco was found tied up and shot in the back of the

SEEN THIS MAN?—State, city police have issued an appeal to anyone who may have seen slain gambler Dominick Alloco after 6 p.m. Tuesday to call Investigator G. A. Loomis or Det. Capt. James Cavoti at Police Bureau, 232-7070, or Henrietta substation, BR 1-4646. Police will accept anonymous calls.

**February 27, 1965 Democrat and Chronicle**

**Dominick "The Deacon" Alloco** was a mafia muscleman. He was a gambler who "owed" huge sums of money to other mobsters. Because of that reason, he was not welcome at most of the gambling establishments in Rochester at the time.

He was tied up and shot in the head, then dumped in a field near Walworth, New York on **February 23, 1965**. He allegedly was "playing the snitch" to the Sheriff at the time as well.

—D&C Photo by Jim Laragy

Body of Dominick Alloco is viewed by investigators in field near Walworth.

**The Body of Dominick Alloco being viewed by investigators. He was found tied up and shot, in field near Walworth.**

In fact, Alloco was allegedly reporting directly to top city and state police officers. His murder was regarded by police as a message from the "syndicate" to "stoolies" that informing would not be tolerated. **(182)**

## Lippa Starts Felony Term as Gambler

Joseph Lippa, 48, of Madison St. was sentenced on **March 30, 1965** to concurrent terms of one year and nine months after pleading guilty to two gambling charges. County Court Judge George D. Ogden imposed the one-year term on Lippa's plea to a felony count of operating a policy business. The concurrent term was imposed on a plea to possession of lottery slips, a misdemeanor.

The heavy-set gambler was arrested May 30, 1964 at his Prospect Street market on 14 charges. The other charges were dropped. Underworld ties were denied before sentencing, Lippa's attorney Leon Armer, made an appeal for leniency, saying, "There has been a great deal in the local press and other places concerning Mr. Lippa in past months, but I feel it's only fair for me to point out to this court that from any knowledge that I have been able to acquire, Mr. Lippa ... has not been any member of, nor has he any connection with, what is best known as the organized criminal underworld."

While admitting that Lippa "violated the law," Armer emphasized that Lippa was not a part of "what one could call the sinister, devious and evil organized criminal underworld." Did removal of Lippa from the scene mean the end of his policy operation? Police doubted it. Police members of the Vice Control Unit who had been close to the Lippa 'bank" for years said that it would be only a matter of days before the big west side operation was under way again.

While certain of the identity of two probable successors, police intended to await developments before cracking down again on the operation. Despite his lengthy criminal record, Lippa had done time in Monroe County Penitentiary only twice. The record of his many appearances in court was dotted with dismissals involving "defective information" or "illegal search." The banker's dossier showed that he had a positive genius for avoiding jail. Former County Judge John P. Lomenzo gave him nine months in the penitentiary in March, 1963, on three gambling counts; the terms ran concurrently. He was out in six months. Two years before that, Lippa drew four months on two counts of receiving stolen property. **(145)**

# Valenti Seeks Permission to Run Rochester's Rackets

On **May 23, 1965**, at or around 11 a.m., Rochester Police officers Lucien J. DiGiovanni and John A. Lipari met one Frank Valenti in the rear of a cigar store at 121 State Street, Rochester, New York. That meeting lasted approximately one hour and ten minutes. Neither DiGiovanni or Lipari reported that meeting to any officer in the police department in the City of Rochester, either orally or in writing.

The meeting ultimately led to the resignations of both vice squad detectives. They resigned instead of getting demoted to patrolmen for lying about their meeting with Frank Valenti. **(181)** Lucien J. DiGiovanni and John A. Lipari both resigned June 15, 1965. A panel was appointed and an investigation was then conducted to investigate the reasons for the resignations. **(180)**

## New York Mafia Bosses Meet At Funeral Chapel

NIAGARA FALLS GAZETTE

Magaddino Chapel Crime Parley Site

Four days later, on **May 27, 1965,** Rochester underworld "Boss," Frank Valenti met with five other Western New York Crime Syndicate Members at the Magaddino Funeral Chapel in Niagara Falls, New York.

Sometime after his arrival at the funeral chapel, Frank Valenti went to the home of Stefano Magaddino located at 518 Dana Drive, Lewiston, N.Y. Stefano Magaddino was the "Boss" of the Buffalo Mafia Crime Family. The other mobsters who visited the funeral home at 1338 Niagara St. on that day were Samuel Rangatore, John Cammilleri, Antonino Magaddino, Peter Magaddino and Joseph Bongiorno, said the Commission.

Those facts were contained in a report released by the State Commission On Investigation, which conducted a 10-month investigation of crime in Western New York. According to the 72-page document, Frank Valenti went to Niagara Falls four days after he met with two Rochester detectives. The Commission did not state why Valenti went to that city, nor did it state that the six men met together at the funeral home.

However, the Commission did say, "It was generally known that the crime syndicate in Western New York with which Valenti had long been identified by law enforcement authorities recognized as its head, Stefano Magaddino of Niagara Falls."

**Magaddino Funeral Chapel, 1338 Niagara Street Niagara Falls, NY**

"Magaddino was also known as Don Stefano or The Old Man by members of his group, which includes such individuals as Peter Magaddino, Antonino Magaddino, Joseph Bongiorno, John Cammilleri, Fred Randaccio, Pasquale Natarelli, Steven Cannarozzo and Samuel Rangatore."

# Mobsters Called To Testify Before Investigation Commission

**Antonino Magaddino, Samuel Rangatore, Peter Magaddino and Stefano Magaddino**

In an attempt to figure out what happened at that **May 27, 1965** Mafia meeting at Stefano Magaddino's funeral chapel, the State Commission On Investigation subpoenaed the mobsters who attended. The Commission specifically mentioned that 57-year-old Samuel G. Rangatore of 31st St., Niagara Falls, had been identified variously as a courier and consultant in the syndicate. Antonino Magaddino, 67, of 1528 Whitney Ave., a brother of Stefano; Peter A. Magaddino, 48, of 1103 22nd St., a son of Stefano, and Joseph S. Bongiorno, 48, of 6831 Pine Ave., a nephew of Stefano, were questioned by the Commission about the events of **May 27, 1965**. All refused to testify on the ground that their answers would tend to incriminate them.

John Cammilleri and Rangatore, both testified before the Commission after being granted immunity from prosecution, both admitted that it was "likely" that they visited with the Magaddinos some time on that day. However, both denied having seen Valenti in Niagara Falls, according to the report.

Rangatore was questioned for approximately 45 minutes on July 7, 1965 in the offices of his lawyers in the United Office Building here. The Commission listed the events leading up to that interview as follows: "For months Rangatore evaded examination by the Commission by submitting a variety of medical excuses. Finally, after court action by the Commission to compel his appearance, Rangatore was examined under a grant of immunity.

"He admitted being present in Rochester over the weekend of **May 23, 1965** (the weekend Valenti met with the detectives). However, he stated that he did not know Valenti and did not see him during that time. That particular phase of the matter was still under investigation by the Commission."

The report, which was signed by Commission members Jacob Grumet, Myles J. Lane, John W. Ryan Jr. and Goodman A. Sarachan, centered on a scandal that broke more than a year previous in Rochester.

"It appears that gambling remained a going and profitable business" in that city, the bi-partisan Commission said. Commenting on Valenti's background, the Commission said that when he returned to Rochester in the fall of 1964, it was his intention to re-establish himself as the leader of syndicate operations in the Rochester area. "As a first step," the report said, "he sought and obtained the approval of the syndicate leader 'Don' Stefano Magaddino of Niagara Falls."

The Commission added that the principal phase of its operation was to be an organization of bookmakers who were to pay a percentage of their profits to the syndicate in return for "protection" which Valenti offered to provide. "Evidence obtained during the Commission's investigation demonstrated that Valenti had a fertile and productive field in which to operate . . ."

In another reference to Stefano Magaddino, in the report, the Commission said there is "no reason to doubt the general accuracy" of a report that ***Valenti was directly under Magaddino*** in the organizational structure of the Western New York criminal syndicate. ***Valenti was placed in that position by Lucian Digiovanni, formerly detective supervisor of the Rochester Vice Control Unit.***

It was detectives Lucien Digiovanni and John Lipari who met with Valenti in Rochester. The report called the meeting "misconduct of the most serious nature," on the part of the police officers, and said it warranted strict disciplinary action. But "that was not done," the report noted. Digiovanni and Lipari were dropped from duty and submitted their resignations during the furor when the case first became public. However, they were later put back on the police force. (146)

COOLING HEELS—Former Detective John Lipari, left, and Detective Lucien DiGiovanni were kept waiting yesterday until State Crime Commission hearing got under way in city's Hall of Justice.

**Detectives Lucien DiGiovanni (right) and John Lipari (left) wait outside of the Hall of Justice in Rochester, New York. They were waiting to testify before the State Crime Commission on October 13, 1965**

# Mobsters Called To Testify Before Investigation Commission

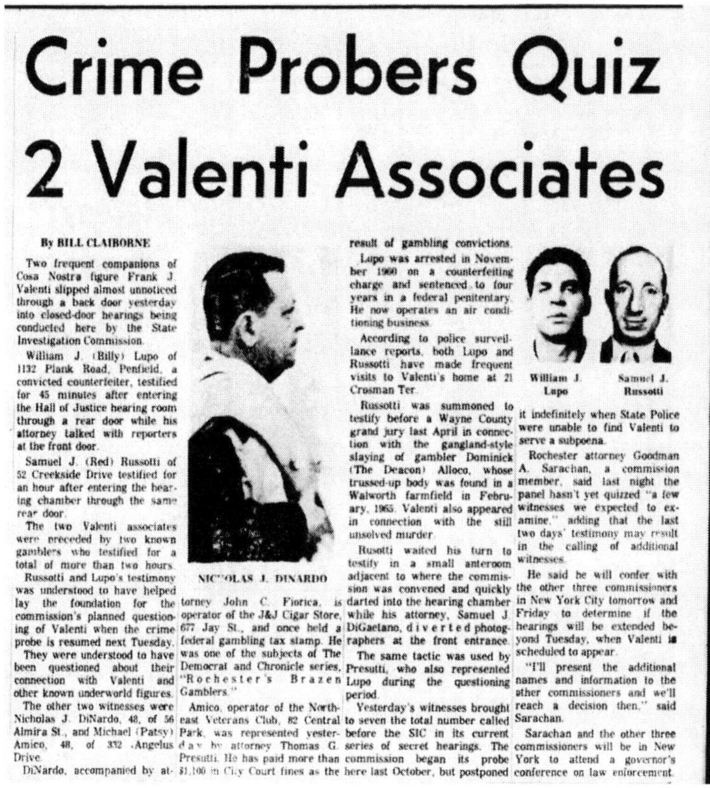

# Crime Probers Quiz 2 Valenti Associates

By BILL CLAIBORNE

Two frequent companions of Cosa Nostra figure Frank J. Valenti slipped almost unnoticed through a back door yesterday into closed-door hearings being conducted here by the State Investigation Commission.

William J. (Billy) Lupo of 1132 Plank Road, Penfield, a convicted counterfeiter, testified for 45 minutes after entering the Hall of Justice hearing room through a rear door while his attorney talked with reporters at the front door.

Samuel J. (Red) Russotti of 52 Creekside Drive testified for an hour after entering the hearing chamber through the same rear door.

The two Valenti associates were preceded by two known gamblers who testified for a total of more than two hours.

Russotti and Lupo's testimony was understood to have helped lay the foundation for the commission's planned questioning of Valenti when the crime probe is resumed next Tuesday.

They were understood to have been questioned about their connection with Valenti and other known underworld figures.

The other two witnesses were Nicholas J. DiNardo, 48, of 56 Almira St., and Michael (Patsy) Amico, 48, of 332 Angelus Drive.

NIC''OLAS J. DINARDO

DiNardo, accompanied by attorney John C. Fiorica, is operator of the J&J Cigar Store, 677 Jay St., and once held a federal gambling tax stamp. He was one of the subjects of The Democrat and Chronicle series, "Rochester's Brazen Gamblers."

Amico, operator of the Northeast Veterans Club, 82 Central Park, was represented yesterday by attorney Thomas G. Presutti. He has paid more than $1,100 in City Court fines as the result of gambling convictions.

Lupo was arrested in November 1960 on a counterfeiting charge and sentenced to four years in a federal penitentiary. He now operates an air conditioning business.

According to police surveillance reports, both Lupo and Russotti have made frequent visits to Valenti's home at 21 Crosman Ter.

Russotti was summoned to testify before a Wayne County grand jury last April in connection with the gangland-style slaying of gambler Dominick (The Deacon) Alloco, whose trussed-up body was found in a Walworth farmfield in February, 1965. Valenti also appeared in connection with the still unsolved murder.

Rusotti waited his turn to testify in a small anteroom adjacent to where the commission was convened and quickly darted into the hearing chamber while his attorney, Samuel J. DiGaetano, diverted photographers at the front entrance.

The same tactic was used by Presutti, who also represented Lupo during the questioning period.

Yesterday's witnesses brought to seven the total number called before the SIC in its current series of secret hearings. The commission began its probe here last October, but postponed it indefinitely when State Police were unable to find Valenti to serve a subpoena.

William J. Lupo

Samuel J. Russotti

Rochester attorney Goodman A. Sarachan, a commission member, said last night the panel hasn't yet quizzed "a few witnesses we expected to examine," adding that the last two days' testimony may result in the calling of additional witnesses.

He said he will confer with the other three commissioners in New York City tomorrow and Friday to determine if the hearings will be extended beyond Tuesday, when Valenti is scheduled to appear.

"I'll present the additional names and information to the other commissioners and we'll reach a decision then," said Sarachan.

Sarachan and the other three commissioners will be in New York to attend a governor's conference on law enforcement.

**Democrat and Chronicle April 20, 1966**

On **April 19, 1966**, two of Frank Valenti's top men in the Rochester Mafia were called to testify before the State Investigation Commision. William Lupo testified for about 45 minutes and Samuel J. "Red" Russotti testified for about an hour.

Two other witnesses who testified were Nicholas Dinardo, operator of J&J Cigar Store and a Federal Tax Stamp holder, and Michael "Patsy" Amico. Amico was the operator of the North East Veterans Club, a suspected gambling parlor.

There was a total of seven witnesses called before the SIC, the State Investigation Committee, that day. (146)

# The Disappearance of John J. "Broadway" Cavagrotti

**John J. Cavagrotti**

In 1967, John J. “Broadway” Cavagrotti ran a gambling business from his car, but the police found out and suggested that he stop. With little else to do, Cavagrotti stepped up his long and costly penchant for card-playing. Snuffy's was the place to do it. Fresh off of a horse race win, Cavagrotti was $88 richer and he wanted to collect.

**Democrat and Chronicle**
**Rochester, New York**
**Sunday April 25, 1982**
**Page 121**

Cavagrotti had parked his car, a 1958 Lincoln sedan, on Bay Street near the gambling joint. But he didn't like to drive it far because it had no reverse gear. Inside Snuffy's, a dingy place officially known as the Northeast Businessmen's Improvement Association, Cavagrotti hailed a man he knew. Could he bum a ride to Finger Lakes? he asked. The man agreed and they left Snuffy's. The last time Cavagrotti was seen, he was in the passenger seat of that man's car, driving down Bay Street, at 2:30 p.m.

The driver of that car was Salvatore "Sammy" Gingello, who later would become “Underboss” of Rochester's Mafia, before he was killed by a bomb planted under his car. Police reports indicated he was, at that time, a small-time hood who had muscled into a couple of gambling joints, including Snuffy's.

Early in 1967, Gingello had walked into a shop on North Goodman Street run by Cavagrotti and his brother Sam. From now on, Gingello announced, he was co-operator. It was a tough pill to swallow for the brothers, but there was little they could do except grouse to their friends and customers, police intelligence reports said after Cavagrotti's disappearance. It was not a marriage made in heaven.

The shop was supposed to sell novelties but the police hadn't caught on, because they kept raiding the place and confiscating horse betting slips and telephones. It was a two-story cinder-block building where you could buy a drink, play the ponies or try your luck at cards. Sometimes, the luck wasn't so good; in 1964 police raided the place after the wives of some regulars complained that their husbands were blowing all of their money there.

Card-playing was the most popular pastime at Snuffy's, and the boys there spent most of their time playing poker, blackjack and gin. The high-stakes card game was poker. You could get into a blackjack game for only $40, but you needed up to $2,000 to start playing poker. Cavagrotti played. And played. Before long, police say, he lost big. "He was in debt up to here," said a police officer, holding his hand to his scalp.

Enter September 21, 1967 the last day of summer and sticky hot. Cavagrotti got to Snuffy's about noon. When he left with Gingello two hours later for Finger Lakes Race Track, his car was still parked on Bay Street. Cavagrotti never cashed in his winning tickets at Finger Lakes. He didn't show up later that afternoon to pick up his son Michael at a local high school, as he was supposed to do. Five days later, Cavagrotti's wife Yolanda filed a missing-person report with police. It noted that her husband was 5 feet 10 inches tall, weighed 190 pounds and had balding gray hair, blue eyes and a light complexion.

Cavagrotti's car was found in an empty lot off Bay Street, near Snuffy's, its front against a fence. Police felt Cavagrotti wouldn't have put the car there because he knew the reverse gear didn't work. Police stepped up their surveillance of gambling joints and the nervous gamblers posted doormen to watch for raids so betting slips could be destroyed or hidden. Searchers checked out Toronto after hearing a rumor Cavagrotti might be there. They turned up nothing. They questioned Gingello, the driver of the car in which Cavagrotti was last seen. Although they felt Gingello was involved, they could prove nothing.

Police had little doubt that Cavagrotti was dead. But who was the killer, and how did he dispose of the body? A favorite theory of police was that Cavagrotti's last resting place was under the concrete lanes of the Keeler Street Expressway between Goodman Street and St. Paul Boulevard, which was being built then. "I didn't give up hope for a long time," says Cavagrotti's wife. "My son Michael and John had a real good relationship.

Before his disappearance, an emissary from the mob had told John Cavagrotti to pay off that debt and stop talking publicly about "mob pressure," according to sources at three law enforcement agencies. The novelty shop closed a few days later. Snuffy's was the last place Cavagrotti, was seen alive. The sun was bright and hazy when John J. "Broadway" Cavagrotti stepped out of Snuffy's gambling joint on Bay Street the. afternoon of Sept. 21, 1967. In two hours, it would be raining. Cavagrotti, 54, had been a convicted gambler known as "Broadway" because he was a flashy dresser. (147)

## Blow Aimed at Gamblers

The State Street Social Club was located at 532 State Street. **Frank DiPonzio** was the operator. The Northway Social Club was located at 234 Portland Ave., **Charles and Murphy Russo** were the operators. The Caserta Social Club was located at 44 Lake Ave., **Orlando Lompo, Angelo DeMarco, Pat DiPolito and Pat Decesare** were the operators.

Police had lost cases against the Caserta Social Club despite testimony that all-night blackjack games were held there. A judge ruled police were unable to prove that the "house" was taking a cut. The State Street Social Club had been closed about six weeks since police waged a harassment campaign by making repeated daily inspection visits there and at other suspected gambling spots.

The Northway Social Club, which was once reported to be the spot for heavy gambling activity, had also been closed for brief periods. Jake Russo, a brother of the two Russos who were the operators of the Northway, was a key figure in the operation there before he disappeared in the autumn of 1964. He hasn't been seen since. Another gambler, **John "Broadway" Cavagrotti**, 54 also disappeared 3 years later.

The plan to attack the chartered club gambling problem was conceived more than a year previous. Police had waited until ample convictions were obtained. All but two of the cases resulted from arrests made that year. One dated as far back as January 1967. That case had just recently been disposed of.

Also a new weapon was tested, Chemical Mace, the police reports said. Sam Cavagrotti had the dubious distinction of being the first person in Rochester to be subdued with the new tear-gas device when arrested. He was charged with assault and his brother, John, was charged with possession of gambling records and keeping a place of gambling.

The assault did not set well with the men of the Mafia. It was one thing to get busted and take your arrest like a good soldier, police reports said. It was quite another thing, police said, to "pop off on a cop." John Cavagrotti already owed money to the mob. He had guaranteed some "layoff bets" which were a protective device where one bookie who receives a large number of bets on one event will pass along some of the risk to another bookie.

In Cavagrotti's case, he had chosen poor risks and had lost his shirt. The clubs whose charters police sought to lift were: The Young Boxers' Athletic Club, 21 South Ave., **Wilfred Lawrence** the said operator. The Venetian Social Club, 627 Clinton Ave. N., **Anthony Falzone** the said operator. The Northeast Veterans Club, 88 Central Park, **Michael, Angelo and Samuel Amico** the said operators. Northwest Men's Club, 677 Jay St., **Nicholas Di-Nardo** the said operator. The Northeast Home Improvement Assn., 257 Bay St., **Joseph "Snuffy" Grock** the said operator and the Sixteenth Ward Veterans Club, which had operated in the now defunct Goodman Novelty Shop, 1313 Goodman St. N., with **Salvatore Gingello** the said club president.

All six premises had been the scene of repeated police gambling raids in recent years. Richard Dutcher of the attorney general's staff here said he will try to begin contacting the suspected gamblers this week. He said he must first learn who the officers are in the corporations which run some of the businesses. If police were successful in their requests, the city would be left with only three other charter clubs they claim were used as fronts for gambling. **(148)**

## Ricky Visconte Is Murdered

A man well-known to police was shot to death and dumped from a car at Hayward Avenue and Fourth Street on **March 11, 1969**. Investigators identified him as Enrico G. "Ricky" Visconte, 40, who had been living at 228 Verona St.

He was slain about a half hour after hc dropped his mother off at a bingo game. He was shot in the head and hip and was pronounced dead at the scene. The slaying occurred between 7:20 and 7:30 p.m.

Several persons in the area reported hearing three shots fired. They supplied police with a description of a car seen driving away from the intersection and of

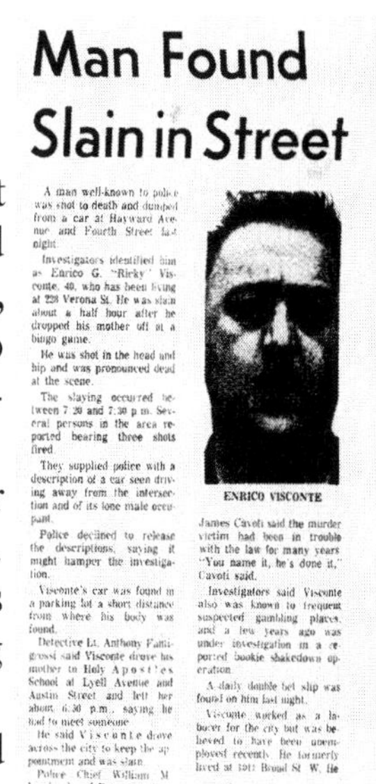

**Man Found Slain in Street**

A man well-known to police was shot to death and dumped from a car at Hayward Avenue and Fourth Street last night.

Investigators identified him as Enrico G. "Ricky" Visconte, 40, who has been living at 228 Verona St. He was slain about a half hour after he dropped his mother off at a bingo game.

He was shot in the head and hip and was pronounced dead at the scene.

The slaying occurred between 7:20 and 7:30 p.m. Several persons in the area reported hearing three shots fired.

They supplied police with a description of a car seen driving away from the intersection and of its lone male occupant.

Police declined to release the descriptions, saying it might hamper the investigation.

Visconte's car was found in a parking lot a short distance from where his body was found.

Detective Lt. Anthony Fantigrossi said Visconte drove his mother to Holy Apostles School at Lyell Avenue and Austin Street and left her about 6:30 p.m., saying he had to meet someone.

He said Visconte drove across the city to keep the appointment and was slain.

Police Chief William M. Lombard and Detective Capt.

ENRICO VISCONTE

James Cavoti said the murder victim had been in trouble with the law for many years. "You name it, he's done it," Cavoti said.

Investigators said Visconte also was known to frequent suspected gambling places, and a few years ago was under investigation in a reported bookie shakedown operation.

A daily double bet slip was found on him last night.

Visconte worked as a laborer for the city but was believed to have been unemployed recently. He formerly lived at 1012 Broad St. W. He

Please turn page

**Democrat and Chronicle March 12, 1969**

its lone male occupant. Police declined to release the descriptions, at the time, saying it might hamper the investigation. Visconte's car was found in a parking lot a short distance from where his body was found. Detective Lt. Anthony Fantigrossi said Visconte drove his mother to Holy Apostles School at Lyell Avenue and Austin Street and left her about 6:50 p.m., saying he had to meet someone.

He said Visconte drove across the city to keep the appointment and was slain. James Cavoti said the murder victim had been in trouble with the law for many years. "You name it, he's done it," Cavoti said. Investigators said Visconte also was known to frequent suspected gambling places, and a few years previous, he was under investigation in a reported bookie shakedown operation. A daily double bet slip was found on him the night he was killed. Visconte worked as a laborer for the city but was believed to have been unemployed recently. He formerly lived at 1011 Broad St. W.

When Charlie Monachino was arrested in 1975 and turned informant, he made a statement to Rochester Police detectives concerning Ricky Visconte. He said that Jimmy The Hammer had a thing for Ricky's girlfriend. **(149)** Jimmy also told his girlfriend Rose Rotundi that he had murdered Ricky Visconte and a girl on Haywood Avenue in Rochester while they were riding in their car. **(150)**

# *Chapter 14*
# Murders, Bombings, Arson and Other Mob Business

## El Marrocco's Restaurant Torched By The Mob

In 1975, Rochester Mafia Soldier, Angelo Monachino was identified by his brother Charles, as being a participant in two murders. Charles Monachino, who was not a "made" Mafia member like his brother, became an informant for the Rochester Police Department in order to avoid going to prison for other unrelated charges.

**An advertisement for the El Marrocco Nightclub located at 884 Emerson Street.**

Angelo Monachino, after being picked up by the police for questioning, became fearful that the other Mafia members would think that he was "informing" like his brother, and try to kill him. After thinking it over, Angelo decided his chances were better with the government than they were with his own "organization." Angelo Monachino became an "informant," testifying to scores of crimes committed by himself and others within the Rochester Mafia. His testimony would put many members of Rochester's La Cosa Nostra behind bars for many years. He testified at many trials and at several Senate hearings.

During Angelo Monachino's testimony before the United States Senate in 1978, he stated the first arson fire that he was aware of that the mob was involved in was at the El Marrocco Restaurant in **late January of 1970.**

El Marrocco's was a nightclub located at 884 Emerson Street in Rochester, New York. It was operated by Pat Marrocco, who was a friend of Rochester Mafia Soldiers Angelo Monachino and Gene DiFrancesco. Prior to arson, Pat Marrocco had been arrested several times for operating an after hours establishment that served liquor past 2 a.m.

Pat Marrocco was having trouble paying his bills and he had borrowed money from several people. Marrocco discussed "torching" the restaurant with Mafia Soldier, Gene DiFrancesco, but Frank Valenti, Rochester's Mafia "Boss," wanted to see the insurance policy before that decision was made. Eugene DiFrancesco would always make sure that his "clients" updated and maximized their insurance policies before the fires were set.

The night before the fire, Angelo Monachino went to the El Marrocco. Pat Marrocco took Monachino upstairs and showed him the remodeling that he was doing. The entire second floor had been ripped apart. The walls had been torn open. One wall had been knocked out, the moldings had been stripped away and the baseboards were ripped out and arranged like a teepee. The second floor had been set up so that the fire would draft up and through the roof. The following morning Monachino said that he heard on the radio that El Marrocco was burning.

The system used in the "Arson For Hire" business was pretty simple, according to Monachino. The mob would demand 25% of the final insurance payment for the loss, getting 25% of that upfront. They took 6 & 1/4% of the insurance payment before they did anything. After they torched the building they got the rest of their 25%. The mob split their share of the proceeds with 25% going to the people who set the fire, 25% going to the man who brought the assignment in (finders fee) and the rest (50%) went to Frank Valenti.

Monachino said, that the problem with this formula was that the "torches" hardly ever got paid. When asked by Senate Committee Investigators why he never complained about not getting paid, Monachino said, "Jimmy The Hammer" complained; look what they did to him: they killed him."

**Eight men accused of arson plot**

By SHERIDAN LYONS

Sheriff's Detective Robert Russello, left, leads Joseph Nalore into court

**Fire Chief Joseph Nalore (right) being led into court to be arraigned for arson. April 9, 1976 Democrat and Chronicle**

Angelo Monachino also testified that the risk of getting caught setting these fires was extremely low due to several factors including having a high official of the fire department on their side. **(185)**

The high official of the fire department turned out to be Fire Chief Joseph Nalore, who was twice charged with arson, but acquitted both times.

# William "Billy" Lupo Is Murdered

In 1970, Salvatore "Sammy G" Gingello, a mob soldier under Frank Valenti, had custody of approximately $100,000 of the organization's money. That money was ostensibly collected as "deposits" for a scheduled charter flight to Las Vegas on a gambling junket organized by local mob members. The money was allegedly stolen right out of Gingello's house. William Lupo was conveniently (for the setup) Gingello's next door neighbor.

Gingello reported this theft to the local police. The speculation by investigators based on circumstances and informant information was that Salvatore Gingello and "Underboss" Samuel "Red" Russotti conspired to place the blame for the alleged theft on William Lupo. It was suspected that the organized crime hierarchy would think that Lupo was involved in that theft, and then they would order Lupo to be murdered.

In **April 1970**, William Lupo was shot to death in Rochester, N. Y. He was found slumped behind the steering wheel of his car, shot in the head four times. It was noted at the time that Salvatore "Sammy G" Gingello immediately replaced Lupo as "Capo" of the strong arm unit of the Valenti Crime Family. The last vestige of the Jake Russo era was eliminated with Lupo's death. At the time of his death, Billy Lupo was under federal investigation for loan sharking. Angelo Monachino would eventually be charged with his murder five years later. **(151)**

D&C Photo by Len Maxwell
Police Technical Sgt. Robert Tacito looks at Lupo vehicle. Arrow shows where bullet hit.

**Rochester Police look at Billy Lupo's vehicle. The arrow shows where the bullet entered.**

Body of William Lupo lies behind shattered windshield.

**Lupo's body was slumped behind the steering wheel.**

# Upstate New York Mob Leaders Hold Meeting In Batavia, N.Y

In the **summer of 1970**, Buffalo, N.Y. mob leaders met with the leaders of the Rochester mob in Batavia, New York. Batavia was known as a quiet, relatively crime-free community, but for several days in **June 1970**, the city was the "Mafia capital" of upstate New York home of the Valenti Crime Family.

**Rochester mobster Frank J. Valenti, left, leaves State Police headquarters in Batavia with a state police investigator on June 2, 1970, en route to his arraignment in Batavia City Court. Valenti, along with three other mobsters and two construction officials were arrested at a downtown Batavia restaurant and charged with loitering. (187)**

It began around lunchtime on Tuesday, **June 2, 1970** when state police, acting on a telephone tip, raided a downtown Batavia restaurant. Six men were taken into custody. Police charged them with loitering because they allegedly "failed to give a reasonable account of their actions" when questioned at the restaurant.

These weren't ordinary suspects. Among those rounded up were Fred Sebastian, 64, of Niagara Falls and Albert Marks, 51, of Brighton, both of whom were active in the Western New York construction industry.

Police identified the other four suspects as Mafia chieftains in the notorious Western New York crime family headed by Stefano "The Undertaker" Magaddino. The then ailing Magaddino's territory included his hometown of Niagara Falls, as well as the cities of Buffalo, Rochester, southern Ontario and even parts of Pennsylvania and Ohio.

The best known of these suspects was Frank J. Valenti, 58, of Henrietta, described as the Rochester Mafia "Boss" and a Magaddino "Lieutenant." The other Mafia leaders were Roy Carlisi, 61, and Joseph Fino, 55, both of West Seneca; and Rene Piccaretto, 45, of Pittsford.

As reporters and TV crews flocked to Batavia to cover the story, the main question on everyone's mind was, what brought all these high-powered mobsters and construction officials to Batavia? Several theories were advanced. One possibility was the mob leaders were trying to exert influence over the construction trades to end strikes then taking place in Buffalo, Rochester and the Falls. Hence the meeting with the two construction chiefs.

Police also theorized that the Batavia meeting may have involved a "reorganization of the Western New York La Cosa Nostra setup," according to The Daily News. The 78-year-old Magaddino, reportedly near death, was said to be stepping down as Western New York boss and the Rochester mob was preparing to break away from the Buffalo Mob. Maybe it was a combination of factors. Later on **June 2, 1970**, the six men were arraigned in Batavia City Court and then allowed to return to their homes. They would be back the following week.

More information soon filtered out. The Rochester Times Union reported on **June 3, 1970** that the previous day's meeting apparently wasn't an isolated event. Mafia leaders had been holding monthly meetings in Batavia for at least six months, the paper said, usually on the last Wednesday of each month. State Police denied knowledge of any such monthly gatherings, reiterating the previous report that they were only acting on a telephone tip. Unfortunately for the State Police, their case against the six men began to unravel within days. Early the following week, loitering charges against Sebastian and Marks were dropped for lack of evidence.

A few days later, City Court Judge Charles F. Graney dismissed the charges against Valenti, Carlisi, Fino and Piccarretto on similar grounds. Fino's attorney Thomas Calandra of Brockport had argued that the loitering charge was unconstitutional because it violated the right to peaceably assemble, to remain silent, to gather with whom you wish and the right to privacy. The judge agreed and the mobsters were allowed to go free. But one message was made clear, even if it wasn't stated openly. These men were not welcome to return to Batavia at any time, for any purpose. As far as can be determined, they never did.

Buffalo Crime Family "Boss" Stefano Magaddino was the most powerful mob boss in Western New York history, although he apparently wasn't as close to death as journalists had surmised in 1970. He lived until 1974. But his influence had waned considerably by then. (152)

Stefano Magaddino

The Rochester mob headed by Frank Valenti did indeed break away from the Buffalo mob in 1970 and aligned itself with the Pittsburgh crime family. Valenti remained Rochester boss until 1972, then served time in prison for extortion before moving to Texas and Arizona. He died in 2008 at age 97.

To its credit, Batavia has never been a "mob town," notwithstanding the events of **June 1970**. It continued to be a community of hard-working individuals from many ethnic backgrounds, all of whom have contributed greatly to the city's development. (153)

## Rochester Mafia Family Breaks Away From the Buffalo Mafia Family

Sometime during 1970, after Frank Valenti's organization had grown considerably in comparison to that of Jake Russo, Valenti confronted Stephano Maggadino, Boss of the Buffalo Mafia Crime Family, in Buffalo, N.Y., and advised him that the Valenti family would no longer be subordinate to Buffalo, N. Y., authority and that Frank Valenti's contacts and allegiance would be with John Sebastian LaRocca in Pittsburgh, Pa.

Due to the strength of the Valenti organization, the relationship (son-in-law) of Stanley Valenti to Antonio Ripepi and the failing health of Stephano Maggadino, this move remained uncontested. Maggadino was allowed to retain 15 percent of the gambling operation in Rochester, N. Y., at the sufferance of Valenti, and Frank Valenti operated basically as an independent unit until his forced retirement in June of 1972.

# William T. Constable Is Murdered

**William T. "Billy" Constable,** was murdered on **December 14, 1970** by Jimmy "The Hammer" Massaro, for allegedly attempting to muscle in on mob enterprises.

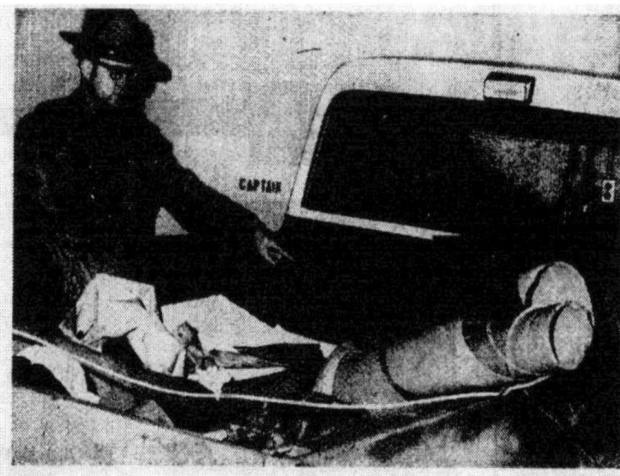

D&C Photo by Marge Van Iseghem

Mystery Vehicle

Trooper R. G. Wistner points to the spot where the body of a Rochester contractor, William T. Constable Jr., was found in the back of his pickup truck in Victor Saturday. Constable had been shot in the head. Story is on Page 1A.

**New York state Trooper, R.G. Wistner points to the spot where the body of William Constable was found in the bed of his pick-up truck.**

He was an employee of Angelo Monachino, who owned Bar-Mon Construction. Bar-Mon construction had been associated with Frank Valenti, "Boss" of the Rochester Mafia. Valenti was the owner of several of Bar-Mon's bulldozers. Angelo Monachino was also a "made" member of Rochester's Mafia.

Charles Monachino fingered his brother Angelo and Albert DeCanzio for the Billy Constable murder, although Jimmy "The Hammer" pulled the trigger.

Monachino and DeCanzio were indicted on April Fools Day 1975 along with Gene DiFrancesco and Frank Valenti for the murder. Angelo Monachino was freed on bail and the charge against DeCanzio later was dropped. Both DeCanzio and Monachino later became government informants and both of them were placed into the Federal Witness Protection Program.

### Slaying, Giant Liquor Theft 'May Be Linked'

By JAMES B. STEAR

Police say a giant liquor theft two weeks ago may be linked to the murder of a Rochester contractor whose frozen body was found in rural Victor Saturday afternoon.

Some of the stolen liquor was recovered yesterday, and a large force of state and city police, FBI men and Treasury agents was said to be close to making several arrests.

At the same time, it was learned the murder victim, William T. Constable Jr., had once been a subcontractor at the city-owned Emerson Street landfill, working for a firm linked with local Cosa Nostra Boss Frank Valenti.

The firm, Bar-Mon Construction Co., did bulldozing work at the landfill from mid-April to early June under an emergency contract with the city. Some of Bar-Mon's bulldozers originally were purchased by Valenti.

Bar-Mon, in turn, subcontracted some of its work to Barcom Construction Co., owned by Constable.

City officials said last night they were not aware of Constable's involvement in the landfill work.

Constable was last seen alive last Monday, just after he went to the city controller's office asking when the city was going to pay Bar-Mon so he could get his share.

Actually, the city had paid Bar-Mon several days earlier. Angelo Monachino, Bar-Mon president, said he hadn't had a chance to give Constable a share.

The liquor theft that police said may be linked to Constable's death occurred Dec. 7 at Eastern Freight Ways, Inc., 1631 Mt. Read Blvd.

About 230 cases of liquor valued at $14,000 were taken from a parked trailer. FBI men and Treasure agents from the Alcohol and Tobacco Tax Unit entered the case because the theft involved interstate commerce.

Thirty cases of liquor were recovered yesterday, but authorities refused to say where. State Police said in a statement:

"Locations where the stolen liquor was recovered are being withheld pending further

Please turn page

**Dec. 21, 1970 Democrat and Chronicle**

In the article on the right, authorities said that William Constable's death may have been linked to a recent liquor theft, but they did not elaborate.(183) In the article above left, the police call the killing a "gangland execution" intended to be a warning to other hoodlum elements. (184)

### State Police Term Slaying 'Execution'

CANANDAIGUA (AP)—State Police Wednesday called the slaying of William T. Constable Jr., 35, of Rochester, "a gangland execution intended as a warning to hoodlum elements."

Constable's body was found in his pickup truck near the hamlet of Fisher Dec. 19. Troopers said they found $7,000 cash and the phone number of a reputed Cosa Nostra chieftain in Constable's wallet.

**Dec. 24, 1970**

# The Columbus Day Bombings

Democrat and Chronicle

Federal, County Buildings, Churches Ripped by Bomb

The disappearance of Jake Russo., the murder of William Lupo, and the ever-increasing organized crime activity generated by Frank Valenti did not pass unnoticed. During the period 1967 through 1970, Frank Valenti and his associates became subject to intense scrutiny by Federal, State, and local law enforcement agencies. That pressure was accompanied by a high degree of local publicity, which resulted in making Frank Valenti pursue a course of action designed to remove investigative pressures, and the resulting publicity, from himself and his colleagues, and at the same time perpetrate acts of violence against individuals who proved uncooperative and resisted Valenti's attempts to influence their activities.

On **October 11, 1970**, Frank Valenti ordered and directed the manufacture of dynamite bombs by Eugene DeFrancesco, Angelo Monachino, and others. Once prepared, Frank Valenti directed that the bombs be placed and detonated at locations selected by him, with two purposes in mind; to direct law enforcement efforts toward terrorist groups and to intimidate selected individuals. The bombs were detonated at the selected locations, which included a Baptist church, the home of a union business agent, the Monroe County Office Building, the U.S. Courthouse and Federal building, and a Methodist church.

The explosions occurred during the early morning hours of **October 12, 1970** (Columbus Day), and came to be identified by the local news media and subsequently the public and law enforcement personel as the infamous "Columbus Day Bombings." The bombings effectively diverted the attention of law enforcement and news media to other areas besides organized crime. This series of bombings served to remove Valenti and his henchmen from the pages of the local papers, and resulted in a significant shift of investigative priorities for all law enforcement agencies in Rochester, N.Y.

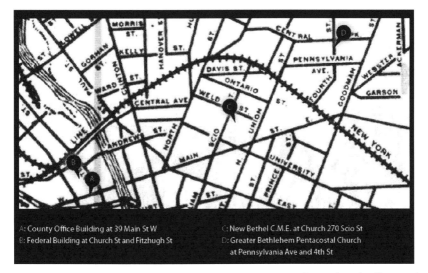

A: County Office Building at 39 Main St W
B: Federal Building at Church St and Fitzhugh St
C: New Bethel C.M.E. at Church 270 Scio St
D: Greater Bethlehem Pentacostal Church at Pennsylvania Ave and 4th St

As a result of this initial success, Frank Valenti directed that additional bombings take place; on **October 27, 1970**, explosions occurred at two synagogues. On **November 6, 1970**, another synagogue was bombed. On **November 25, 1970** (Thanksgiving), a black Islamic mosque and black Bapist church were bombed. On **December 14, 1970**, the residence of a Monroe County Court Judge was bombed at Valenti's direction.

Again Frank Valenti's efforts were rewarded in that the frequency of the exposions, and the extensive damage which resulted served to occupy the attention of the news media. The nature of the targets of the bombs caused the majority of investigative effort to be directed toward the various radical groups, known militants, and antiwar protesters, with a past history of violent activity.

Five years later, investigative efforts ultimatety revealed the true source of the bombing incidents which occurred In Rochester during 1970. Frank Valenti, Anthony Gingello, Salvatore Gingello, Thomas Didio, Angelo Vaccaro, Dominic Celestino, Eugene DeFrancesco, and Rene Piccarreto were indicted on July 24, 1975, by a Federal Grand Jury in Rochester, N.Y., in connection with the bombing incidents. Frank Valenti sought and obtained, on the grounds of ill health, a severance and was not tried. Eugene DeFrancesco was found guilty of Federal charges relating to the bombings.

All other defendants were found not guilty. DeFrancesco was sentenced to 11 years in Federal prison. On February 15, 1979 Frank Valenti pleaded guilty to illegal possession of a destructive device (bomb) and was sentenced to serve 3 years probation. Valenti was already imprisoned as a result of unrelated federal charges at the time. Probation was to be served upon Valenti's release from federal prison in June 1980. (156)

## Angelo Monachino and Vincent Massarro are "Made" Into The Rochester Mafia

**Angelo Monachino**

**Vincent "Jimmy the Hammer" Massaro**

Angelo Monachino and Jimmy "The Hammer" Massaro were officially "made" and sworn into the Rochester Mafia in **February of 1971** at a gathering at Frank Valenti's farm.

Monachino first met Valenti through Eugene Di-Francesco. It was Di-Francesco who encouraged Monachino to join the organization. DiFrancesco told him "it would be in his best interest to join" (the organization). Monachino was told that if he joined, it would help him in his construction business. Monachino said, he "also knew that not joining would hurt him in other ways."

After performing numerous jobs for Frank Valenti, including several arsons, Angelo Monachino was asked to join the organization and was officially sworn in, in **February of 1971**. (157)

## Frank Valenti's "Elite Crew"

During the Frank Valenti regime, there was a departure from what was considered the "normal" organized crime family structure. Valenti appointed an underboss, consigliere and capos, similar to other families. However, Valenti also formed a personal unit of soldiers under "Capo" Dominic Chirico. Dominic Chirico and that group were responsible directly to Frank Valenti. The members of that unit were identified as Dominic Chirico, Thomas

Didio, Dominic "Sonny" Celestino, Angelo Vaccaro, Ross (Rosario) Chirico, Vincent Massaro, Spike LaNoverra, Eugene DeFrancesco, and Angelo Monachino.

Each of those members had areas of responsibility within the group. Dominic Chirico served as "Capo," as noted, but also acted as Fank Valenti's chauffeur and personal bodyguard. Angelo Vaccaro and Dominic Celestino operated dice and card games. Spike Lanoverra, Eugene DeFrancesco, and Thomas Didio operated the loan sharking and extortion aspect, providing the "muscle." Angelo Monachino operated a construction company, involved with fraudulent contracts and influencing labor union members, specifically Teamsters Local #398 members and Officers. Vincent Massaro operated generally as an arsonist. Rosario Chirico, although peripherally involved in, counterfeiting and a loansharking operation, was primallly responsible, for handling stolen cars and providing weapons for the entire Valenti operation.

From 1969 through 1972, Rosario Chirico removed or caused the removal of serial numbers from an untold number of rifles, shotguns, and handguns and distributed them throughout the Valenti organization. Additionally, Rosario Chirico directed the alteration of these firearms to accept firearm silencers manufactured at Chirico's place of business, Trolley Collision. These silenced and untraceable firearms were designed solely for the purpose of assassination.

Also during this period, Rosario Chirico contracted for the manufacture of a device that would remotely detonate an explosive by radio signal. After much experimentation and modification, the radio signaling equipment was successfully used to remotely detonate explosives. On at least one occasion, a device of this nature was used to blow up a motor vehicle.

During Valenti's tenure, this select group would commit crimes on the direct orders of Frank Valenti, and the proceeds of those crimes would be given directly to him only. Valenti consistently utilized that loyal group for his personal enrichment. For example, during the period 1969 through 1972, that group committed at least eight major "arson for profit" fires in the metropolitan Rochester, N.Y. area. The fires were arranged by Frank Valenti and the proceeds were retained by him and not contributed to the general fund of the organization. (11)

The use of that elite crew and more specifically the lack of sharing of funds generated by this crew would eventually lead to the overthrow of Frank Valenti by his immediate subordinates. Furthermore that crew would be the backbone of the splinter group called the "B Team" which remained loyal to Valenti when the Rochester Mafia split in half and the notorious Rochester Mob Wars began.

At least three members of that elite crew would eventually be murdered, another shot and wounded, some would be beaten, and others would become government informants.

## Missing Lippa Cash

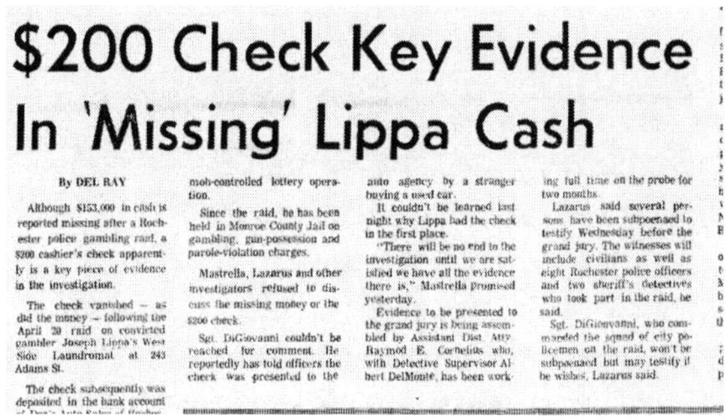

$200 Check Key Evidence In 'Missing' Lippa Cash

By DEL RAY

Although $153,000 in cash is reported missing after a Rochester police gambling raid, a $200 cashier's check apparently is a key piece of evidence in the investigation.

The check vanished — as did the money — following the April 20 raid on convicted gambler Joseph Lippa's West Side Laundromat at 243 Adams St.

The check subsequently was deposited in the bank account

mob-controlled lottery operation.

Since the raid, he has been held in Monroe County Jail on gambling, gun-possession and parole-violation charges.

Mastrella, Lazarus and other investigators refused to discuss the missing money or the $200 check.

Sgt. DiGiovanni couldn't be reached for comment. He reportedly has told officers the check was presented to the auto agency by a stranger buying a used car.

It couldn't be learned last night why Lippa had the check in the first place.

"There will be no end to the investigation until we are satisfied we have all the evidence there is," Mastrella promised yesterday.

Evidence to be presented to the grand jury is being assembled by Assistant Dist. Atty. Raymod E. Cornelius who, with Detective Supervisor Albert DelMonte, has been working full time on the probe for two months.

Lazarus said several persons have been subpoenaed to testify Wednesday before the grand jury. The witnesses will include civilians as well as eight Rochester police officers and two sheriff's detectives who took part in the raid, he said.

Sgt. DiGiovanni, who commanded the squad of city policemen on the raid, won't be subpoenaed but may testify if he wishes, Lazarus said.

**Rochester, New York**
**Democrat and Chronicle**

Although $153,000 in cash was reported missing after a Rochester police gambling raid, a $200 cashier's check apparently was a key piece of evidence in the investigation. The check vanished as did the money following the **April 20, 1971** raid on convicted gambler Joseph Lippa 's West Side Laundromat at 243 Adams St. The check subsequently was deposited in the bank account of Dee's Auto Sales of Rochester Inc., a used-car agency at 1199 Ridge Road E., Irondequoit.

Records in the Monroe County Clerk's Office show that a certificate to do business under the name Dee's Auto Sales at 1199 Ridge Road E. was issued in 1968 to Anthony F. DiGiovanni and Lucien J. DiGiovanni. In 1969, the certificate was discontinued and Dee's Auto Sales of Rochester was incorporated.

Anthony and Lucien DiGiovanni were brothers. Police Sergeant Lucien DiGiovanni had recently been suspended without pay by Police Commissioner John A. Mastrella and he was charged in a departmental action with failure to turn in a revolver seized in the raid on Lippa's place.

Mastrella said a hearing on the departmental charge against Sgt. DiGiovanni would be held by **Sept. 30, 1971**. In the meantime, a Monroe County grand jury was impaneled immediately to investigate "all the circumstances surrounding the raid," District Attorney Jack B. Lazarus said. More than $20,l00 in cash and $17,500 in checks confiscated in the raid were turned in to the police property clerk's office, but Lippa was reported to have said that another $153,000 was missing. Joseph Lippa, long associated with gambling in Rochester, was described by one police official as the "banker."

As a direct result of some "missing" cash after the police raid on Lippa's gambling establishment, several persons were subpoenaed to testify before the grand jury. The witnesses included civilians as well as eight Rochester police officers and two sheriff's detectives who took part in the raid. Sgt. DiGiovanni, who commanded the squad of city policemen on the raid, wouldn't be subpoenaed but may testify if he wishes, Lazarus said.

Mastrella, Lazarus and other investigators refused to discuss the missing money or the $200 check. It was never determined why Lippa had the check in the first place. "There will be no end to the investigation until we are satisfied that we have all the evidence there is," Mastrella promised at the time.

Evidence presented to the grand jury was assembled by Assistant District Attorney Raymod E. Cornelius who, with Detective Supervisor Albert DelMonte, had been working on the mob-controlled lottery operation. After the raid, Lippa was held in the Monroe County Jail on gambling, gun-possession and parole-violation charges. **(158)**

## Reputed Rochester La Cosa Nostra "Capo" Richard Marino Becomes A Trustee Of Rochester, N.Y. Teamsters Local #398

**Richard Marino**

In 1972, Richard Marino, Rochester LCN Family "Capo" (captain), and Local #398 Union Steward, became a Trustee of Teamsters Local #398. Richard, who attained his job through the help of Sammy Gingello, reputed Rochester La Costra Nostra Family "Underboss", would later become Business Agent of Teamsters Local #398 as well. **(159)** Marino would also later replace Sammy Gingello as "Underboss" of the Rochester Mafia in 1978 after Gingello was killed by a car bomb.

## Dick Marino Is Appointed Delegate to Joint Council #17

On **January 4, 1972** Richard Marino (Teamsters Local #398) was appointed as a Delegate to Teamsters Joint Council #17 after former Delegate Joseph Maurici (Teamsters Local #398) resigned his position of Council Delegate. **(160)** To obtain that position, a person must be at least a Business Agent or Officer in his Local Union, Teamsters Local #398. Marino was given the oath of office by Teamsters Joint Council #17 President Joe Catalano on **May 11, 1972**. **(161)**

## Thomas Marotta Gets "Made" In the Rochester Mob

**Thomas Marotta**

It's unclear who decided that Marotta should join the criminal ranks, perhaps Gingello or Marotta's cousin Thomas Didio, another Rochester mobster. But by the early 1970s, Thomas Marotta had been welcomed into the family. In late 1971 or early 1972, court records are unclear on the date, the initiation became official.

One day Sammy Gingello told Thomas Marotta to prepare for a swank evening out. He said, "Get dressed up tonight, we gotta go somewhere," Marotta recalled in a conversation captured in a December 2000 undercover videotape. Instead of club hopping, Gingello took him to the Henrietta home of Rochester Mob "Boss" Frank Valenti.

More than 30 people, including a local college professor, awaited Marotta in a large basement, to ask whether he wanted to officially join the mob, Marotta recalled on the videotape. In Valenti's basement, the mob adhered to an induction ceremony common with the national crime syndicate La Cosa Nostra. Valenti, or another local mafioso of prominence, pricked the trigger finger of the new member. The blood would be drained onto a tissue. The bloodied tissue would be handed to the inductee, then set afire. The newly "made" member would hold the tissue as it burned away.

Marotta acknowledged on the videotape that he agreed to become one of the local family, then connected to New York's prominent Bonanno Crime Family, and underwent the standard rite. Still, he had his doubts about some of those sitting in judgment of his criminal worthiness. "I sat around with three guys I know are stool pigeons, and they're OK'ing me," he said.

Sacrosanct rules were made evident at the Henrietta induction. You revealed no secrets, you engaged in no illegalities without the knowledge of the mob powers-that-be, and you watched whom you slept with. "You don't mess around with any of the wives or girlfriends of any men in the organization," Joseph "Spike" Lanovara, who was "made" at Valenti's home months before Marotta was, once testified about the initiation.

Angelo Monachino, another "made" man, also talked about the risks of breaking the rules. "If you divulge any secrets, or anything else, it could even become your death," he testified. (162)

# *Chapter 15*
# There Is a New Boss in Town

## Samuel Russotti, Rene Piccarreto and Salvatore Gingello Take Control Over the Rochester Mafia

**Samuel Russotti "Boss"**

**Rene Picarreto "Consigliore"**

**Sam Gingello "Underboss"**

In 1972, Frank Valenti was confronted by Rene Piccarreto, Samuel "Red" Russotti and Salvatore Gingello, who accused him of skimming money from the organization for his own personal use. It had been discovered by the others that Valenti was buying property in Arizona, and investing in various businesses in the Phoenix, Arizona area. Valenti readily admitted to keeping certain monies for himself, but assumed that he would be supported by his associates in Pittsburgh, Pa.. He also assumed that Dominic Chirico and his cadre of soldiers would protect him from any personal harm. (163)

In May 1972, Samuel Russotti, Rene Piccarreto and Salvatore Gingello approached Frank Valenti (Boss of the Rochester Mafia) for the second time and demanded that he return the money that he had stolen from the other members of the Rochester mob and turn over all records of the organization to Samuel Russotti. Valenti was also told that it was time for him to "retire."

The trio had accused Valenti of "skimming the profits." Valenti did as he was told but he immediately ordered Dominic

Chirico, Valenti's body guard and "Capo," to eliminate the trio, as they were threats to his administration. Chirico relayed the command to his crew but they refused to carry it out. The trio, Samuel Russotti, Rene Piccarreto and Salvatore Gingello, had earned the respect and loyalty of many of the family members and Chirico's crew feared that the trio's followers would retaliate. **(164)**

Dominic Chirico's soldiers made no attempt to murder Russotti, Piccarreto, or Gingello because they were aware of Valenti's misconduct and the superior strength of mob members who were loyal to Russotti, Piccarreto, and Gingello.

Salvatore Gingello, upon his succession to the position previously held by William Lupo, and with the concurrence of Samuel "Red" Russotti, had recruited a large number of new members without the knowledge or consent of Frank Valenti. Those new recruits, were loyal to Gingello, and they greatly outnumbered those individuals loyal to Frank Valenti and were a viable factor in forcing Frank Valenti from power.

Subsequent events led law enforcement officers to believe that Thomas Didio (a member of Dominic Chirico's group) advised his cousin, Thomas Marotta, a close associate of Gingello, of Valenti's intentions to have Russotti, Piccarreto, and Gingello killed. Upon learning this, Rene Piccarreto consulted with his contact in the Bonanno crime family and after advising him of Valenti's intentions, requested the support of the Bonanno family in removing Frank Valenti from power by whatever means necessary. **(165)**

## Rochester Mobster Dominic Chirico Is Gunned Down on Raines Park

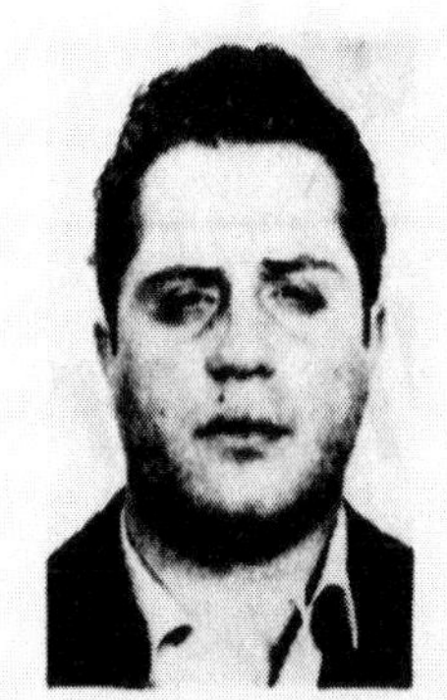
DOMINIC CHIRICO

But the murder of Frank Valenti was not sanctioned, due to his seniority and influence with organized crime members in Pittsburgh, Pa., and throughout the United States. Instead, on **June 5, 1972**, Dominic Chirico, the only "Capo" loyal to Valenti, was shotgunned to death in front of his girlfriend's apartment on Raines Park in the City of Rochester. Witness testimony and subsequent changes in the structure of the Rochester organization allowed investigating officers to speculate with some degree of accuracy that the murder was perpetrated by soldiers directed by Salvatore Gingello, with the assistance of Thomas Didio. That killing was a message to Frank Valenti that he could be next if he did not accept retirement.

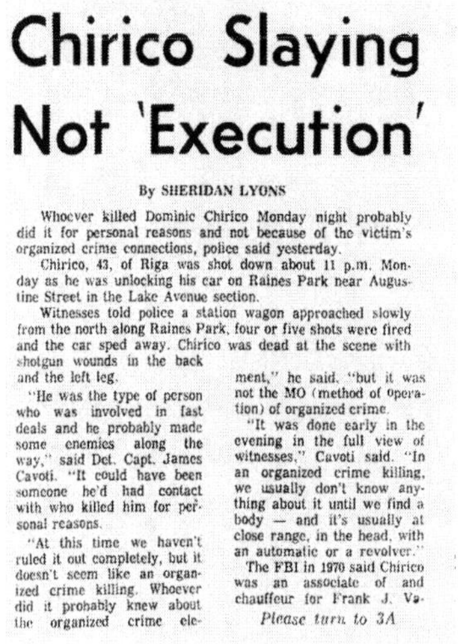

# Chirico Slaying Not 'Execution'

By SHERIDAN LYONS

Whoever killed Dominic Chirico Monday night probably did it for personal reasons and not because of the victim's organized crime connections, police said yesterday.

Chirico, 43, of Riga was shot down about 11 p.m. Monday as he was unlocking his car on Raines Park near Augustine Street in the Lake Avenue section.

Witnesses told police a station wagon approached slowly from the north along Raines Park, four or five shots were fired and the car sped away. Chirico was dead at the scene with shotgun wounds in the back and the left leg.

"He was the type of person who was involved in fast deals and he probably made some enemies along the way," said Det. Capt. James Cavoti. "It could have been someone he'd had contact with who killed him for personal reasons.

"At this time we haven't ruled it out completely, but it doesn't seem like an organized crime killing. Whoever did it probably knew about the organized crime element," he said, "but it was not the MO (method of operation) of organized crime.

"It was done early in the evening in the full view of witnesses," Cavoti said. "In an organized crime killing, we usually don't know anything about it until we find a body — and it's usually at close range, in the head, with an automatic or a revolver."

The FBI in 1970 said Chirico was an associate of and chauffeur for Frank J. Va-

*Please turn to 3A*

The following day, Frank Valenti was confronted at the Red Lion Inn, Rochester, N.Y., and ordered to leave town, by Samuel "Red" Russotti, Rene Piccarreto, and Salvatore "Sammy G" Gingello.

Shortly after those confrontations, Frank Valenti moved from Rochester, N.Y., to Phoenix, Ariz. With the removal of Frank Valenti, Stanley Valenti prudently removed himself as well, concerning himself with a flourishing produce business and select illegal enterprises outside the city of Rochester, N.Y.

Samuel "Red" Russotti assumed the position of "Boss" vacated by Frank Valenti and Rene Piccarreto retained the position of "Consigliere." Salvatore "Sammy G" Gingello was elevated to the position of "Underboss" in the Rochester organization. With the support of the Bonanno Crime Family, Russotti, Piccarreto, and Gingello severed the tenuous ties that Pittsburgh organized crime members had over the Rochester Crime Family when Frank Valenti was in power. (167)

Angelo Vaccaro left the Rochester, N.Y., area shortly after the murder of Dominic Chirico and former soldiers of Chirico were separated and placed under newly designated "Capos" by Samuel "Red" Russotti. Oddly, Thomas Didio, a former soldier of Dominic Chirico, was elevated immediately, and given additional responsibilities in the organization. During the period 1972 through November 1973, Vincent "Jimmy the Hammer" Massaro (arsonist for Frank Valenti) continued to commit arson fires at the direction of the new leadership under Samuel "Red" Russotti.

The 1972 murder of Dominic Chirico was the 7th gangland type slaying in the Rochester area since 1960. (188)

## Charges Against Police Sgt. Lucien DiGiovanni are Settled in "Secret Deal"

Rochester Police Sgt. Lucien DiGiovanni was indicted after a grand jury investigation into reports that more than $100,000 in cash disappeared during a gambling raid at Joe Lippa's West Side Laundrymat, 243 Adams St. He plead guilty to a charge of tampering with evidence in a gambling raid but seven other charges against him were dropped. **(167)**

One county representative called the plea bargain a "secret deal" that did a disservice to the people involved. **(189)**

In the other police-action case, Regan, always on the offensive in a heavily Republican county, labeled the settlement of charges against Police Sgt. Lucien DiGiovanni a "secret deal" that did a disservice to the people involved.

DiGiovanni, indicted after a grand jury investigation into reports that $100,000 or more in cash and checks disappeared during a gambling raid at Joe Lippa's West Side Laundramet, 243 Adams St., pleaded guilty Oct. 13 to a charge of tampering with evidence in a gambling raid, but seven other charges against him were dropped.

Lazarus replied that "plea bargaining" is accepted by "the American Bar Association and the U. S. Supreme Court as a necessity in our criminal justice system."

**November 5, 1972**
**Democrat and Chronicle**

## Valenti's Heir Rene Piccarreto

# Rene Piccarreto—Valenti's Heir

By THOM AKEMAN
*D&C Staff Writer*

Silently and secretly, 49-year-old Rene J. Piccarrelo has taken over the Rochester Mafia leadership from public figure Frank J. Valenti, 61.

Falenti stepped down when a bodyguard was slain, and the threaty-voiced, cigar-smoking Piccarreto, — long the loyal number-two man here — moved up.

Valenti retired shortly after 11 p.m. June 5, 1972, when one of his three bodyguards, Dominick Chirico, 44, was shot dead in Rochester, police authorities on the Mafia say.

Chirico's shotgun slaying was a warning to Velenti that someone had been hired to kill him, the authorities say.

Killing a bodyguard as a warning is a courtesy the Mafia extends to men who have given long years of loyalty.

Valenti retired without resistence when Chirico was killed, the authorities say.

MORE THAN TWO YEARS AGO, Valenti admitted five men, including Chirico, the the decision-making inner council of the Mafia here, the authorities say.

The five, all hoodlums and younger than the other Mafiosi, were believed to be violent and hadn't inherited their rights to belong to the council. Authorities theorized they were "muscle men" being brought in to fight a threatening gang war.

Who held the contract on Valenti, who ordered it and who ordered Chirico killed isn't clear, say nine investigators from six law-enforcement agencies, most of whom are assigned to investigate gangland activities here.

Whether Piccarreto seized the leadership, stepped into it, was promoted into it or was pushed into it isn't clear either.

A THREE-WAY GANG WAR AT that time was Dividing the Mafia family that controls the rackets in upstate New York, authorities say. That family long had been headed by Stefano Magaddino, an 82-year-old Sicilian immigrant whose operation is based in Buffalo.

The Buffalo power struggle may have spilled into Rochester, police authorities say.

The Mafia, which took control of gangland activities here less than nine years ago under Valenti's leadership, is part of the Magaddino family, the U.S. Justice Department has said.

But Valenti until fall 1964 was a member of the Joseph Bonanno Mafia family

Please turn to 3A

RENE J. PICCARRETO
. . . polite, soft-spoken

**April 29, 1973**
**Democrat and Chronicle**

Silently and secretly, 49-year-old Rene J. Piccarreto had taken over the Rochester Mafia leadership from public figure Frank J. Valenti, 61. Valenti stepped down after Chirico's shotgun slaying, a warning to Valenti that someone had been hired to kill him. Killing a bodyguard as a warning is a courtesy the Mafia extends to men who have given long years of loyalty. Valenti retired without resistance when Chirico was killed, the authorities said. **(190)**

## The Irondequoit DMV Robbery and the Murder of Ernie White

**Ernest White, DMV robbery suspect was found with 3 bullets in his head.**

In early 1973, Al DeCanzio, Charles Monachino and others, planned a robbery of the Irondequoit, N.Y. office of the Department of Motor Vehicles. They carried out that crime on **March 30, 1973**. The actual crime was committed by Ernest White and Reginald Hawkins, using White's car for transportation.

During the robbery White and his car were identified by witnesses and a warrant for his arrest was issued. The conspirators feared that White would talk if he was arrested and they summoned him to the garage of the construction company where they worked. Telling him that they intended to make it look as if he had been kidnapped, and thus allay suspicion of him. DeCanzio and Monachino tied up White with his permission, placed him in the trunk of a car belonging to DeCanzio's wife, and then DeCanzio fired three bullets into White's head. The body was dumped into a manhole, near the Clarissa Street Bridge (1) where it was discovered several months later.

The principal witness at DeCanzio's murder trial was Charles Monachino. After receiving immunity, Monachino testified in detail concerning the robbery of the motor vehicle office and the murder of White. Throughout the investigation, in his testimony before the Grand Jury and at trial, Monachino contended that although he knew after the robbery that White would be killed sometime, he did not know that the murder was planned on the night it occurred. Based upon Monachino's testimony, the trial jury was told that if Monachino was an accomplice in the White murder, his testimony must be corroborated.

After DeCanzio's conviction became final, Monachino recanted and swore that his testimony at the trial was false. He claimed that in truth he had participated in a meeting held prior to the killing at which White's murder was planned. This additional fact was highly significant for if Monachino had helped to plan the killing and participated in it, as he now contends, he was an accomplice as a matter of law and defendant was entitled to an appropriate charge that Monachino's testimony was not sufficient to convict unless it was corroborated.

The testimony of one other witness at DeCanzio's murder trial, that of Thomas Wheeler, was also important to the disposition of that proceeding. Wheeler was being held in the Monroe County Jail on a rape charge at the same time that DeCanzio and

## Warrant Issued in $21,689 Theft

Irondequoit police yesterday issued an arrest warrant for a man in connection with the March 30 robbery of a Monroe County License Bureau office in Irondequoit.

Ernest David White Jr., 32, whose last known address was given as 708 Parsells Ave., is wanted on charges of first-degree armed robbery and first-degree grand larceny, police said.

He is charged with entering the license bureau at 726 E. Ridge Road in Hudson-Ridge Plaza with another man and robbing the bureau of $21,689 in cash and checks, police said.

Police have not identified the other suspect. White should be considered armed and dangerous, police said.

Police said White became a suspect through a police investigation and identification of pictures by witnesses.

The robbery came 35 minutes after the office had closed for the day. Lawrence J. Masters, manager of the bureau, told police he had locked the back door to the one-story building and couldn't explain how the bandits entered the office.

A 1970 black Chrysler that police said had been used in the robbery was found, 30 minutes after the holdup, in a driveway at 1137 E. Main St.

Police said White was the owner of an auto body shop at that address.

ERNEST D. WHITE JR.

Reginald Hawkins (White's partner in the robbery of the motor vehicle office) were there. Wheeler testified at DeCanzio's murder trial that DeCanzio and another inmate planned to kill Hawkins in jail and that DeCanzio asked him to act as a lookout while they did it. After DeCanzio's conviction, Wheeler also recanted his story and swore that officers of the Monroe County Sheriff's Department lured him into his trial testimony by physical abuse and by promising to help him obtain a favorable sentence on his rape charge.

After DeCanzio’s conviction became final, he instituted a proceeding seeking to vacate his conviction because of misconduct by the police and the prosecution and because of newly discovered evidence i.e., Monachino’s recantation. DeCanzio was granted a new trial.

# *Chapter 16*
# The Hammer Conspiracy

## Vincent "Jimmy The Hammer" Massaro Is Murdered

**Vincent "Jimmy the Hammer" Massaro**

In **September and November 1973**, Vincent Massaro complained to other organization members and some individuals outside the organization that he was not being paid enough for his efforts. Massaro's specialty was "arson for hire." During November 1973, Samuel "Red" Russotti had a meeting at the residence of his sister in Rochester, N.Y. The participants at that meeting were: "Red" Russotti, Rene Piccarreto, Salvatore Gingello, Richard Marino, Thomas Marotta, Sam Campanella, Eugene DeFrancesco and Spike LaNoverra.

A decision was made at that meeting by the upper echelon of the Rochester Mafia to order the murder of Vincent Massaro. Eugene DeFrancesco and Spike LaNoverra were then ordered to commit that murder, as a test of loyalty, since they had previously been soldiers under Dominic Chirico. DiFrancesco and LaNoverra were unable to accomplish the killing within the few days that they were given to do so.

So, another meeting was called and Angelo Monachino was ordered to attend. At that second meeting, Russotti, Gingello, Piccarreto, Marino, and Marotta ordered Angelo Monachino to assist Lanoverra and DiFrancesco in the murder of Massaro. Angelo Monachino was a close friend of Vincent Massaro as well as a former Chirico soldier.

On **November 23, 1973**, with the aid of Angelo Monachino and Spike LaNoverra, Eugene DiFrancesco shot Vincent Massaro to death in the Bar-Mon Construction Co. garage, premises owned by Angelo Monachino. Massaro was killed with a handgun, equipped with a silencer provided by Rosario Chirico.

On **November 28, 1973**, Officer John Donlon of the Rochester, NY Police Department made a grisly discovery in the trunk of a car parked at 203 Atkinson Street in the city of Rochester. The body of reputed Rochester mafia member Vincent "Jimmy the Hammer" Massaro was found dead with half of his face blown off, stuffed in the trunk of his own car. He had been shot eight times in the head at close range. **(169)**

## Failed Omerta -The Early Informants

Francis J. Pecora was a professional shoplifter who was arrested in **August of 1974** for the theft of $8,000 in diamond rings from a Present Co. store in Penfield, NY. While he was free on bail, sheriff's deputies were called to Pecora's home to handle a domestic disturbance. Once there, Pecora's wife alerted the deputies to some slightly "warm" guns and appliances that were also in the home. Francis Pecora was taken into custody for further questioning.

Rather than face possible jail time, Francis Pecora became an informant and then fingered William P. "Jake" Zimmerman as a fellow shoplifter and receiver of stolen goods. Under direct orders from Rochester Chief of Detectives, William C. Mahoney, Pecora traveled to Buffalo, NY, on **December 18, 1974** and stole $1,200 worth of merchandise from various stores. He then sold it all to Jake Zimmerman at his home in Gates, NY. At 8:30 PM the next evening, Sheriff's Detectives knocked on Zimmerman's front door and arrested him for possession of stolen property.

Zimmerman, who was known by police for selling stolen goods to Mafia members, was not about to take the rap either. He too became an informant and he fingered one Russell Russo, another possessor of stolen property. Russell Russo was more than eager to help detectives. He was willing to tell them about the March 30, 1973 robbery of the Dept. of Motor Vehicles in Irondequoit, NY. **On January 17, 1975** Russo signed an affidavit implicating Charles M. Monachino, whom he described as his best friend, and Monachino's brother Angelo. Russo would later claim that Assistant D.A. Patrick Brophy, Detective John Kennerson and Chief of Police William Mahoney wrote what they wanted on the affidavit and then forced him to sign it.

Monachino was then picked up by police. Once in custody, Charles Monachino turned out to be very cooperative as well. In return for immunity from prosecution, Monachino signed an affidavit claiming that Albert J. DeCanzio engineered the DMV robbery and then killed Ernest White. Albert DeCanzio was no small fish, he worked for the Mafia. He had been a driver, mechanic, cook and confidant of Frank J. Valenti, former "Boss" of the Rochester Mafia.

DeCanzio went on trial for killing Ernest White in **April of 1975**. The star witness was Charles Monachino, who testified that he witnessed Al DeCanzio shoot Ernest White to death on April 1, 1973. Monachino also claimed that he was unaware of DeCanzio's intention to do so. DeCanzio was convicted of the murder.

In exchange for a shorter sentence for the White murder, DeCanzio became the next police informant in early **June of 1975**. DeCanzio implicated Angelo Monachino and other Rochester mob members for several unsolved arsons as well as the notorious Columbus Day Bombings.

Angelo Monachino was then arrested. He was offered immunity from at least one murder and several other charges if he would talk. He talked. Angelo Monachino backed up DeCanzio's stories on the arsons and the bombings. Monachino then implicated several reputed high level mobsters in the death of Jimmy "The Hammer" Massaro.

Many more arrests followed. On **June 27, 1975**, six men were charged with the Massaro murder. On **June 30, 1975** two mob members, one of them a lawyer, were charged with plotting to kill Sheriff Lombard. On **July 10, 1975**, a Chili dentist was arrested for arson. On **July 18, 1975** two more men were indicted for killing Massaro. On **July 25, 1975** eight men were indicted for the Columbus Day 1970 bombings. Finally six more men were arrested on arson charges. All of these arrests were a direct result of the informant testimony of Al DeCanzio, Angelo Monachino and others.

Unfortunately, most of those charges would be dropped due to a lack of evidence, or the defendants were found not guilty. Of all those arrested, Gene DiFrancesco was found guilty on two charges and Valenti, Roncone and Uchie were convicted of lesser charges. (3)

## The Hammer Conspiracy

In June, 1975, detectives from the Monroe County Sheriff's Office arrested Joseph Lanovara and Angelo Monachino and charged them with complicity in the 1973 murder of one Jimmy Massaro. Those suspects thereafter cooperated with law enforcement authorities in the continuing probe and implicated six individuals, alleged to be members of organized crime, in the planning and ordering of the gangland-style execution.

Under New York State law, however, criminal convictions may not be based upon the uncorroborated statements of accomplices. Because they lacked the requisite independent verification of the information given by Lanovara and Monachino, who were participants in the crime, members of the Monroe County Sheriff's Office embarked upon a scheme to concoct such evidence.

More specifically, it appeared that Chief of Detectives William Mahoney induced Detective William Marks and Detective Lieutenant John Kennerson to assert that while conducting routine surveillance in November, 1973, they observed their cooperating witnesses in the company of the six suspects at the dates, times and places attested to by Lanovara and Monachino.

Notes and surveillance logs were then fabricated to buttress these claims. Based upon accomplice testimony as corroborated by Marks and Kennerson, the six defendants were convicted of murder. Those six defendants were almost the entire leadership of the Rochester Mafia at the time. A short time later, two more Mafia members were arrested for the Massaro murder, placing the entire leadership of the Rochester Mafia behind bars. (4)

## Leaders Of Rochester Mafia Sentenced For the Massaro Murder

Library
Jan. 14, 1977 — Three men convicted of the gangland murder of Vincent "Jimmy the Hammer" Massaro are led to a courtroom for sentencing. From the left in foreground are Samuel "Red" Russotti, Rene Piccarreto and Salvatore "Sammy G" Gingello.


**Above, "Red" Russotti, Rene Piccarreto and Sammy Gingello are being led to the courtroom for sentencing in the Massaro murder case.**

The informants' testimony resulted in Samuel "Red" Russotti, Salvatore Gingello, Rene Piccarreto, Gene DiFrancesco, and Thomas Marotta being convicted on November 11, 1976 of murder and conspiracy.

The mobsters all received sentences of 25 years to life in **January 1977**. Richard Marino, Teamsters Local #398 Business Agent, was tried separately a short time earlier, found guilty and received a similar sentence.

## Mobsters Go to Prison

On **January 14, 1977**, Samuel "Red" Russotti, Rene Piccarreto, Salvatore "Sammy G" Gingello, Richard Marino, Thomas Marotta and Eugene. DeFrancesco, were imprisoned for 25 years to life as a result of their conviction in Monroe County Court for the November 23, 1973 murder of Vincent "Jimmy the Hammer" Massaro. The incarceration of those individuals resulted in a virtual elimination of all vestiges of leadership within the Rochester Mafia. In their absence, a temporary "Boss" was chosen to ensure the continuation of the "enterprise."

D&C Photo by Burr Lewis

Rene Piccarreto (second from left), Thomas Marotta and Eugene DiFrancesco (right) arrive at Attica.

## Massaro murderers get long prison sentences

By MARCIA BULLARD
*D&C Staff Writer*

Five alleged members of the Rochester Mafia convicted of murder were sentenced to lengthy prison terms yesterday in Monroe County Court.

Three of the five were taken to Attica prison about an hour after the sentencing, and two others remain in the county jail on a federal detainer while awaiting a trial in federal court in Buffalo.

The five men were convicted Nov. 10 of murdering Vincent "Jimmy the Hammer" Massaro in 1973 because Massaro reportedly had violated the rules of organized crime.

Four of the men were sentenced to maximum terms of 25 years to life in prison, and one received the minimum sentence of 15 years to life.

Judge Eugene W. Bergin said he hoped the sentences "will act as a deterrent to those who follow in your places in the structure of organized crime in this city." If anyone doubted the existence of a Rochester Mafia, "those doubts should have been resolved" during the eight-week trial earlier this fall, Bergin said.

Those receiving the maximum sentence, and their alleged positions in the local Mafia, are Samuel "Red" Russotti, 63, the boss; Salvatore

### They exit smiling

**January 15, 1977**
**Democrat and Chronicle**

**The picture on the left shows Rene Piccarreto, Thomas Marotta and Eugene DiFrancesco arriving at Attica State Prison in New York to begin serving their lengthy prison sentences for murdering "Jimmy the Hammer" Massaro.**

# Didio Promoted To "Acting Boss"

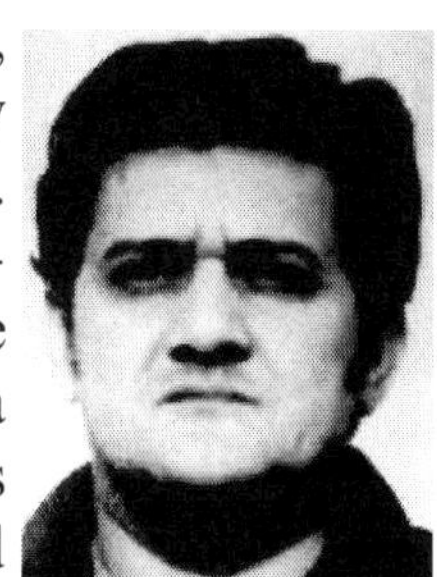

**Thomas Didio**

Thomas Didio was a bodyguard, chauffeur, and confident of Salvatore "Sammy G" Gingello, and a cousin of Thomas Marotta. Didio was placed in control of "The Organization" by Samuel "Red" Russotti and Salvatore "Sammy G" Gingello. Didio was previously a "Soldier" under Thomas Marrotta. He was known primarily for his intimidating size and "slow wit." It was believed that Didio's blood relationship to Thomas Marrotta would insure that the wives and families of the defendants (of the Massaro murder) would be provided for and that Didio's limited mental capacity would allow the defendants to control Didio, and the organized crime operation from their jail cells.

Once he was in power, Didio did not prove to be receptive to orders from Russotti Piccarreto, or Gingello. Didio did not provide financial support for the defendants families either, despite his relationship to Marotta. Organized crime members loyal to Russotti and Gingello were reduced in status and removed from union positions and no-show jobs by Didio. That caused a great deal of resentment and dissension within the organization.

In the **Spring of 1977**, a fund-raising event was held for the benefit of the imprisoned mob leaders. It was alleged that Didio diverted a large sum of the money that was raised, at this event, for his own personal use.

Sensing the discontent within the organization, Thomas Didio sought counsel with Stanley Valenti, and through him received guidance from Frank Valenti, who was incarcerated at the Springfield Medical Center for Federal Prisoners, Springfield, Mo. It was believed that the Valenti's viewed the current circumstances as an opportunity to regain control of the Rochester organized crime operations. In **July 1977**, Angelo Vaccaro returned to Rochester, N.Y., from Texas, at the request of Thomas Didio.

During **midsummer 1977**, Didio loyalists Samuel Campanella and James Canarozza were added to the list of persons allowed to visit with Frank Valenti with the notation "to be allowed only when accompanied by Stanley Valenti." Campanella and Canarozza were both Business Agents for Teamsters Local #398 in Rochester, NY and Campanella was Vice-President of that union at that time.

During approximately the same period, Gingello loyalist John Fiorino visited the imprisoned mob bosses in jail. Reliable information revealed that by the **late summer of 1977**, the imprisoned former mob bosses decided that it was time to remove Thomas Didio from his position of power. (5)

## The Meeting at the Blue Gardenia

In September of 1977, Thomas Didio was on top of the world. He was the "Acting Boss" of the Rochester Mafia. All five of his superior officers in the organization, the same ones that gave him his job and title of "Acting Boss," were all still in jail. They had been there for nine months already and were going to be there a very long time, since each had received 25 years to life for their roles in the Massaro murder.

Didio had a solid backing that included Sonny Celestino, Angelo Vaccaro, Frank Frassetto, Rosario Chirico, Anthony Chirico, Sam Campanella and James Canarozza. Each had pledged their allegiance to Didio. They had all been secretly meeting with Stanley Valenti and were taking advice from Frank Valenti, who was due to be released from prison at any time.

The leaders of the Pittsburg, Pennsylvania Mafia in the La-Rocca Family, whom the Valentis were close to, assured Frank and Stan Valenti that there would be no outside interference in any potential power struggle in Rochester by any of the existing Mafia crime families.

With those thoughts in mind, Thomas Didio, Angelo Vaccaro and Sonny Celestino went to meet some "A Team" representatives so that they could discuss the future of the "organization" that they all belonged to. The meeting was held at the Blue Gardenia, one of the mobsters' favorite hangouts.

When Didio, Vaccaro and Celestino arrived, they were confronted by a larger group of "A Team" representatives that included John Fiorino, Joe Rossi, Thomas Taylor, Joseph LoDolce and others unknown.

On direct orders from Sammy Gingello, whom the "A Team" representatives had been talking to in prison, Thomas Didio was informed that his promotion to "Acting Boss" of the Rochester Mafia had been rescinded! Effective Immediately!

Didio, who had no intention of stepping down as "Boss," did not respond well to those orders. An altercation ensued and Didio, Vaccaro and Celestino were then all severely beaten and ejected from the restaurant. They immediately went into hiding...

## ...and the Rochester Mob Wars began!!

1) 10-11-79 Democrat and Chronicle "DeCanzio Dodges Courtroom Blows"
2) 67 AD 2d. 111 (1979) DeCanzio vs. Kennedy
3) April 13, 1979 Democrat and Chronicle "Cops against cops and the mob went free"
4) Http://openjurist.org/629/f2d/723/united-states-v-berardi
5) May 2,5, 1980 Senate Hearings pg.439-440
6) Senate Hearings, Permanent Subcommittee on Investigations May 2,5, 1980 page 440
7) Senate Hearings, Permanent Subcommittee on Investigations May 2,5, 1980 page 440
8) Democrat and Chronicle July 7, 1978
9) Senate Hearings, Permanent Subcommittee on Investigations May 2,5, 1980 page 441
10) Senate Hearings, Permanent Subcommittee on Investigations May 2,5, 1980 page 442
11) Senate Hearings, Permanent Subcommittee on Investigations May 2,5, 1980 page 443
12) ROCHESTER DEMOCRAT AND CHRONICLE Sunday, March 12, 1978
13) Rochester, N.Y. Democrat and Chronicle April 13, 1979
14) ROCHESTER DEMOCRAT AND CHRONICLE Sunday. April 23, 1978
15) Senate Hearings, Permanent Subcommittee on Investigations May 2,5, 1980 pg. 444
16) Democrat and Chronicle May 20,1978 Mob War Revives With A Bang
17) ) OPINION OF The INDEPENDENT REVIEW BOARD IN THE MATTER OF THE HEARING OF ROBERT TRIANO November 22, 1999 page 6
18) Democrat and Chronicle May 23, 1978 Latest Mob Blast Rocks Local Club
19) Democrat and Chronicle May 23, 1978 Latest Mob Blat Rocks Local Club
20) May 23, 1978 Democrat and Chronicle Any of 7 Could Be Next Target
21) Democrat and Chronicle May 26, 1978 2 More Inches and He Would Be Dead
22) Democrat and Chronicle June 10, 1978 Bomb Threat Empties Bar
23) Senate Hearings, Permanent Subcommittee on Investigations May 2,5, 1980 (page 446)
24) Democrat and Chronicle July 7, 1978 Mob leader killed inside Victor Motel
25) Rochester, N.Y., Democrat and Chronicle, July 7, 1978 Didios Death weakens Mob Insurgents
26) Rochester, N.Y., Democrat and Chronicle, July 20, 1978 Grand Jury indicts 2 mob suspects
27) Democrat and Chronicle November 2, 1978 Mob Pressure Drives 2 away.
28) November 17, 1978 Democrat and Chronicle 5 Plead Innocent To Bomb Charges
29)OPINION OF The INDEPENDENT REVIEW BOARD IN THE MATTER OF THE HEARING OF ROBERT TRIANO November 22, 1999 page 6
30)Democrat and Chronicle December 1, 1978 "Teamster officers"
31)Senate Hearings, Permanent Subcommittee on Investigations May 2,5, 1980 page pg. 435-436
32)Democrat and Chronicle March 6, 1979 Informant could link Mafia to bombings
33)Rochester, New York Democrat and Chronicle Apr. 13, 1979
34)ROCHESTER DEMOCRAT AND CHRONICLE Tuesday, Apr. 17, 1979 article "The Who's Who of characters in bombing probe" page 3B D&C photo by Joe Watson
35)Democrat and Chronicle November 1, 1979 Mobster Describes Bombing
36)Rochester Democrat and Chronicle Sunday, January 6, 1980 Page: Page 21
37)Rochester, N.Y. Democrat and Chronicle January 31, 1980 All 7 found Guilty in Mob war Trial
38))Rochester, N.Y. D&C March 12, 1980 Judge to Bombers "A Vicious Conspiracy"
39)647 F.2d 224 UNITED STATES of America, Appellee, v. William BARTON, Anthony Chirico, Rosario Chirico, Dominic "Sonny" Celestino, Betti Frassetto, Frank Frassetto and Angelo Vaccaro, Defendants-Appellants. *Nos. 357 and 402 to 406, Dockets 80-1096, 80-1102, 80-1103,80-1116, 80-1117 and 80-1130.* United States Court of Appeals, Second Circuit. *Argued Nov. 19, 1980. Decided March 27, 1981.* Rehearing Denied April 27, 1981.
40)725 F.2d 16114 Fed. R. Evid. Serv. 1418 UNITED STATES of America, Appellee, v. Michael A. PELUSIO, Thomas A. Pelusio, Defendants-Appellants. *Nos. 422, 346, Dockets 83-1175, 83-1179.* United States Court of Appeals, Second Circuit. *Argued Oct. 31, 1983. Decided Dec. 22, 1983*
*41)*Rochester, New York Democrat and Chronicle article
42) Democrat and Chronicle July 30, 1980 Informant To Aide New Probe

43) Democrat and Chronicle October 16, 1980 Man Guilty of Causing Blast
44)Democrat and Chronicle November 18, 1980 Man Shoots Self to Death at Downtown Social Club
45)Democrat and Chronicle March 27, 1981 Reputed Mobster Surrenders, Denies Bank Theft Counts
46)Democrat and Chronicle November 6, 1981 Witnesses Describe Sucker Punch
47)December 18, 1981 Democrat and Chronicle Victim Was Informant
48)December 19, 1981 Democrat and Chronicle New Mafia War Feared
49)February 4, 1982 Democrat and Chronicle Judge Rules Mistrial In Stebbins Arson Case
50)Democrat and Chronicle January 7, 1982 Club Fire Believed to Be an Accident
51)February 23, 1982 UPI Archives (http://www.upi.com/Archives/1982/02/23/Mad-Dog-Sullivan-the-son-of-a-detective-and/7269383288400/)
52)ROCHESTER DEMOCRAT AND CHRONICLE March 10, 1982 page 2
53)Democrat and Chronicle March 14, 1982 Grand Jury to Hear of Assault
54)March 23, 1982 Democrat and Chronicle Fire Damages Club Linked to Mob
55)May 26, 1982 Democrat and Chronicle Man Linked to Local Mob Shot to Death at Coin Store
56)Democrat and Chronicle June 9, 1982 Torpey and Taylor Arrested
57)SUNDAY DEMOCRAT AND CHRONICLE, ROCHESTER, N.Y.. NOVEMBER 27, 1983
58)August 18, 1982 Democrat and Chronicle Sullivan: I'm No Hit Man
59)August 29, 1982 Democrat and Chronicle Case of Mistaken Identity, Wrong Man Slain
60)August 28, 1982 Democrat and Chronicle Gangland Retaliation Feared
61) Rochester, New York Democrat and Chronicle September 4, 1982 page 10 article "Pelusio Leads Mob Faction?" By David Galante
62) September 24, 1982 Democrat and Chronicle Sullivan Found Guilty in Fiorino Slaying
63) 725 F.2d 16114 Fed. R. Evid. Serv. 1418 UNITED STATES of America, Appellee, v. Michael A. PELUSIO, Thomas A. Pelusio, Defendants-Appellants. *Nos. 422, 346, Dockets 83-1175, 83-1179.* United States Court of Appeals, Second Circuit. *Argued Oct. 31, 1983. Decided Dec. 22, 1983*
64) Rochester Democrat and Chronicle article, Man of the Mob: The Making and Breaking of Tom Marotta by Gary Craig, Staff Writer for the Democrat and Chronicle. Article appeared on 4-25-04 pg 1A
65) November 11, 1982 Democrat and Chronicle Organized Crime Tied to 2 Local Unions
66) Democrat and Chronicle November 28, 1982 New Club Is Suspected Gambling Front
67) December 16,1982 Democrat and Chronicle 2 Indicted in Union Assault
68) March 11, 1983 Democrat and Chronicle Torpey Guilty on Four Charges
69)Rochester, New York Democrat and Chronicle April 28, 1983 article "Brucato Charged With Lying to Grand Jury" page 12
70)Democrat and Chronicle May 28, 1983 Clues Sought In Shooting at Mob Linked Social Club

71)Rochester Democrat and Chronicle November 12, 1983 Men Questioned after Marotta Shooting
72)Rochester, New York Democrat and Chronicle article "Men Questioned After Marotta Shooting" dated November 12, 1983 page 1B
73) November 16, 1983 Democrat and Chronicle Policeman Tells of His Close Call on Night Fiorino Slain
74) March 11, 1983 Democrat and Chronicle Court Refuses to Grant Immunity
75) December 9, 1983 Democrat and Chronicle Fiorino's Widow Takes the Witness Stand
76)January 3, 1984 Democrat and Chronicle Mistrial for Torpey, Taylor
77)SUNDAY DEMOCRAT AND CHRONICLE, ROCHESTER, N.Y., SEPTEMBER 16, 1984 pg. 28
78)Rochester, New York Democrat and Chronicle September 30, 1984 page 21
79)October 2, 1984 Democrat and Chronicle Informant Testifies on Motel Killing
80)October 22, 1984 Democrat and Chronicle Rackets Trial Goes to Jury This Week

**81)OPINION OF THE INDEPENDENT REVIEW BOARD IN THE MATTER OF THE HEARING OF ROBERT TRIANO NOVEMBER 22, 1999 PAGE 6**

**82)DECEMBER 18, 1984 DEMOCRAT AND CHRONICLE 7 IN MOB CASE GET STIFF TERMS**

**83) UNITED STATES V. THOMAS TAYLOR, NO. 84-126, W.D.N.Y., 5/15/84**

84)Rochester Democrat and Chronicle November 12, 1983 2 Clubs Raided, 9 people arrested
85)February 3, 1987 Democrat and Chronicle A Dark Tale of Hit Men in the Mob
86)July 30, 1987 Democrat and Chronicle "Charlie The Ox" Enters Guilty Plea
87)August 7, 1987 Democrat and Chronicle Greece Man's Plea Closes 1985 Truck Bombing Case
88)September 19, 1987 Democrat and Chronicle Mob Figure Gets 15 Years for Bombing
89)July 30, 1987 Democrat and Chronicle "Charlie The Ox" Enters Guilty Plea
90)October 3, 1987 Democrat and Chronicle 51 Page Indictment
91)October 3, 1987 Democrat and Chronicle 51 Page Indictment
92)DEMOCRAT AND CHRONICLE ROCHESTER. N.Y. SATURDAY, OCTOBER 3, 1987
93)October 8, 1987 Democrat and Chronicle Hitman Named In 3 Killings
94)October 9, 1987 Democrat and Chronicle Important Federal Witness Sentenced to a Five Year Term
95)October 15, 1987 Democrat and Chronicle Amico Denied Bail In Mob Case

96)May 1, 1988 Democrat and Chronicle 3 Illegal Gambling Clubs Shut by Police in Raids
97)August 31, 1988 Democrat and Chronicle  Judge scolds Mobster
98)November 2, 1988 Democrat and Chronicle Amico May Testify at Mob Trial
99)November 3, 1988 Democrat and Chronicle Tapes in Mob Case Called
Most Important Witnesses
100)November 4, 1988 Democrat and Chronicle 3 linked to mobster initiation
101)November 8, 1988 Democrat and Chronicle Mob trial witness recalls gambling payments
102)November 9, 1988 Democrat and Chronicle Strong Arm Tactics Described
103)November 17, 1988 Democrat and Chronicle Piccarreto Wrote he was Mafiosa
104)November 13. 1988  Democrat and ChronicleTrial Throws Light on Rochester's Gambler Underworld
105)November 13. 1988 Democrat and Chronicle Trial Throws Light on Rochester's Gambler Underworld
106)SUNDAY DEMOCRAT AND CHRONICLE  ROCHESTER, N.Y. NOVEMBER 13. 1988
107)December 1, 1988 Democrat and Chronicle Fear Not in The Cards Witness Says
108)December 7, 1988 Democrat and Chronicle Medics Take Witness From Court
109)December 1, 1988 Democrat and Chronicle Mob Turned Upside Down
110)http://articles.mcall.com/1990-08-02/news/2759500_1_indicted-grand-jury-organized
111)Opinion of the Independent Administrator in regard to Angelo Misuraca hearing: 11-20-90, Opinion dated March 6, 1991 and Judges order signed July 16, 1991
112)Opinion of the Independent Administrator in regard to Angelo Misuraca hearing: 11-20-90, Opinion dated March 6, 1991 and Judges order signed July 16, 1991
113)OPINION OF THE INDEPENDENT REVIEW BOARD IN THE MATTER OF THE HEARING OF ROBERT TRIANO Dated: November 22, 1999
114)Rochester, New YorkDemocrat and Chronicle Sunday April 21, 1991 Page 77
115)DEMOCRAT AND CHRONICLE. ROCHESTER, N.Y.,  SATURDAY, DECEMBER 7. 1991
116)Rochester, New Democrat and Chronicle:  Saturday, January 25, 1992 Page: 1
117)http://www.nytimes.com/1993/06/30/obituaries/samuel-russotti-81-was-reputed-head-of-mob-in-rochester.html

118)Opinion of the Independent Review Board for Joseph LoDolce Dated: September 16, 1997

119)IRB Decision of the IRB for Robert  Traino

120) Democrat and Chronicle 2-23-97 "Leader defends Local's actions"
121) Proposed charges against Charles Ross dated 10-14-96
122)Proposed charges against Charles Ross dated 10-14-96 page 2
123) Decision of the IRB 9-16-97 in regard to Joseph LoDolce
124)Proposed IRB charges against Charles Ross dated 10-14-96 page 7
125)Rochester, N.Y. Democrat and Chronicle August 10, 1959
126)Rochester, N.Y. Democrat and Chronicle August 10, 1959
127)Rochester, NY Democrat and Chronicle August 13, 1959 FBI Investigates Teamsters Here
128)Democrat and Chronicle 3-25-48 "Some Hats Change for Easter-Some Don't.
129)Democrat and Chronicle 5-18-48 "5 Arrested in Numbers Game Raid"
130)Democrat and Chronicle October 5, 1963 Local Teamster Chief Indicted on Accepting Pay-offs from employers
131)Democrat and Chronicle 10-13-64 Union Officials Kickback Trial Begins Today
132) Democrat and Chronicle October 9, 1963 Thousands in N.Y. Mob Valachi Tells Inquiry
133)October 10, 1963 Democrat and Chronicle "Local Police Doubt "Cosa Nostra" Link Here
134)Rochester, New York Democrat and Chronicle December 14, 1964 "Where is Jake Russo? Valenti's Enforcer Missing
135)Democrat and Chronicle Rochester, N.Y. October 17, 1964 "Buscemi Convicted in Builder Payoffs"
136)Democrat and Chronicle Rochester, N. Y. Nov. 19, 1964 "Teamster President Stripped of Offices
137)New York Times December 5, 9, 1964 'Paper is Enjoined on Police Record' and 'Pretrial News Case Is Delayed Upstate'
138)ROCHESTER, N.Y. DEMOCRAT AND CHRONICLE Monday, Nov. 30, 1964 article "'Stamped' Gambler Number Two" page 17
139)ROCHESTER DEMOCRAT And Chronicle Thursday, Dec. 3, 1964 article on page 18
140)ROCHESTER. N. Y., Democrat and Chronicle FRIDAY, DEC. 4, 1964 Clerics Rap Gamblers stamps or No
141) ROCHESTER. N. Y., Democrat and Chronicle FRIDAY, DEC. 4, 1964
142) New York Times December 20, 1964 'Rochester Upset By Mafia Report"
143)Rochester Fears Underworld War by Charles Grutzner, New York Times article December 15, 1964
144)Democrat and Chronicle January 31, 1965 article "It's Arrest #26 For Joe Lippa" page 8
145)March 31, 1965 Democrat and Chronicle article Lippa Starts Felony Term as Gambler page 13
146)Democrat and Chronicle April 20, 1966 Crime Probers Quiz 2 Valenti Associates
147)Democrat and Chronicle Rochester, New York Sunday April 25, 1982 page 121
148) Rochester, New York Democrat and Chronicle July 1, 1968 article "Blow Aimed at Gamblers" page 1

149) The Hammer Conspiracies by Frank A. Aloi 1982 page 65
150) The Hammer Conspiracies by Frank A. Aloi 1982 page 207
151) Senate Hearings, Permanent Subcommittee on Investigations May 2,5, 1980 page 434
152) June 3, 1970, Daily News. Upstate New York Mob Leaders Hold Meeting in Batavia
153) Batavia June 3, 1970, Daily News Hidden History: mobsters arrested in Batavia, By Mark Graczyk
154) Rochester, New York Democrat and Chronicle October 12, 1970
155) Rochester Democrat and Chronicle April 13, 1979
156) Senate Hearings, Permanent Subcommittee on Investigations May 2,5, 1980 page 435
157) pg 38 of the 1978 Senate Hearings Permanent Subcommittee on Investigations August 22, 1978
158) Rochester, New York Democrat and Chronicle article "$200 check key evidence in Missing Lippa Cash" dated September 3, 1971 page 1
159) article "Wilson to Receive Humanitarian Award" Labor Independent Newspaper December 12, 1972
160) Minutes of JC#17 dated January 4, 1972
161) Minutes of JC#17 dated May 11, 1972
162) Rochester Democrat and Chronicle article, Man of the Mob: The Making and Breaking of Tom Marotta by Gary Craig, Staff Writer for the Democrat and Chronicle. Article appeared on 4-25-04 pg 1A
163) Senate Hearings, Permanent Subcommittee on Investigations May 2,5, 1980 page pg.436
164) http://tonycd23.tripod.com/
165) Senate Hearings, Permanent Subcommittee on Investigations May 2,5, 1980 page 437
166) Senate Hearings, Permanent Subcommittee on Investigations May 2,5, 1980 pg. 43
167) Democrat and Chronicle November 5, 1972 Lucien DiGiovanni article
168) Sunday, April 29, 1973 Rochester Democrat and Chronicle page 1
169) The Hammer Conspiracies by Frank Aloi 1982 page 14
170) Senate Hearings, Permanent Subcommittee on Investigations May 2,5, 1980 pg. 438
171) Opinion of the Independent Review Board in the Matter of Robert Triano pg. 4
172) 1978 Senate Hearings
173) Democrat and Chronicle article titled "They Never Say he was a Family Man
174) Democrat and Chronicle article titled "Marotta says he didn't see assailant" April 13, 1983
175) August 4, 1983 Democrat and Chronicle slain leaders ambition may have led mob to order his death
176) November 11, 1983 Democrat and Chronicle "Marotta gunned down again"
177) Opinion of the IRB in regard to Robert Triano dated November 22., 1999 page 9
178) Memorandum and Order concerning Angelo Misuraca dated July 16, 1991

179) Opinion of the IRB in regard to Robert Triano dated November 22., 1999 page 8
180) Democrat and Chronicle August 18, 1965 page 4A "Majority's Report on Police Probe"
181) Democrat and Chronicle September 2, 1965
182) Democrat and Chronicle February 27, 1965 "Alloco's Last Pal sought by Police" and February 25, 1965 Gamblers murder regarded as syndicate message
183) December 21, 1970 Democrat and Chronicle "Slaying, giant Liquor theft may be linked"
184) December 24, 1970 Democrat and Chronicle "State Police Term Slaying Execution"
185) September 13,14, 1978 Senate Hearings (Arson for Hire)
186) Democrat and Chronicle March 13, 1966
187) clipping from the June 3, 1970, Daily News.
188) June 6, 1972 Ex Con gunned to death
189) November 5, 1972 Democrat and Chronicle
190) April 29, 1973 Rochester Democrat and Chronicle Page 1
191) Rochester Democrat and Chronicle May 23. 1980 "Frank Valenti to be Paroled"
192) November 10, 1982 Democrat and Chronicle Mob insiders squeal; Federal jury indicts 10
193) Rochester, New York Democrat and Chronicle Monday, Nov. 30, 1964 "Stamped Gambler #2"
194) Democrat & Chronicle February 22, 1997 Leader defends local's actions
195) Democrat and Chronicle article "Slain gang leaders ambition may have led mob to order his death

# Rochester Mafia Membership List

**Members, Associates and Murder Victims**

Murdered

**Dominick Alloco**

**Angelo Amico**

**William Barton**

**Dominic Celestino**

**Salvatore Campanella**

**James Canarozza**

Murdered

**John J. Cavagrotti**

**Anthony Chirico**

Murdered

**Dominic Chirico**

**Rosario Chirico**

**Anthony Columbo**

Murdered

**William Constable**

**Albert DeCanzio**

Murdered

**Tom Didio**

**Eugene Di-Francesco**

**Sam DiGaetano**

**Louis DiGiuilio**

**Angelo DiMarco**

Murdered

**John Fiorino**

**Betti Frassetto**

**Frank Frassetto**

**Joseph Geniola**

**Anthony Gingello**

Murdered

**Sam Gingello**

**Charles Indovino**

**Joey LaMendola**

**Joseph LaNovera**

**Joe Lippa**

**Joseph LoDolce**

Murdered

**William Lupo**

**Richard Marino**

**Thomas Marotta**

Murdered

**Vincent Massarro**

**Joseph Mastrodonato**

Murdered

**Nicholas Mastrodonato**

**Angelo Monachino**

**Charles Monachino**

**Joseph Nalore**

Anthony Oliveri

Donald Paone

Murdered

Gerald Pelusio

Thomas Pelusio

Loren Piccarreto

Rene Piccarreto

Vince Rallo

Joseph Rossi

Murdered

Jake Russo

Samuel Russotti

Rodney Starkweather

Leonard Stebbins

Joseph Sullivan

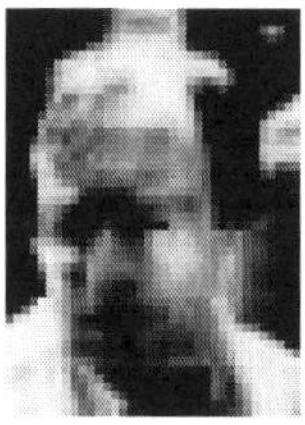
Dominic Taddeo

Thomas Taylor

Joey Tiraborelli

Thomas Torpey

Murdered

Dino Tortatice

John Travigno

Joseph Trieste

**Angelo Vaccaro**

**Frank Valenti**

**Stanley Valenti**

Murdered

**Ricky Visconte**

Murdered

**Ernest White Jr.**

**William Zimmerman**